SUMO

A THINKING FAN'S GUIDE TO JAPAN'S NATIONAL SPORT

by

DAVID BENJAMIN

Illustrated by Greg Holfeld

TUTTLE Publishing

Tokyo │Rutland, Vermont│ Singapore

for Annie & Swede

"Books to Span the East and West"

Tuttle Publishing was founded in 1832 in the small New England town of Rutland, Vermont [USA]. Our core values remain as strong today as they were then—to publish best-in-class books which bring people together one page at a time. In 1948, we established a publishing outpost in Japan—and Tuttle is now a leader in publishing English-language books about the arts, languages and cultures of Asia. The world has become a much smaller place today and Asia's economic and cultural influence has grown. Yet the need for meaningful dialogue and information about this diverse region has never been greater. Over the past seven decades, Tuttle has published thousands of books on subjects ranging from martial arts and paper crafts to language learning and literature—and our talented authors, illustrators, designers and photographers have won many prestigious awards. We welcome you to explore the wealth of information available on Asia at www.tuttlepublishing.com.

Published by Tuttle Publishing, an imprint of Periplus Editions (HK) Ltd.

www.tuttlepublishing.com

Copyright © 1991, 2010 Periplus Editions (HK) Ltd.

Library of Congress Cataloging-in-Publication Data

Benjamin, David, 1949-
  Sumo : a thinking fan's guide to Japan's national sport / by David Benjamin.
    256 p., [16] p. of col. plates : ill. (some col.) ; 21 cm.
  Includes bibliographical references and index.
  ISBN 978-4-8053-1087-8 (pbk.)
  1. Sumo. 2. Sumo--Japan. I. Title.
  GV1197.B46 2010
  796.812'5--dc22

2009030880

ISBN: 978-4-8053-1087-8

Distributed by

North America, Latin America & Europe
Tuttle Publishing
364 Innovation Drive
North Clarendon
VT 05759-9436 U.S.A.
Tel: 1 (802) 773-8930
Fax: 1 (802) 773-6993
info@tuttlepublishing.com
www.tuttlepublishing.com

Japan
Tuttle Publishing
Yaekari Building 3rd Floor
5-4-12 Osaki Shinagawa-ku
Tokyo 141 0032
Tel: (81) 3 5437-0171
Fax: (81) 3 5437-0755
sales@tuttle.co.jp
www.tuttle.co.jp

Asia Pacific
Berkeley Books Pte. Ltd.
3 Kallang Sector #04-01
Singapore 349278
Tel: (65) 6741-2178
Fax: (65) 6741-2179
inquiries@periplus.com.sg
www.tuttlepublishing.com

Revised and updated edition
26 25 24 23   7 6 5 4 3   2301VP
Printed in Malaysia

Contents

Introduction 7

CHAPTER 1
The Pit 19
"Death Valley" 23
Rhythm and Recognition. 24

CHAPTER 2
Big Al, Mad Dog, Tokyo Rose and the Silver Spoons . . . 29
Nomenclature: Proper and Improper. 32

CHAPTER 3
The "Grouping Urge":
  Blubberbutts and Thoroughbreds 43
Left/Right/Up/Down and All That. 45
Genus and Species. 49

CHAPTER 4
Backstage: Choking Up in the Church 57
Napoleon and Konishiki 59
The Locker Room 65
Aprons and Ads 68
The Meditations of the Beast. 70

CHAPTER 5
The Sumotori Rag: Pose-striking, Time-killing and
  the Eight Forms of Screwing Around 73
The Importance of the Overture 77

"Kokoro" and KITSH............................ 79
The KITSH Pecking Order 81
Eight Ways to Screw Around..................... 83

CHAPTER 6
Tachiai: Hookers, Bulldozers, Boxers, Stranglers,
    Matadors and Low-down Yankee Liars............ 97
Jumpers and Receivers 99
Bohr's Constant vs. The Human Factor............. 101
"Fast Is Good, Heavy Is Better" 104
The Five Styles of *Tachiai* 106
To Live and Die at *Tachiai*...................... 110

CHAPTER 7
The Fistfight at the Malamute Saloon and
    Other Japanese Cultural Treasures 113
The Expert 114
Hands, Feet and Angles......................... 116
The Guy in the Pajamas 121
The Finish.................................... 123
Extra Terms.................................. 129

CHAPTER 8
The Ripsnorter in Nagoya 133
Chiyonofuji's Ghosts........................... 135
Asahifuji's Jinx 138
The Match 144

CHAPTER 9
Afterward: "Keep Up Appearances Whatever You Do".. 153
The Membrane of Sportsmanship 155
The Rite of Withdrawal......................... 159
The Interview 163

CHAPTER 10
The Basho Beat:
"Give That Rhythm Everything You've Got" 171
Banzuke: Confucian Confusion 173
The Real Ranks: Upper Echelon 175
The Real Ranks: Down Below.................... 180
The Weight of Concentration 185
Good Basho, Bad Basho 187

CHAPTER 11
Tank This One for the Gipper................... 189
Little Spoon, Tamaryu, and the Politics of Mono-ii 192
A Sense of Honor 196
"Yaocho Doesn't Exist" 199
The Last-Day Blues........................... 202
How to Take a Dive 206
The Rite of Passage........................... 207

CHAPTER 12
The Statistical Imperative 211
The Data Deficit 214
Rating the Rikishi 215

CHAPTER 13
Whither Sumo... Especially With All These *Gaijin*? ... 225
The Mongol Hordes 226
Cracks in the Façade.......................... 231
An American Solution......................... 232
Just a Game 241

Acknowledgments............................ 245

Glossary 247

Index..................................... 251

Introduction

"Well, it's kind of interesting, but they're so fa-a-at!"

Every real fan creates his sport in his own image.

Me, I'm a sumo fan. Been that way since '87. Long time. And what's sumo to me?

Well, it's ballet and it's bullfighting...
— blundering and grace...
— dignity and buffoonery.

It's lightning and molasses...
— suet and gristle....
— the monstrous and the minuscule...
— the loner and the mob.

It's choreography and spontaneity...
— honor and corruption...
— the cerebral and the Neanderthal...
— basketball and judo...
— football and the balance beam.

It's frogs and princes...
— clerics and clowns...
— Br'er Rabbit and Br'er Bear...
— d'Artagnan and Quasimodo...
— silk and mud...
— tits and ass...
— incense and beer.

Sumo is, minute for minute, split-second for split-second, the quintessential spectator sport. It's sudden and violent, with almost no rules. One guy against the other and the ref (most of the time) is just another pretty pair of pajamas. The only guy who'll ever blow a whistle is the drunk in the 53rd row.

And sumo — no question — is the best sport there is if you're prone to imagine yourself in there, swinging away — because all these guys are out of shape...

- because you've got little guys going up against humongous guys — and winning!...
- because fat guys take on guys who look like Schwarzenegger (the movie star, not the Governator), and beat 'em!...
- because women pour out of the bleachers to touch you! (So what if they're all 58 years old? They're women!)

Sumo is a joy to discover and a fascination to pursue. I came to it as a TV sports fan — one of the millions of *kotatsu*-potatoes who admits I can't begin to play the game as well as those jocks on the screen, but who insist we know it better than the players. Or at least as well... as some of them...

... once in a while.

It is from that point of view that I write this book. There exist, in sumo circles, many others — especially *gaijin* (foreigners) — who enjoy the sport from a perspective that, although I often deplore it, is equally fertile. They tend to treat sumo as a mystic cultural treasure of Japan that also offers its cognoscenti an infinite source of in-group gossip.

I remember when I met Doreen Simmons, the reigning queen of *gaijin* sumo experts in Tokyo. I told her I was writing a sumo book and she fixed on me a suspicious and proprietary squint. What sort of book? She wanted to know.

"Well, from the point of view of the sports fan."

Doreen smiled with relief and lowered her deflector shields. "Well," she said, "I don't care about *that*."

Sumo is the only sport in the world in which the foremost expert need not know, or care, about what happens when the athletes are actually in action. Imagine a book about the World Cup in which the road to the championship is a mere backdrop for discussions — in much finer detail — of Ronaldo's top ten iTunes, or Ronaldinho's orthodontia.

But in sumo circles, this is the norm. Much of the interest, among foreigners, dwells on a tiny, weird backstage domain, a cloister, "the sumo world," in which its participants circulate — bedtimes, hairdos, hobbies, medical history, marital aids...

I have begun to suspect that this unnatural focus on background — rather than competition — plays a major role in the odd, grotesque image of sumo outside Japan. To me, before I began to see sumo as a sport, and not such a weird sport at that, it struck me as half Oriental conundrum, half disgusting joke. This tends to be a pretty common perception among *gaijin*.

But wait! This sense of mild distaste isn't just a *gaijin* bias. As democratic citizens, the Japanese people are not obligated, as they might have been under Tokugawa or Tojo, to quietly revere sumo as a Shinto sacrament. Long before they reach adulthood, today's sophisticated Japanese apply entirely private and arbitrary (read: "normal") criteria to decide whether they really enjoy watching fat men grab each other's love handles and do the lambada.

Even in Japan, sumo — like pickled plums, noodle-slurping and urinating in public (all popular facets of Japanese culture) — is an acquired taste. Among most Japanese, a fondness for sumo grows slowly in the reluctant psyche — which explains why the average age of a sumo crowd at the Ryogoku Kokugikan in Tokyo (sumo's Madison Square Garden) is nearer fifty years than twenty.

Reiko Komiya, a housewife of my acquaintance and a woman of vehement opinion, typifies sumo's acceptance problem among even the natives. When she was a young girl in Niigata, there was no television. Sumo wrestlers were disembodied radio heroes. Reiko's favorite was Akinoumi, archrival to the immortal Futabayama.

For years, she crouched beside the crystal set and followed the trials of Akinoumi like Ralphie Parker enthralled by Little Orphan Annie. And then, a miracle! Her parents took Reiko, just then becoming a teenager, to Tokyo to see her sumo idols in the flesh. But...

Ew, gross! Too *much* flesh. "I was so disappointed," she said, her face still — almost 50 years later — reflecting that moment of deflation. "They were so fa-a-at." Reiko, since, has recovered her affection, but only after a long interval of apostasy.

Western observers, bred in cultures where "you can never be too rich or too thin," share Reiko's childhood antipathy to blubber. We complicate this with the suspicion that there is something vaguely obscene in the brief glimpses of sumo that seep now and then through the chrysanthemum curtain. Phidias and D.H. Lawrence both gave us graphic depictions of young men entwined in combat, but ah, these striplings were lissom, chaste, and handsome — unsullied (except in the prurient mind) by even the vaguest intimation of, well...

Hush, it is unspoken. We are forbidden to suggest it, lest we invite the wrath of sumo's purists. But it lurks, anyway, in the backs of our minds. Naked men. With breasts. Jiggling. Embracing. Touching each other...

Remember. For most of us aging foreigners, what was the first sumo we ever saw? Five seconds once a year on ESPN2, right? It seemed like the camera angle was always the same. You're sitting there on the couch beside your impressionable five-year-old daughter and suddenly you're both looking up at the world's biggest ass, its coloring a whiter shade of pale, with these wormy bands of cellulite and little pimply flecks. And the only consolation is that the worst part — the middle — is (barely) covered with... Jesus, what is that? A diaper?

And then this immense *tuchis* — you remember? — to which is attached Jabba the Hutt, flings itself forward into a similar mutant. Here's where you notice that they both have these short pudgy arms, and they start to grope at each other, like manatees in heat...

And then — whew! — ESPN's five seconds of sumo is up. It ends abruptly, probably because it's unfit for family viewing. God, what if they ripped off each other's diapers?

Well, those are vivid memories — and hard to erase. But there's more to sumo (thank God) than this weird vision of two gay lumberjacks undressing each other in a sandbox. That, after all, is a fleeting misperception. So forget it. Try to picture sumo, instead, as fun — first of all because it conveys such simplicity and innocence.

Fundamentally, it's kid stuff.

I can't think of a sport more childish than sumo. When you're a sumo wrestler, you get to live in a clubhouse where no girls are allowed. You're encouraged to eat all you want and have "thirds" on dessert. You nap all afternoon, and drink beer all night. When you play, you get to take off all your clothes and roll in the dirt. And a whole match hardly ever takes more than 10 seconds; so you're never late for dinner. You never have games in the rain, the snow, or the hot sun. You never have to think about what's good for the "team," and as long as you keep getting bigger and fatter, you don't even have to pay attention to the coach.

Sumo is the only sport in the world that allows you to be a superstar and a snackhound at the same time — which, of course, creates a magical affinity between the jock on the TV screen and the slob sitting in front of it. Y'see? Sumo isn't just fun. It's hog heaven!

"Sure," you say, "but if only they weren't so fa-a-at..."

Why do people keep coming back to contemplate those vast flanks of adipose tissue — staring, judging? Well, because fat is sumo's two-headed nickel, its draw and its flaw. Fat is to sumo as chin music is to baseball... as the offsides rule to soccer... as race is to basketball... as the specter of Darryl Stingley and Jack Tatum to pro football... as Death itself to boxing. First, you learn to live with it. Later, but only with a conscious effort, you come oddly to appreciate it.

Try to get this into your head. This isn't your aerobics class. This is Japan, where the fat and the sylphlike, the whale and the butterfly, Rosie O'Donnell and Paris Hilton, share the same aesthetic universe and coexist in perfect harmony. The Japanese see little dissonance in aesthetic paradox, which is why a sumo wrestler usually marries a woman no larger than his right thigh.

Fortunately, there are three ways to overcome the irrational anti-fat (and secretly homophobic) bias that prevents the full, idiotic enjoyment of sumo. These are as follows:

1) THINK Japanese. Unlike Westerners, Japanese tend not to fret if a little boy goes through his formative years eating like a septic tank and swelling up like a corn-fed shoat. Remember that this is an island nation whose Depression started two years early, in 1927, and lapped right over into more than ten years of wartime austerity, which was followed by a post-war famine that consumed another decade. These people starved for 30 years.

   So, let's hear it for fat boys, the showpieces of the Japanese economic miracle. "Things are looking up, Hiroshi! There goes another kid who looks like the Michelin man."

2) BECOME Japanese. The sumo world, according to popular legend, is a closed world, unchanged for centuries. Its intricacies, unfathomable to the outsider, are a lens to peer into the mystery that is Japan. But to behold Japan through this pinhole, you must learn Japanese and then master the special patois of sumo, throw yourself into research and memorize lists of the great wrestlers and champions of the past. Introduce yourself to *oyakata* (stable masters) and attend practices. Meet the wrestlers, ingratiate yourself with the Sumo Association, wangle yourself a free pass to all the *basho* (tournaments), immerse yourself in the private lives, the gossip, the scandals, the daily routine, the emotional burdens, and the physical discomforts of the sumo wrestlers.

This, of course, is more exertion than most employed people have time for, and it poses the danger
that you'll become more Japanese than the Japanese —
thus rendering yourself offensive to everyone, regardless of race, color, or national origin.

Nevertheless, there is a surprisingly large group of
foreigners in Japan (known, in English as sumo nerds
and, in derisive Japanese, as *otaku*) who have taken
this vicarious route to enlightenment.

3) OSMOSIS, or casual exposure, is a more felicitous way
to learn sumo's delights. This method's most endearing feature is that it doesn't require you to be Japanese
or to go native. Any *gaijin* who spends more than a
few weeks in Japan inevitably notices little flashes of
sumo popping up in daily life. In the morning on the
subway, he sees sumo photos in sports tabloids and
weekly magazines. He'll probably notice *The Japan
Times'* English coverage of each *basho*. TV provides
sumo highlights on the news. From time to time, a few
sumo nerds get together to publish a magazine for a
while, until it perishes either from insolvency, illiteracy,
or staff dissension. While I was living in Japan, the late
Sumo World was sumo-nerd Scripture.

And then, there are the *rikishi* (wrestlers) themselves. You
encounter them on the street. They're not like Western athletes, who either avoid public contact or go out only in dis-
guise. Sumo wrestlers are obvious. Decked out in their official
garb of bathrobe and shower thongs, they roam the streets of
Tokyo like ambulatory roadblocks, foraging in the daytime
for *chankonabe* (their favorite food) and at night for nookie
(their favorite pastime).

By far the average person's most likely exposure to sumo is NHK-TV. The *basho* are held six times a year (in all the odd-numbered months), and the national television network broadcasts not only every one, but the whole thing, from wire to wire, for 15 days, including weekends — with no commercial interruptions. Faced with this year-round sumo immersion on Japan's most important TV source, the average channel-hopper usually ends up seeing quite a bit of sumo whether he had planned to or not. And he notices gradually that he is becoming inured to those physical anomalies of the sumo wrestler that once seemed so repellent.

In these repeated glimpses, unsightly fat becomes mere physical bulk, the necessary armor of battle between giants. At the same time, the *rikishi,* who seem at first to be indistinguishable larger-than-life Japanese archetypes, evolve into smaller, more likeable creatures: individuals, odd characters, regular guys? Heroes, even. As this happens, curiosity plants its seed, and the passion — especially among those previously addicted aficionados of the ring, the mat, the gridiron or the rink — grows!

If you, too, have ever felt this tingle of sumo curiosity, then this book is for you.

But heed this warning. If you regard sumo not as a sport — to watch and to cheer, to handicap and bet on, to shout for your favorites, and hiss your personal villains — then perhaps you'd be happier with a do-it-yourself rock gardening manual. In any case, skip this book. There are many volumes that perpetuate the stuffy image of sumo preferred by its traditionalists (who dominate the Sumo Association). In this book, I have intentionally violated the conventional approaches to sumo that seem especially cherished by the confraternity of *gaijin* groupies.

Sumo, for example, began as a form of gladiatorial entertainment to amuse the captive royal court in Kyoto, and assumed a measure of seriousness by mimicking Shinto religious ritual. Essentially, it began its history as more spectacle than sport — no more significant than its present-day parallels — ice dancing, pro wrestling, synchronized swimming, soap-box derby, Cirque du Soleil, et cetera. Sumo, however, had developed a measure of competitive regularity by the mid-1920's, before which Sumo Association records tend to be spotty. As tournaments entered the national calendar, *rikishi* evolved into genuine athletes whose foremost interest was not to appear picturesque, awesome, or roly-poly, but to win — and by their efforts thus to (a) make a living and (b) entertain the fans. Alas, even today, sumo retains a host of traditions, sanctions and unwritten rules that hinder the athlete's progress. But these bureaucratic intrusions prevail despite — not because of — the wrestlers' commitment to their job.

Among all the injustices imposed on sumo, the worst, I think, is to regard it merely as a cultural pageant. For a fan, this presumption is plainly impractical. I guess it might be possible to delight in ritual throughout one whole day of sumo. Maybe as long as 36 hours. But if, after watching 20 or more bouts, you haven't grasped the intense drama of each confrontation, or discovered the special, personal style of even one *rikishi,* you will soon weary of culture and go back to your Stephanie Plum.

I've written this book for fans, or folks who want to be fans. The game's the thing; it's the joy of sumo. All the showbiz and cultural trappings — whether they're pretty, or strange, or funny, or just plain tedious — fade into the background once two *rikishi* face each other across the ring.

Like just about every other good spectator sport, sumo is fun because you can ignore the buildup, the publicity, the post-mortem analyses and the prejudices of your fellow fans, and just watch. The more you watch, the more you know and the less you need to depend on self-appointed experts (like me) to tell you whether we're having fun yet.

Herein, then, is freedom from expert opinion! I will guide the casual but astute fan through the stages of sumophilia. We will go from ignorance to obsession, but we'll stick mainly to those aspects of sumo that emerge inevitably from seeing it on TV — or, if you must, Movietone News.

If this approach seems personal, it is. This is how I learned sumo, by myself in the privacy of my own rabbit hutch, and I think it's the best way.

CHAPTER 1

THE PIT

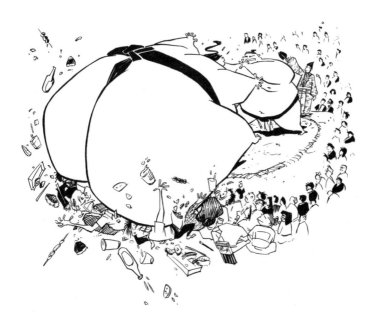

The typical sumo novice gets a first taste of the sport in one of two ways. Mine came at home, where I spend my days writing. I turned to NHK's sumo broadcasts as respite from work and from the vast wasteland of Japanese daytime TV. I wasn't eager to watch fat guys with greasy hairdos mauling each other in public, but after six hours of staring at a computer screen, even sumo is welcome relief.

Such chance encounters on the boob tube have spawned a legion of *gaijin* (foreign) sumophiles and at least one Japanese fan: my wife Junko, who, before my influence, ranked sumo on her list of "Favorite Things" just above a Novocain injection into the roof of her mouth. However, I'm afraid more people discover sumo the other way, which is when some culture vulture hauls you down to the Ryogoku Kokugikan (go ahead, try to say that three times fast!) to see the waltzing whales in the flesh. This is not the ideal first encounter with sumo, although I do recommend periodic visits to the Kokugikan, if you can get there. There's nothing like physical contact with the smell, feel, flavor and noise of sumo. If Ryogoku, however, is your first full blast of sumo (without a session or two of TV orientation), you're in danger of being grossed out — as Reiko Komiya was — or suffering sensory overload.

At the arena, at first blush, the ring is not the thing. Look around. If you bought the affordable seats in the upper deck, you have a great vantage point to drink in the spectacle spread out before you. The crowd arrives gradually, wanders and visits, and chatters endlessly. Here is the aspect of sumo that television can't convey. A day at the sumo matches is Japan's Chautauqua. It's town meeting time. It's the parish pancake breakfast.

Ushers, dressed in ancient costumes whose sleeves drape almost to the floor, shuffle constantly, guiding spectators, serving beverages and piles of food to the fans in the high-priced box seats that circle the sandbox (*dohyo*, actually). Food is incessant at the sumo matches. And expensive.

Traditionally (every explanation in sumo begins with the word, "traditionally"), the box seats are "owned," managed and doled out by teahouses. In order for me to occupy a box seat for one day's sumo, for example, my wife made a connection with a fellow worker from Shitamachi (the old, picturesque part of Tokyo). Her neighbor was a second- or third-generation member of the "support group" for the Dewanoumi *sumobeya* (sumo stable), which is, of course, affiliated with a certain Tokyo teahouse.

(If you're not keeping up with all this, don't worry. Sumo, like many things Japanese, is swollen with arcana that transfix *gaijin* and paralyze them with awestruck absorption. The Japanese, who prefer to use sumo for day-to-day amusement, tend to bypass such bullshit and go straight to the good stuff.)

For a one *tatami*-mat box, which holds four Japanese-size people, the price is in the range of $1,000. For that, you are treated to enough food to keep you bloated for the next 48 hours, and as much beer, *sake* or whiskey as you can fit into the box among your legs, bags, coats, umbrellas and gifts.

Gifts? If this is Japan, there must be *omiyage!* To show their gratitude for your purchase of the tickets, the teahouse unloads into your laps four shopping bags, stuffed with sumo souvenirs — most of it food and most of it yummy (if you only had an appetite left!). These gifts compete for space with you, your personal effects, and the growing accumulation of empties, used *yakitori* sticks, half-consumed *obento* (box lunches) and other flotsam. Just about the time you begin to feel your first pangs of claustrophobia, oops! Hey! It's over — perfectly timed! The last match arrives at the same moment, it seems, when you couldn't endure — for even ten more minutes — sitting there, numb-legged, holding yourself erect and supporting the slumped form of the old man in the next box who has polished off his tenth bottle of Asahi Super Dry and fallen noisily asleep on your shoulder.

If the idea of strangers falling asleep on your shoulder bothers you, you shouldn't be in Japan. But, even if you didn't manage a box seat and didn't collect three or four cubic meters of *omiyage* and the person next to you stays awake, there's still plenty of atmosphere at the Kokugikan to distract you from the actual sumo.

Let's return to the cheaper seats in the upper deck. Lean over the railing and scan. The box seats and "sand seats" close to the *dohyo* are a mosaic of aging Japanese. Very few children.

You might spot (the NHK cameramen always do) a few young women, who've come as guests of an aunt or uncle. There are always several uncomfortable, squished-looking *gaijin* businessmen in rumpled suits. But mostly, this is an *obaa-san/ojii-san* (Grandma and Gramps) occasion. The *obaa-san* tend to be overdressed in their brightest frocks and beaded sweaters. The *ojii-san* are slightly underdressed in baggy pants, tweed coats and knit shirts; they look like horseplayers hanging around the paddock (many of them, on other days, are).

Listen to the constant buzz, the bursts of ladies' laughter and the bark of masculine grunting (Japanese men speak in the manliest male argot this side of Texas), and you might — if you shut your eyes — imagine that you've come upon an enormous combined Tupperware Party and Lions Club convention. Many of these people come for the sumo, but many don't know sumo nearly as well as the TV fans watching at home. Live sumo is a once-a-year social occasion, a pretext for friends and relatives to gather at one place, eat, drink, and jabber. In Tokyo, a city of incessant and almost painful tension, the Ryogoku Kokugikan is one of the few truly leisurely scenes you'll ever witness. The old man who falls asleep halfway through the wrestling or turns to his companion to say, "When does Musashimaru (who retired in 2003) wrestle?" is an integral part of the experience in Ryogoku — where the January, May, and September *basho* occur — or in Osaka in March, Nagoya in July, Fukuoka in November.

Sumo is a 15-day picnic six times a year, and the wrestlers just happen to be part of it — for many, an insignificant part.

After you've drunk in all this atmosphere, and it doesn't take long, you haven't really missed much of the action. Down there. On the *dohyo*. Way down there. (Opera glasses are a popular accessory at the sumo matches.) As you peer down at that small, brightly lit mound of dried mud and sand, you should feel a tingle of recognition — I mean, if you (like me) are really a fan, and not just a voyeur sopping up one more facet of Oriental mystery.

A word should pop into your mind, a word that hearkens back to high school sports. You recognize this arena for what it is. This is a pit!

"Death Valley"

In modern sports, certainly at the professional level, pits have become almost extinct. Certain venues, like "Death Valley" in Clemson, South Carolina, or Soldiers Field in Chicago, or Cameron Indoor Stadium at Duke University, or "The Pit" itself, the old basketball court at the University of New Mexico, sometimes earn the label, but they are only a mild facsimile. A real pit is where the only dividing line between fans and players is a wall of flesh and a thin veneer of self-restraint. A pit is a place where fans breathe on the players and the players spray sweat onto the throng. A pit is where fans and players are so close that they stand knee-deep in the same pool of emotion and feed each other with anger, fear, outrage, and exultation. A pit smells, feels, looks, and roars like a figment of Dante's imagination.

Ostensibly, the Ryogoku Kokugikan presents no such infernal terrors. Everybody loves the sumo wrestlers. But in shape and atmosphere, this is a pit. No other major sports arena in the world seats its fans quite so close to the brink of the playing field. A look down above the *dohyo* is a wondrous sight. The sand of the *dohyo* dazzles beneath the TV lights. The ring, or *tawara,* is a circle (made of rice bales) inside a square. The edge of the square drops off precipitously to a narrow aisle — and beyond that, in all directions, you got people. Every day, sumo wrestlers fly off the *dohyo* — 300, 400, 500 pounds of hurtling blubber — into the laps of the fans.

And how do the fans react? They laugh, they hoot! They slap the careening monsters on the shoulders and mop the sweat from their clothes. Sumo has no dividing line. Wrestlers coming and going shoulder their way through spectators who clog the aisles to pat their backs and thrill in their proximity. Sumo is a pit sport, and this place, the Ryogoku Kokugikan, is the ultimate, perfectly symmetrical, klieg-lit, high-tech, air-conditioned Pit. If there is a better sporting palace, more ideally suited for the texture and emotion of its sport, it isn't on this planet.

Rhythm and Recognition

Once you've developed a sense of this place and let it infect you, then, eventually, you notice the sumo itself. The essence of watching sumo, properly, requires that you slip into its rhythm. A day's sumo moves to its own beat, and you feel the beat best only when you're at the Pit.

Second best (and very close), is the NHK live broadcast every day, which follows the action from start to finish, saturates the viewer with instant replay and never breaks the mood with beer commercials.

For those whose jobs do not allow them a two-week vacation six times a year to follow the *basho*, there are highlights on the late news, which I avoid. All you see is the main matches of the day, none of the Class A, and B, and C matches. None of the circling and pawing and scowling. Just the clash, the struggle and the fall. It's like watching "Baseball Tonight" on ESPN. All those homers, but not a single hit-and-run — that ain't baseball, Mel!

Better you should record the live broadcast on your DVR and play it back after supper and *furo*, ideally with your feet under the *kotatsu* and — near at hand — a six-pack and a nice bag of dried squid.

Sumo is a stalking dance, and the stalking begins early in the day, with a long series of bouts among lower level — *jonokuchi, jonidan, sandanme* and *makushita* — wrestlers, the kids in dull brown belts. These warm-up matches are rush-ed. They last little longer than a highlight clip. And the ritual chest-thumping that characterizes sumo is forbidden among the scrubs. But they are part of the beat. The stalking dance whispers its rhythm first in the morning hours, every day of each *basho*.

As the day's wrestling progresses upward in rank, the matches lengthen, the dance slows. And the audience feels the deepening gravity of the drama on the *dohyo*. There are two upper divisions in sumo, *makuuchi* (the top) and *juryo*. In soccer, the equivalent would be first and second division; in baseball, the Majors and Triple-A. Unlike baseball, though, the Majors in sumo divide up into further permutations. The official upper-division sumo ranks, starting from the pinnacle and proceeding downward, are: *yokozuna, ozeki, sekiwake, komusubi,* and *maegashira*.

The gangs of *makuuchi* and *juryo* wrestlers, respectively, start their matches with a parade. Before they fight, they get to throw salt and drink holy water and spit. The matches slow down. The endless buzz of socializing fades momen-tarily when each clash finally erupts. The rhythm slows as the matches become more important. Tension builds, every seat in the arena finally fills, and the Pit falls dead silent when the monsters collide.

For those of you watching at home, working or reading or munching, there are sudden moments of suspension. "Wait. *Jikan desu*! (Time's up!)"

Without all the strutting and dawdling, glowering and pos-ing, the extraordinary drama of sumo would boil down to fat men with dirty feet trying to push each other's noses into their brains. No other sport so effectively, so seductively — in the midst of its own delivery — glorifies itself. No other sport has sumo's melodramatic contrast of stasis and explosion. Base-ball, another game of waiting, staring and posing, comes closest, perhaps, but never — like sumo — guarantees, even once, a desperate, decisive climax more than 30 times every day.

Foreplay, if you will, and orgasm.

Even to the newcomer, the atmosphere — mounting drama surrounded by a Golden Agers picnic — is the first, obvious charm of the sport. It can seduce you into coming back or, more economically, tuning in again. And again.

By and by, a deeper grip takes hold. As you sit there, faithfully feeding on the day's action in the sandbox, some of those formless dumplings become vaguely familiar. You notice shapes, hairlines, habits, tics. Tits. Asses. In all that pawing and groping, especially if you've been a fan of some sport sometime in your life, you begin to see patterns. And it occurs to you.

"Wait a minute. Looka that! These guys are making moves! These tubs have style!" Well, some of them do. Toyonoumi, in all his career, never had a clue.

There! You see what happens? You start to learn their names!

But I get ahead of myself. Nobody catches names right away. The first day of sumo, either at the Pit or on the tube, is a blur. But if you were lucky that day, you were intrigued. You got used to the fat and decided that all these guys were not homosexual showoffs (And if so, what the hell? So was Rock Hudson). You enjoyed (or so you say) the rituals. You felt the beat, noticed the drama. You caught the first symptoms.

You might even be so intrigued after one day — or two — that you decide to study up. There are plenty of sumo guides out there — both on paper and online. They tend toward a numbing sameness but, nevertheless, they're eventually necessary. The one universal feature of all the guides is how much of their information — slit, gutted and spread out in gory detail — is superfluous and pedantic. And boring. Which is why you should take my advice and don't read the guide before you catch the fever. Without passion, all sports lore is gibberish.

The game is the thing. Tune in. As you watch every afternoon on NHK (or, in the U.S., TV Japan), you pretty soon find yourself studying the daily listings on *The Japan Times* sports pages, or on the Sumo Association's not-bad website (http://www.sumo.or.jp/eng). You try to remember their names.

OK, let's see... KotoinazumaKitakachidokiKushimaumiKoboyamaKonishikiKotonishikiKasugafujiKyokuDOzanKyo-kuGOzan... Kee-rist!

It doesn't really work. But that's OK, because you start to recognize them in other ways. Little things pop up and give personality to the names (like Allen Iverson's countless tattoos, or Brett Favre carrying his receiver off the field after a touchdown). You notice differences. Look. This one's sort of cute. That one's unbelievably ugly. This one always wears a baby blue diaper. This one's losing his hair. Is that one's name really Yo Mama? And that one...

"God, who *is* that one? He's sweating like a pig!"

CHAPTER 2

BIG AL, MAD DOG, TOKYO ROSE
and the Silver Spoons

Forget the sweaty one for a minute. He's unique, he's cute, and he's funny. But he's a putz. He isn't gonna do it for you.

Thing is... you gotta connect.

In your first day of watching sumo — especially if you're live and on-the-scene — it's likely you will note almost nothing of the competitors themselves, especially if you're too far from the *dohyo* to notice how sweaty the sweaty one is. However, although the whole scene passes you by in a sort of pinkish haze, you need to awaken to at least one extraordinary wrestler. One hulk must catch your eye and fire your imagination.

Person-to-person. It's how you connect.

The one who did it for me was the one who, I contend, was the greatest of them all: Chiyonofuji. Chiyo or "the Wolf" as the press liked to call him, retired in May of 1991. He was a wrestler who bore the unmistakable mark of immortality, like Joe Louis or Michael Jordan. He quietly forced the entire sumo galaxy to revolve around him. Other wrestlers tried, for a while, to emulate his regimen, physique and style, but they were pale imitations. When I began to succumb to the pleasures of sumo back in 1987 there was no one even close to Chiyonofuji.

For one thing, he looked different. He had, for instance, no boobs — just a smooth, granite slab of pectoral muscle. No jellied blankets of suet rippled beneath his skin. His belly, a small hard bulge above his belt, did not bounce like a cantaloupe in a nylon bag. His arms were not the elbowless sausages with baby-fists that seem obligatory among sumo wrestlers. His arms, really, were the striking feature of Chiyonofuji's aspect. They reminded me of the coal miners with whom I once worked, round-shouldered mountain men whose arms were a paradox of mass and dexterity. Such arms are not huge and distended like those on the denizens of Gold's Gym. But they are heavy — too heavy, certainly, to lift with a normal human shoulder — with bulges at forearm and bicep that never seem to relax, as though they'd been artfully packed with riverbed stones. Yet, such arms — coal-miner, Chiyonofuji arms — swing and flex with a feathery lightness. Chiyonofuji carried truncheons, but moved them like wings.

Chiyo, even without the usual indulgence one grants to the swollen face of the large athlete, was handsome. Not matinee-idol beautiful, but handsome. He affected none of the theatricality of lesser wrestlers; he was almost trance-like in his demeanor, from the moment he entered the arena and bowed to the ring judges to the instant of his victory when — suddenly — he betrayed himself as perhaps sumo's most expressive, emotional competitor.

One noticed Chiyonofuji, irresistibly, because in his face, his body, his skill, one could see the art and discipline of sumo. From the great artists of the sport, the fan begins to measure his own interest and define his attachment to sumo. He connects.

That connection happens only to sports fans. If it doesn't happen, you never become a sports fan, and you don't understand why some people do. Even among fans, there are vast gulfs of incomprehension, because one human heart has only enough room for a few such passions. The sports with which you don't connect become, at best, alien pastimes. At worst, they are the enemy of sport itself, squandering great athletes, precious natural resources, and valuable air time.

I don't think anyone is immune from the connection, or from its resulting loyalties. But I think you're more susceptible to it if you're a child or, at least, childish. I was both when I made my first real connection — to pro football: specifically the Green Bay Packers. Among the great Green Bay players of that halcyon time, each fan had his own gladiator, his private Packer, a gridiron version of Chiyonofuji who transcended the confusion on the TV screen. Mine?

As I recall, he would seize the ball as a mean little kid might snatch candy from his baby brother, and then he'd plunge into a Gordian tangle of bodies. Gone. Finished. But then — somehow — in a churning, clawing, slobbering frenzy, he would burst out on the other side, dragging people, shrugging them off, and then looking up, looking around. For what?

More people to run into! Instead of running for the open field, he would charge into crowds, assault them, knock them down and step on their heads. He was the quintessential full-back: Jim Taylor. If not Taylor, or Paul Hornung the Platonic halfback, or Ray Nitschke, the archetypal linebacker — or even football! — then Ruth, Williams and Koufax in baseball. Willie Mays! Or Tilden, Sampras, Navratilova in tennis. Tiger Woods in golf. Pele, Bobby Orr, Bill Russell. Some players are so good that you feel it, even if you've never seen the sport before. They seduce you with awe and hold you with compassion. You want them always to be just that great and never grow old. Until you care, vicariously and irrationally, about what happens to the players, there's no point in knowing names, discussing technique, or tracing bloodlines.

The joy of sumo is that, once you have the connection, you're looking at men in jockstraps — much easier to tell apart than whole teams of guys with helmets, numbers, identical uniforms, and Kevlar elbow pads. Each sumo combatant gets a solo shot, every day, to simulate the savagery of the fullback, the grace of the halfback, or the surgical violence of the free safety. This literally naked spotlight helps the fan to learn each wrestler's body, his oddities, tendencies, coach, name — all that useless stuff — surprisingly fast.

Nomenclature: Proper and Improper

OK, let's say you've spotted your private hero and made that connection. What's next?

Well, you cannot hold your head up, as a real fan, if you only recognize one or two favorite studs. You're committed now, and you have to learn them all. You need names. As Butch once said to Sundance, "Who are those guys?"

First, you have to know what to call them, as a group. If you wanna be a serious, know-it-all fan (and who doesn't?) you should probably stop calling them "sumo wrestlers," which is redundant because "sumo" is "wrestling." The most correct term is probably *rikishi* ("big strong bastard"), but lots of experts prefer *sumotori* — which I like, too, because if you bungle the translation badly enough, it comes out as "street fighter" — which nicely denotes the proletarian ambience of sumo. Sumo nerds will also confuse you with the term *sekitori*, which means, simply, a *rikishi* in one of the upper two divisions of sumo (*makuuchi* and *juryo*, remember?).

Actually, Junko and I sometimes just lapse into calling the guys "sumo" (plural: "sumos"), which is a little like calling Alex Ovechkin a hockey puck. But heck, if the shoe fits...

When it's all in the family, on your own TV, you can call a sumo wrestler anything you want (including "sumo wrestler"). If "lardass" strikes your fancy — as in, "Hey, who's that lardass wrestling Hakuho?" — Why not? Especially if you end up cheering for Lardass in his next match. There's something mystical in the act of name-giving, even when you do it in derision. Once you've given this stranger your own private ID tag, you start to care. Somehow, his fate is in your hands.

This is how I came to know, and love, an old warhorse of the *dohyo* named Ozutsu. If ever there were an archetypal fat homely *rikishi*, it was old Ozutsu — who battled tooth-and-nail with every fellow second-rate wrestler, but went down irritably in flames when he faced one of the stars. Ozutsu's dubious distinction was that a disproportionate share of the fat in his body had migrated to his face, puffing it up like a terminal case of mumps and squeezing his lips into a permanent, pudgy, protuberant "O." He looked like a goldfish in a Warner cartoon, so — irresistibly — we began to call him "The Goldfish."

Once we had saddled Ozutsu with that degrading label, we began to watch his matches more closely — and more affectionately. We began to notice his occasional moments of exceptional cunning, and the passion with which he fought, even in a hopeless mismatch.

I didn't know it at the time, but Ozutsu's chosen name is also evocative. "Ozutsu" translates as "Enormous Cannon," or simply, "The Big Gun." Either the Goldfish himself, or his *oyakata* (coach) hung this one on him, for good karma, in 1978, after he'd wrestled — without much distinction — for seven years under another name. Change your name and change your luck! This is standard procedure. The naming of *rikishi*, like T.S. Eliot's naming of cats, is a blend of gravity and comedy, tradition and whimsy. And, like Eliot's cats, everybody has (at least) three names.

Every *rikishi* enters the lists with his family name, provided by Mom and Dad. Eventually, he consults with his *oyakata*, perhaps peruses the honor roll of his *sumobeya* for inspiration from a heroic forebear, perhaps seizes upon some mystic force in the ecology of his home prefecture, to devise his fighting name.

And then, finally, on retirement, for a whole fresh dose of good karma, the *rikishi* adopts a new name — creating confusion that usually lingers for the rest of his life, because people insist on remembering him by his *nom de guerre*. This requires the addition of an obligatory middle name: "Formerly," as in "Futagoyama Formerly Wakanohana," and "Azumazeki Formerly Takamiyama."

Now, back to Ozutsu, who added a fourth name to increase the confusion. In '78, he decided that his first fighting name, "Daishin," was sending out bad vibes. So, presto-chango, he became Ozutsu. To offer another example, in August, 1990, Takanohama (whom we preferred to call "Frankenstein") changed his name to Toyonoumi. We suspected that this happened because people were getting him mixed up with his coach, Fujishima Formerly Takanohana. We also suspect that the name change was specified by Coach Fujishima/Takanohana himself, because he was embarrassed by a too-close association with Frankenstein — who was not really somebody you want to be mistaken for.

Ideally, this fighting-name hocus-pocus provides the *rikishi* with a talisman that sends him soaring into the ring surrounded by the winged blessings of a hundred friendly spirits. Many such fighting names, translated, summon forceful imagery. "Hokutoumi," one of sumo's all-time winners, means — appropriately — "Northern Victory Sea." "Tamawashi" carried the mysterious name "Hawk Ball" — or "Ball Hawk?" Maybe he was a shortstop back at Ulan Bator Junior High. "Kirishima" means "Foggy Island." "Takekaze" translates as (apologies to Christopher Guest) "A Mighty Wind." "Goeido" means "Mighty Road," which prompted Junko and I to nickname him "Route 66." What mightier road, *ne*? And "Asashoryu," the Mongol assassin of the 2000's, comes out lyrically as "Blue Dragon in the Morning."

Others are weird. "Kotoinazuma" (or, as we used to call him, "Baby Huey") comes out as something like "Lightning Guitar." Maybe he was a Chuck Berry fan. We struggled to translate the name of another Mongol, "Tokitenku." Finally, Junko rendered it as "The Temporal Universe." Perhaps Tokitenku chose the name to intimidate his opponents. Subduing the temporal universe would seem a daunting task. And yet, Tokitenku lost lots of matches. And then there's "Itai," who wrestled through the '90's. If you go purely by sound without reading the Japanese characters (which makes Japanese a much funnier language anyway), "Itai" means "Ouch!" — probably the best name ever for a sumo wrestler.

Still other sumo-fighting names are better left untranslated because they sound, well, sissy. "Hananokuni" means "Land of Flowers." And "Toyozakura" comes out as "Oriental Cherry Blossom." Grrr!

For *gaijin* fans, however, and for many Japanese — who need to consult a dictionary to make sense of many sumo names — official *rikishi* nomenclature tends to be polysyllabic and forbidding. Consider, for example, the dilemma posed by trying to pronounce Takamisakari, a simple guy who needs a simpler moniker. We call him "Mad Dog."

"Simplify, simplify!" said Thoreau. Regardless of the sport, jocks are easier to remember, easier to love, even easier to forgive, when they have. simple lyrical labels. Mudcat Grant! Oil Can Boyd! Catfish Hunter! The Cooz! The Assassin! Dr. J! Dr. K! Earl the Pearl! Wilt the Stilt! Shoeless Joe! Cool Papa Bell! And all those Marvins: Marvelous Marvin Barnes, Marvin "The Hitman" Hagler, Marvin "The Human Eraser" Webster! And so on, sonorously.

That said, not every jock is nicknamable. On Steve Garvey or Brett Favre, Dirk Nowitzki or Greg Maddux, a pet name would hang unnaturally, like a dead-trout necktie on a Shiite mullah. But Duke Snider and Moose Skowron would've seemed alien if addressed by their Christian names (William and Edwin). There are others for whom the nickname alone is name enough: Boog, Goose, Whitey, Sweetness, Tiny, Big Daddy, Big Papi, Bad News, Too Tall, Tiger, Hondo, A-Rod, the Bambino, the Mad Stork, the Golden Bear…

The Sumo Association doesn't really encourage the public to invent frivolous pet names for *rikishi*, and Japanese sportswriters and sportscasters are careful to toe that line. Diz and PeeWee do not man the mikes in the sumo league. But all the better. For us compulsive hypocorists, the approval of officialdom is an unwelcome intrusion.

There are more than 60 *rikishi* in sumo's upper two divisions, and Junko and I usually deem fewer than 20 worthy of nicknames. *Rikishi* who deserve nicknames achieve them only as fast as they demonstrate a measure of walk, personality, talk, personality, style, personality…

Herewith, a sample of sixteen *rikishi*, ranging from the mid-1990's to about 2009, whom we came to love, beginning of course, with the sweaty one.

1) The sweaty one was Fujinoshin. The first time we saw him, he was wearing a light blue *mawashi* (belt) which was stained and soaked with perspiration. He probably could've wrung it out into a bucket and gotten enough fluid to float his bathtub ducky. What else to call him? With apologies to Horshack, Barbarino, and Juan Epstein: "The Sweathog!"

2) Ozutsu, for reasons already explained, was "The Goldfish."

3) Akebono, or Chad Rowan, was a tall Hawaiian *yoko-zuna* (grand champion) who grew — atop his thin legs — a spectacular rotundity, around which he wrapped, in his early career, a brilliant orange *mawashi*. We had no choice but to call him "The Great Pumpkin."

4) Ryogoku (not to be confused with the arena) was a middling *maegashira* almost as wide as he was tall, with the density of a wet sandbag. Moving him off the *dohyo* was like trying to shlep a week's worth of the family's waste out to the curb on Monday morning before the garbage truck rolled up. Of course, we called him "Trashcan."

5) Kotoinazuma will always be one of our favorites. We called him "Baby Huey" because he was (relatively) small and huggable, his *mawashi* used to be baby blue and he battled the bigger guys with an irresistible look of infantile determination.

6) In a short period of time in 1989-90, two brothers entered the *juryo* class—with enormous publicity — at a very tender age: Takahanada (then 17 years old) and his older brother Wakahanada (18). Herded along by the press-agentry of the Sumo Association, they achieved swift and immense popularity. They deserved it, of course, because they were very young and gifted, and — most important — their father, Takanohana (whose post-retirement name was Fujishima Oyakata), was a famous former *rikishi* with his own *sumobeya* (stable) and lots of status in the Sumo Association. From the very get-go, these privileged sons were beloved of the gods and programmed for a quick ascent to the pinnacle of sumo — which they attained with blinding speed but under new names, Wakanohana and Takanohana. We called them, simply, the "Silver Spoons." Wakahanada was "Big Spoon," Takahanada was "Little Spoon."

7) Tochinowaka was strong, easily distracted, belligerent, and reportedly a pretty nasty guy at home as well. Best of all, he had a face like a Mafia bodyguard. To fit the image, he needed the right nickname: "Big Al." This didn't make him any more lovable, but at least it wreathed him in a kind of dark glamour.

8) We saw Daishoyama smile once. It was adorable. From then on, to us, he was just "Dimples."

9) Mitoizumi was a special case. You either loved him or hated him. Another *rikishi* whose size far exceeded his ability, he performed nevertheless with an almost insufferable insouciance. He wore a garish *mawashi*,

slapped his own face before every match and, when performing a simple salt-strewing ritual just before the face-off, turned it into a grand production by throwing the entire contents of the saltbox at the ceiling. He smiled impishly whenever he won and limped self-piteously when he lost. Altogether, he was a ham actor and an adolescent show-off. His nickname came to us spontaneously, because he's the sort of character you react to, the minute you see him on TV. You say, "Who IS that asshole?" Hence, even though we came to love the guy, Mitoizumi will forever be "The Asshole."

10) Ryukozan, shortly after completing his first *makuuchi* basho, died at the age of 22, probably of being simply too fat for such a small body. He recalled Maupassant's words, "... Short, perfectly spherical, fat as dripping, with puffy fingers, dented at the joints like strings of sausages ..." More than any *rikishi* we had ever seen, Ryukozan possessed that perfect rotund egg-shape that so often depicts sumo wrestlers in cartoons. In honor of that, we named him "Humpty Dumpty," and in his honor, we retired that nickname. We will only apply it again to a *rikishi* who is as willing as was Ryukozan to risk his life for the sake of the perfect figure.

11) Among the qualities sumo traditionalists cherish in their athletes is an air of stoic dignity rendered in Japanese by the word *"hin,"* and translated into English as "class." The great post-millennium Mongolian *yokozuna*, Asashoryu, proved lacking in this virtue, at least according to most Japanese observers. This

widespread distaste with Asashoryu might have developed because of the fist he thrust toward the ceiling before every face-off. It might be because he often delivered one last extra blow to a defeated opponent. It might be just because he was a foreigner who walked right in and started whomping the bejesus out of the natives. In any case, Junko's judgment of him, useful as a nickname, was "Hinganai." In English: "Ain't got no class."

12) Asashoryu's nemesis, the only guy who could really stand up to him for many *basho*, was his fellow Mongol, Hakuho. Unfortunately, Hakuho totally lacks any distinguishing features or idiosyncrasies. In every *basho*, however, he was the only *rikishi* in a plain brown *mawashi*. We could have called him "Stag Movie," but we settled on "UPS."

As Hakuho's indicates, the use of *mawashi* color is a great mnemonic. For example, among *rikishi* who were active while I was re-writing this book, we called Asasekiryu "Scarlet Ohara" because his was the reddest belt in the history of sumo. We called Yoshikaze "Tokyo Rose" for the lovely rose shade of his *mawashi*, and Kisenosato became "The Eagle" because the maroon of his belt matches the uniforms of Boston College's fightin' Eagles.

13) Iwakiyama, one of sumo's countless journeymen, suffered the early onset of male-pattern baldness, an affliction made conspicuous by sumo's emphasis on big, shiny hair. That complicated gingko-leaf topknot, called a *chonmage*, is hard to put together if your hairline keeps creeping back into your collar

(if you had a collar) — as it did to Iwakiyama. Since his name includes the syllable, "-yama," meaning "mountain," we came to recognize him, as soon as he appeared on TV, as "Mount Baldy."

14) Speaking of mountains, the most mountainous *rikishi* of recent times was a young goliath named Yama-motoyama, which means "The Mountain Under the Mountain." The only appropriate nickname for this kid, who is virtually the size of two mountains (plus he had these really big tits!), had to be "Twin Peaks."

15) Every sumo era needs an "Asshole," a twitchy scenery-chewer who goes bananas over every match. Mitoizumi's successor in this role was a fireplug from Aomori named Takamisakari. Just before facing his foe, "Mad Dog" whacks himself five times about the head and chest, clenches his entire (cute, little) body into a throbbing, florid knot, takes so many deep breaths that he almost keels over, then grabs the traditional handful of salt, turns and throws the salt so hard into the *dohyo* that he leaves a divot. Then he goes out and (usually) gets his ass kicked by someone bigger and younger. He goes away wincing, muttering, shaking his head and stomping his feet in hydropho-bic dejection. When Mad Dog wins, of course, his rabies goes away and he's just a big puppy.

16) The arrival of white guys into the sumo world has opened fresh possibilities in nicknames. Unlike Asian or even Polynesian *rikishi*, the Eastern Europeans who matriculated into the *makuuchi* division in the early 2000's evoke, in the Western mind, Western parallels.

For example, looking at the greasy slick-backed hair and bulging pallor of Bulgarian *rikishi* Kotooshu, I suddenly felt myself drifting back in time to Las Vegas in the 70's. Here, indeed, was the second coming — sans jumpsuit — of "Fat Elvis." Baruto, a tall, fair, austere Estonian whose real name is Hoovelson, is the spitting image of actor/politician "Fred Thompson." And for obvious reasons of similarity, we refer to a Georgian *rikishi* named Kokkai as "Ralph Kramden."

Today, I can impress friends and bore total strangers at parties by rattling off the sanctioned names of virtually every *rikishi* in the upper two divisions of sumo, and attach the names to a face, a bellybutton, a set of mannerisms, a rank, even a *sumobeya* — all because, at the beginning, I taught myself these identities through the shorthand of nicknaming.

By the time you read this book, some of the *rikishi* listed here might have retired, been demoted or — like Humpty Dumpty — died. This is good, because instead of accepting my dumb nicknames you'll be making up your own according to your own impulses. The key is not the names themselves, but the nicknaming habit, which is as old as sport itself. It tends to concentrate your mind. It helps you to examine each player as a distinct personality and watch him — as he goes through his stalking dance — for the word, the term, the description that is his very essence, his message to mankind...

His ineffable effable
Effanineffable
Deep and inscrutable singular Name.[1]

---

1 Eliot, T.S., *Old Possum's Book of Practical Cats*, Harcourt, Brace & World, New York, 1967

CHAPTER 3

THE "GROUPING URGE"
Blubberbutts and
Thoroughbreds

OK, sports fans, now you're up to the point where you're remembering the jocks, and bandying around pet names as though you suck down pints of Yebisu with these guys every night at Kenji's Bar & Grill. The next stage, the inevitable drive, is to "study" them, *rikishi* by *rikishi*. It's what fans do.

Sumo bubblegum cards would be the ideal visual aid, but the Sumo Association would never approve. (See Chapter 13.)

By now, you've no doubt already dug up an English copy of the Sumo Association's official rankings, or *banzuke* (readily available on the Web), which can serve as a combination player roster, batting order and racing form as you watch the matches on TV. Already — where before you saw only Tweedledum and Tweedledee — you've noticed physical differences among the bruisers. And almost as soon as you've learned to separate one from another, you find yourself grouping these guys, seeking common types, categories, species.

This is a natural. It's also been thought of already. The Japanese have for a long time divided *rikishi* conveniently into two types, called *ankogata* and *soppugata*. Creatively translated, these come out in English as "blubberbutts" and "thoroughbreds."

Anko are short, oval-shaped and relatively unlovely. *Soppu* are taller, leaner, more athletic and, well, hunkier. These categories are crude, but ingenious in one sense, because they bespeak the most obvious criterion of judgment, the standard that touches us all when we behold sports: the shape of the bod.

The flesh.

Anko and *soppu* are street words — not profane or obscene, but plain. You will not hear them uttered by NHK's smarmy broadcast team, nor will you often see these two words in the English explanations of sumo, composed by Tokyo's platoon of *gaijin* sumo experts. Nobody, officially, (if they value the backstage pass issued by the omnipotent Sumo Association) talks about blubberbutts and thoroughbreds.

Which is ridiculous, because it just isn't natural. Talking about guys' looks, comparing, handicapping, categorizing their physical appearance, is basic fan intelligence. How else to decide whom to pull for in a game when you've never seen either team? How else to choose up sides for kickball at recess on the first day of school? Show me a sumo expert who doesn't harbor a personal preference for either the blobs or the hunks, and I'll show you a veritable poseur.

Left/Right/Up/Down and All That

However, even NHK flacks and sumo nerds feel the unspoken law of sports that demands some sort of taxonomy, the "grouping urge." Since they eschew the obvious corporal criteria for *rikishi* comparison, the sanctioned experts resort to more esoteric means. They classify *rikishi* by means of their favorite grips.

I'm not kidding.

If you had asked a sumo nerd about, say, Asahifuji, he'd have said that Asahifuji preferred a *migi-yotsu* (right-hand) grip on the other fat guy's belt, while Chiyonofuji, by contrast, was happier with a *hidari-yotsu* (left-hand) grip. Often, said nerd might interject additional phrases that indicate whether the *rikishi* prefers his dominant-hand grip to be under (*shita*) or over *(uwa)* his opponent's corresponding arm.

Nice to know, but goddamn hard to follow. Such classifications aren't as simple as watching a baseball player settle into the third-base batter's box, thereby prompting the safe assumption that he's a right-handed hitter. Sumo matches don't give you that much chance to figure which hand is where.

In a sumo match of, say, five seconds' duration, in which two *rikishi* are spinning in circles, flailing their arms and yanking off each other's *sagari*, determining with the naked eye who got his left arm over the other guy's right arm so he could get his left hand on the right side of the other guy's belt (not to mention which one got his right arm under the other guy's left arm so he could get his right hand on the left side of the other guy's belt) could be just enough of a distraction to ruin the whole five seconds for you. And when it all happens in five seconds anyway, does it really matter where anybody's hands were?

Nevertheless, sumo pedants take pride in pointing out the left/right/up/down orientation of this *rikishi* or that *rikishi*, and bleating triumphantly when the two wrestlers demonstrate their tendencies in combat. If you know this stuff, it's fun showing off. I'm a little ashamed, but I even do it myself. And sometimes, this is vital knowledge. If you know, for instance, that Chiyonofuji never — ever — lost when he got a left-hand, inside grip on his opponent's *mawashi*, you had the key to watching the Champ's matches. Every opponent tried to keep that goddamn left hand away from his belt, and they almost always failed. Chiyonofuji's left hand was in the same league as Sugar Ray Robinson's. But, if the other guy succeeded in fighting off that deadly left, then you had suspense, excitement, magic! — because you knew Chiyo was improvising! To get an idea of how the fan feels when he knows Chiyonofuji is winging it, picture Gene Kelly walking alone in the moonlight with a new tune in his head, or Picasso left by himself in front of a blank white wall with a grease pencil in his hand.

But that's the exception. Often, a *rikishi* simply isn't talented enough to execute his favorite grip more than two or three times in a *basho*. You can watch his every match for two years before figuring out exactly what the hell the poor shnook is trying to do with his hands. Often, two experienced *rikishi* will block each other's favorite grips, forcing both of them to wrestle from weakness rather than strength. But how does the fan know this? None of this esoteric "grip" classification is easy to spot. You can watch sumo for years without discerning this much fine detail.

Nevertheless, among sumo insiders, this *migi-yotsu/hidari-yotsu, shitate/uwate* rigmarole is the Approved Method for grouping the fat guys. Obviously, when you talk about their hands, rather than their tummies, you lend to sumo wrestlers (and their overseers in the Sumo Association) a welcome note of dignity. But the obfuscation and euphemizing that tends to clutter the business of telling the fat ones apart from the sleek ones isn't simply a matter of false dignity.

The strongest reason, I think, for this left-right/up-down riddle, is religious. Sumo's curators, on the Japanese side, are a quasi-priesthood of officious reactionaries, and on the *gaijin* side, they constitute an apple-polishing society of culture mongers. Ideally, these guardians present *rikishi* to the public not as individuals with great big whopping differences in shape, style and personality, but as mute acolytes of national orthodoxy. In this distorted lens, the differences among the *rikishi* are subtleties of wrist and leverage. Otherwise, the players are ideally viewed as homogeneous, a unified group whose victories and defeats are insignificant. Their singular value, in the Shintoist/culturist scheme, is that they preserve a ritual pastime that bespeaks the beauty and impenetrability of things Japanese.

This ideal is not just unrealistic. It's harmful to the sport. Most of the problems of sumo spring directly from this dogma. Fortunately, at least two factors confound the elders' efforts to mummify sumo. First, the *rikishi* themselves are too distinctive and vital to all sing alto in the plainsong chorus. They are competitors. Their matches are not rehearsed sets of responses and genuflections on a sandy altar. The *rikishi* go out there hungry, crafty, and wired.

They wanna win. They grab, jab, gouge, claw, and smack each other in the chops. They do stuff that athletes — real athletes — are supposed to do, can't help but do. They're not dignified, but they're fun.

The crowd comes out because the wrestlers are sincere and the game is wild and woolly — another reality that defies sumo's religionists. The fans know what's going on, and they know it isn't church. They study the jocks. They learn their gestures and idiosyncrasies, divide them up according to bodies, emotions, strength, age, speed, hometowns and home stables, cuteness and ugliness, boobs and bellybuttons, even right-handedness and left-handedness.

This gets us back, finally, to sumo's great standoff — *ankogata* or *soppugata*, to feed or not to feed? There is not a barroom sumo discussion anywhere in Japan that doesn't eventually get around to this timeless, passionate quandary. Muscle or fat. Beauty or blubber. This is Japan's version of Ruth-or-Maris, Aaron-or-Bonds, Kobe or LeBron, Montana-or-Marino, DH-or-no DH.

Begin it a thousand times and it will ignite discussion at the same point and spin it in the same circle. It will engage, with equal claim to authority, the expert and the amateur, the novice and the old-timer, the know-it-all and the pupil, the dilettante and the junkie. The "grouping urge" — always based on the idea that there are two kinds of people — is the fan's dialectic, the wisdom of the playground, the DNA of sports. Fans group jocks instinctively because it's fun. More usefully, the act of classifying jocks connects you more and more deeply, because it teaches you so much! Based on the guy's looks, you can make remarkably accurate assumptions about what to expect from a particular player. Line up all the guards in the National Basketball Association, for instance. The well-schooled hoop fan can — with a high degree of accuracy, simply by comparing their bodies — divide them into the various categories that apply to their position. You have, for instance, point guards, shooting guards, swingmen and defensive specialists, plus your big-guard and your small-guard types, guards who penetrate and guards who pull up. And then, there's the occasional pure genius (Magic Johnson).

And of course — this is the best part — you can be totally fooled. Muggsy Bogues and Charles Barkley were the unlikeliest of basketball players. Maradona never looked like much of a soccer star, and Johnny Unitas? That guy played pro football? You're kidding.

Genus and Species

All of which boils down to the inescapable conclusion that *ankogata* and *soppugata* are, on the one hand, invaluable terms in the appreciation of the sport of sumo, and, on the other hand, simply not enough. Breaking the *rikishi* down to only two categories is, at bottom, sloppy. Your average sumo nebbish — Hokutoriki, for example — is neither fat nor lissom, neither soft nor hard, neither big nor small, and he's almost supernaturally mediocre. He doesn't fit either slot.

I attacked the challenge of *rikishi* taxonomy early in my own sumo education, long before I had ever heard the words *ankogata* and *soppugata*. I tried as many as 12 different classifications, realized I'd gotten carried away and reduced that number to eight. My second cut got me down to five, but it was not a well-sifted five.

Finally, I recognized that properly, beneath the Genus Anko (Blubberbutt), there are two distinct species of *rikishi*, your Hippos and your Butterballs. Beneath the Genus Soppu (Thoroughbred), two species also emerge, your Jocks and your Cabdrivers.

A foolish consistency, however — as Emerson nagged — is the hobgoblin of little minds. As I organized *rikishi* according to my own typology, I noticed some mixing of genus and species. It is rare but possible for an *ankogata* kind of guy — I recall a nose-breaker named Akinoshima, five-foot-nine and built like a panda — to be a Jock. Wesley Unseld, likewise, was a pretty nimble endomorph! And there are numerous examples of the *ankogata* Cabdriver.

In a little more detail, here is the definitive Benjamin Taxonomy of *rikishi* and how you can tell them apart.

1) JOCKS. A Jock is someone who'd be an athlete even if sumo didn't exist. Jocks, despite a perpetual size disadvantage, have always dominated sumo's highest two ranks, *yokozuna* and *ozeki*. Chiyonofuji, for example, who might be the most athletic *rikishi* of the 20th century, ranked — in 1990 — 25th in height among 38 *makuuchi* division wrestlers, and 35th in weight. In 2009, the two reigning *yokozuna*, Asashoryu and Hakuho — at 153 kilograms (337 lbs) each — were slightly below the average weight, 156 kg, in the *makuuchi* ranks.

With Chiyonofuji as their ideal, Jocks defy the perception that all sumo wrestlers are fat boys who flunked the junior high entrance exam and got shipped off to the local sadist by their despairing dads. Sumo's Jocks, in a nutshell, are compact, muscular, usually quick, and shockingly agile for their size.

It's conventional to assert that, as a rule, Jocks tend to be technically more sophisticated than *rikishi* in the other three species, because they must compensate for their weight disadvantage. However, there are actually many Jocks whose wrestling skills are suspect and who tend to rely on a blend of sheer athleticism and brute force. Chiyonofuji's stablemate Hokutoumi — the Jake LaMotta of sumo — was a great example of this category.

2) HIPPOS. The secret of being a Hippo is in your glands. If you're a little taller than the average bear and possess an almost infinite capacity for gaining weight without collapsing from a series of stress fractures all over your grotesque body — and you can still move — you are a rare and unnatural deposit. And you're scary as hell ("Oh my God, Helen! It's moving!"), 'cause hardly any-

body knows what to do with you. Konishiki (real name, Salévaa Atisanoe), a Samoan/Hawaiian behemoth who once weighed in at 264 kg (580 pounds), is the ultimate Hippo. In his time, his only challenger for the title of Weight Watchers' Public Enemy Number One was *yokozuna* Onokuni, who hit 211 kg (462 pounds) before gravity and cholesterol began wreaking revenge on his health. Since Konishiki retired in 1997, the closest anyone has approached to his supreme hippohood has been Japan's biggest-ever native-born *rikishi*, Yamamotoyama, ("Twin Peaks"), who tipped the scales at 248 kg (546 pounds and still growing) in 2009.

Nobody would ever beat Hippos if they could get out of their own way. The TV commentators regularly gush about Hippos being "quick" for their size — a questionable assertion when you realize that no one has really put together a sample group of 500-pound people to find out how quick they are, not to mention the problem of convincing them to all run the 40-yard dash, so you can draw up a bell curve. An NHK color man praising a Hippo for his quickness is the equivalent of his ESPN counterpart saying that a journeyman relief pitcher (like the post-steroid Eric Gagné) is "sneaky fast." With Hippos, quickness is the issue, because it's what they ain't got. Yamamotoyama, for instance, in terms of sheer mass, is four people, and he's only got two legs. Try getting four people with eight legs to move together in a hurry and you have a sense of your average Hippo's mobility. There are escalators that are shiftier.

As Onokuni (who retired in 1991 at age 28) demonstrated also, the burden of bulk tends to erode Hippos' competitive intensity and shorten their careers. Being a Hippo is like being John Wayne's horse — except the son of a bitch never gets off your back. Asashio, for example, a delightful character who qualified as a pygmy Hippo, retired late in 1989 at age 32, after several wretched tournaments. By contrast, Kirishima, a Jock, won promotion in 1990 — at age 31 — to *ozeki*, sumo's second highest rank; and Chiyonofuji was still winning basho in 1991 at age 34. Hippos blossom early and decline young. Jocks are late bloomers.

3) BUTTERBALLS. These are the guys the inexperienced fan thinks of when he pictures sumo. Butterballs are short, fat and mediocre — which is one reason why some people call them Rotarians. The funny thing about Butterballs is you tend to love one on sight or hate 'im — because he tends to resemble either a teddy bear or a mutant hog walking on two legs. Of course, one man's Pooh is another man's Porky. I've developed a grudging admiration for the really ugly Butterballs, like the Goldfish (Ozutsu), and I tend to detest the cute ones.

Guys like the Goldfish or, more recently, Kakizoe, typify one of the insidious charms of Butterballs. More than Jocks, Butterballs step onto the *dohyo* every day with a chronic disadvantage. Although they have succeeded in the cherished sumo aspiration of dumpling themselves into dangerous obesity, they haven't been able to match this inflation with any growth in their natural talent. Day to day, all he ever wants to do is survive. For the essential Butterball, survival depends on his wits, on his knowledge of his opponents, his application of a few favorite moves, and the wisdom never to wrestle beyond his abundant limitations. With self-preservation as his prime directive, the Butterball has long since replaced, in his outlook, the pride of the tiger with the sneakiness of the shithouse rat.

Because they're so round, stumpy, homely and aver-age, it takes time for Butterballs to grow on you. But Butterball love really does blossom. It starts with pity and graduates to sympathy, and then — though you might not feel it happening — you start to identify. You look in the mirror, notice your own spare tire, the old pimple scars, the bags under your eyes, the five o'clock shadow at 11 a.m. You think about all the daily defeats and indignities that grind you into the sand. You look behind that dull stare and see the coyote's furtive gleam. And suddenly it isn't Toyonoshima waddling out in front of all those rice-munching voyeurs to get creamed again by Asashoryu. It's you, and that shiny turquoise jockstrap is all that's left of your ego.

"Come on, you fat goddamn housewife! Don't screw up again!"

4) CABDRIVERS. These are the guys who look like your uncle in Toledo, who never gets up off his ass all day on the job, doesn't get a lick of exercise between bowling nights, and has a chair in front of the TV that nobody else ever sits in. Cabdrivers would be Jocks if they had a little more talent, or muscle, or desire. They could be Butterballs if their fat distribution wasn't so lumpy and irregular. They tend to look like German tourists in body stockings.

Cabdrivers are sumo's meat-and-potatoes, fish-and-chips, boilermaker working stiffs. They're baggy in the gut and they're pretty strong without showing much sign of having a whole muscle anywhere on their bod-ies. They're prone to the sorts of physical ailments we all live with: sore backs (Kimurayama), kidney stones (Takanofuji) and hair loss (Iwakiyama). But aches or no aches, these guys punch in every day, work their

shift, pick the sand off their butts, and grab a six-pack
on their way home.

In sumo, the two glamour species are Jocks (Genus Soppu)
and Hippos (Genus Anko). But these two showpiece classes
do not truly typify the sport of sumo. I think that more than
any other professional sport in the world, sumo is the province of the common man. In one typical *basho*, for example,
using my admittedly subjective classifications, I counted only
ten bona fide Jocks among the 42 top-division *makuuchi*
wrestlers. There were three Hippos, led by the colossal Yamamotoyama, and the rest were working-stiff *rikishi* — 11
Butterballs and 18 Cabdrivers, including two *ozeki*, Kaio (a
Cabdriver) and Chiyotaikai (a Butterball).

Of course, if I were sitting with you in front of the TV, we
might disagree on this distribution, arguing over — for example — whether Kokkai ("Ralph Kramden"), the big Georgian
Cabdriver, merits consideration as a Jock.

In that case, I might assert, patiently, that the measure of
a Jock is more than just athleticism, which is evident in Kokkai's style and physique. Kokkai's problem is that he doesn't
have the heart of a Jock! He gives his full effort only sporadi-
cally, and he lacks the sort of killer instinct that has marked
the true jock ever since Achilles strung Hector's corpse to his
chariot and dragged it around beneath the walls of Troy. I've
actually seen Kokkai try to help a beaten opponent up off the
ground. Pathetic!

But still, you might persist in disagreement — which is
cool. The Benjamin Taxonomy is not authoritative. It lacks
logic. And it's not very respectful. Next time you get to watch
a *basho*, make your own list. Or make up your own categories. If you prefer three groups, or five, or 10, go ahead —
that's the spirit!

Categories, in fact, are pointless without disagreement (which is why the Sumo Association's *ex cathedra* rankings are so dull). Arguments, actually, are the life of the party. One trait that distinguishes the real fan from the dilettante is that he argues at the drop of a hat, or a name, or a stat — instantly, tirelessly and obstreperously. A fan argues about points that can never be settled, about statistics that don't exist, about events that never happened, about imaginary teams.

The "grouping urge" is one of the wellsprings of such fan arguments. More people in, say, Syracuse, in one day, spend more words and energy inventing, revising and disputing sports categories — often punctuated by threats— than the rest of the people in the world burn up on discussions of foreign policy or deficit spending.

(I've called Syracuse. It's true.)

So, if by doubling the available number of *rikishi* categories, I have added even 10 percent to the volume of argument about sumo, well, good for me, because it means I've made the sport more contentious — and therefore more fun for regular people.

You know. The guys down at Kenji's Bar & Grill.

CHAPTER 4

BACKSTAGE
Choking Up in the Church

Most sports reporting is incompetent. I'm entitled to say this, because I've done my own share of nitwit sportswriting.

However, though sportswriters are the caboose of journalism, the fatuity of our output isn't entirely our fault, because sports readers tend toward ignorant expectations. In sports with scores, your average Associated Press postgame roundup begins with the final score and ends by describing a decisive hit or shot or goal that led thereto, or maybe the grand total of Butch Dewlapp, high scorer. In a race, the story inevitably dwells on the last lap, the final 20 meters, the home stretch or the kick to the tape. In boxing, your conventional sportswriter goes straight to the last round, the telling blows, the final knockdown, and — if there's a little space left over for literary flourish — the puddle of blood on the canvas.

Bylined sportswriters have more stylistic freedom, of course, which usually means that they avoid telling you the final score at all, leaving such mundane chores up to the lackey who writes the headlines. It also means that the writer tends to gloss entirely over anything that actually happened in the game, so that he (or she) can proceed directly to an exegesis of the game's "meaning" in the vast scheme of human fates that hang upon the success or failure of the franchise. In either case, you learn very little of what actually happened and, in the worst case, you learn far too much about a witness who — at least according his testimony — was there.

In sumo, this cycle of insipid reportage — especially in English — is narrower, making it all the more oppressive, and abysmally bereft of information. Usually, the post-match analysis is finished when your ringside reporter gives the benediction, which comes in the form of a sesquipedalian phrase signifying the technique that finished off the loser. This polysyllable succinctly defines the relative positions of the two *rikishi* at the moment the match ended. It is literally the last word on the battle, and it is dispensed with reverence by the commentators.

All sports fans relish the moment of climax, the cathartic leap from struggle to decision, but the hardcore fan wants more. Gimme the score and name the winner, tell me the grip and measure the distance, but then I wanna know: What was the "turning point?" When did the Big Mo shift? When did the victor smell blood? When did the loser flinch? These are questions that inspire the disputation of sports and turn spectator into scientist. Such issues transcend the mere brute clash of athletic competition and place sports among mankind's more exalted intellectual pursuits — geopolitics, military strategy, philosophy, the weather, James Bond movies, etc.

Napoleon and Konishiki

For instance, your typical sportswriter, covering, say, the Battle of Waterloo, would have hung the whole story on Blucher's dramatic arrival from "the heights round Frischemont" to rescue Wellington and send Napoleon's army into rout. Even Victor Hugo called this, momentarily, "the turning-point." But then, he went on to place much more emphasis on an earlier shift in the battle's balance, when Napoleon's magnificent 3,500 mounted cuirassiers, under Milhaud, charged the plateau of Mont-Saint-Jean. As he gave the order [Hugo recalled], Napoleon "ordered a dispatch-rider to ride posthaste to Paris with the news that the battle was won."

Talk about chutzpah, huh? Picture Tom Coughlin ordering the fat lady to sing at halftime of Super Bowl XLII!

But Coughlin had a flat field and a hot quarterback. Milhaud was a horse of another temperature. Neither Milhaud, nor Ney, Kellermann, Delord, Wathier, nor even Lefebvre-Desnouette had troubled to scout the battlefield properly and to see that huge crevasse on the approach to Mont-Saint-Jean, the sunken country lane that ran between Braine-l'Alleud and Ohain — where one-third of the attacking cavalry plunged to their deaths.

"It was the beginning of the defeat," said Hugo during the days of Napoleon. These are the words of a thinking fan who studies the game and reads the agate.

Most New York fans, reviewing the Red Sox extraordinary comeback victory in the 2004 American League Championship Series, would dwell on Curt Schilling's heroic "bloody sock" performance in Game 6, or perhaps, David Ortiz' momentum-shifting 12th-inning home run in Game 4. But a real fan would go back a little further, to the ninth inning of Game 4, when Sox manager Terry Francona sent utility outfielder Dave Roberts to first base to pinch-run for Kevin Millar. Roberts' subsequent steal of second, after three close pickoff tries by Yankee relief ace Mariano Rivera, made it possible for Roberts to score on Bill Mueller's base hit. That one extra base was the key that finally, after 86 years, dispelled the Curse of the Bambino. In turn, that moment was only possible because of a quiet trade-deadline transaction in July, in which Red Sox general manager Theo Epstein sent obscure minor-leaguer Henri Stanley to the Los Angeles Dodgers for Roberts.

As Epstein's prescient transaction shows, turning points can occur days before the Big Game, or months or years — often unseen or unheard of by the hapless fan who swallows the pap dished out by journeyman sportswriters. This is starkly true in sumo, whose action is so dizzyingly brief that, indeed, the decisions and errors of strategy can often be found in the prelude to the match.

Consider, for example, the most important match of the 1990 Natsu (summer, i.e., May) Basho, between Chiyonofuji and Konishiki. For both *rikishi*, a great deal was at stake— but more so for Chiyonofuji. The great *yokozuna* was battling against time and posterity. He was close to his 35th birthday, and the speculation that he would soon retire was growing ever louder. Takamiyama, Konishiki's *oyakata* (head coach) had declared before the *basho* that Chiyo was over the hill. Chiyonofuji was already the winner of 30 *basho* and in the previous one he'd become the first *rikishi* in history to win 1,000 matches. But in the stubborn memory of the sumo world, Chiyonofuji would remain an ever-so-slightly soiled immortal if he failed to match Taiho's all-time record of 32 tournament championships.

The Natsu Basho title was within Chiyonofuji's grasp as he prepared for his Day 14 match against Konishiki. He was 12-1, tied for the lead with Asahifuji. Of course, Konishiki was a hell of a hurdle to clear. Konishiki outweighed Chiyo by a cool 244 pounds.

Never mind. Konishiki could be had.

One day, at his sumo-motif *chankonabe* restaurant in Komagome, I discussed that very match with Shinko, a former *sekitori* who had wrestled both Chiyonofuji and Konishiki. Shinko explained the relationship between Chiyonofuji the master and Konishiki, the young, emotional giant. "Put Chiyonofuji against Konishiki ten times in practice, every day, and every day Chiyonofuji will win nine times. If they wrestled on the first day of every *basho*, Konishiki would never win. Never."

Coming into Day 14 of the Natsu Basho, Chiyonofuji had not shown his age. He looked really *genki*, a strange word that means "healthy" in Japanese but in Sumo-speak means more — confident, well-focused, finely-tuned, and lucky.

Until Day 11, Konishiki had kept pace with the leaders. Then, consecutive losses to Kushimaumi and Asahifuji had killed his chances for a *yusho* (tournament win). If Konishiki had snagged this *yusho*, it would have put him squarely in line for promotion to *yokozuna*, a rank to which no *gaijin* had ever ascended. The three defeats postponed that goal, but he still needed a good *basho* record to merit a shot at *yokozuna* the next time out in July. Nevertheless, though he needed to keep winning, Konishiki faced less pressure than Chiyo.

Also to Konishiki's advantage, he had recently begun to reverse Chiyonofuji's longstanding dominance. Chiyo's overall record against Konishiki was 18-8, but Konishiki had beaten Chiyo three straight. The first in that streak was in the November 1989 Kyushu Basho, when a terrified Konishiki had shocked Chiyonofuji on Day 11, en route to the first *yusho* of his career. Chiyonofuji won the next *basho* but lost his match with Konishiki. Konishiki beat him again in March.

When they finally faced off and charged on Day 14 of the 1990 Natsu Basho, the pattern seemed unaltered. The slap of flesh, a moment of tension and then Konishiki bulled Chiyonofuji off the *dohyo*. But this time, there was a difference. The turning point was already in the past.

This match was over a long time before it started. Let's go back.

In the (November) Kyushu Basho, six months before, the rhythm and electricity of a great athletic battle hung over the *dohyo* and intensified as Konishiki and Chiyonofuji met. Konishiki struggled mightily, against an old pro and his own fear. To watch him — to watch both *rikishi* — was moving and memorable. The turning point came in the first seconds of the fight, when Chiyonofuji's deadly left hand darted toward Konishiki's belt — once, twice, three times. And again! Each time, with great windmill swings of his right arm, Konishiki batted away Chiyonofuji's left.

Konishiki sacrificed his own devastating charge and he fought one-handed. He gave up most of his offense to defend himself against the certain defeat in Chiyonofuji's left. Only when Konishiki had parried Chiyonofuji's fourth thrust could he move in, turn the match in his favor and ride Chiyonofuji off the *dohyo*.

Now jump forward. Six months later in the Natsu Basho, the hoped-for drama of Chiyonofuji/Konishiki was non-existent. Konishiki's first charge backed Chiyonofuji immediately to the brink. Chiyonofuji bounced several times at Konishiki, kept his left arm curled ineffectually against his chest and made only one sluggish thrust with his right hand. The match was a turkey. Chiyonofuji backpedaled, lost and sat down. Konishiki had had a tougher match four days before against Oginohana, a rookie in his third *makuuchi* tournament who finished the *basho* with a 4-11 record.

So what happened?

The word that explains that disappointment is one that every American sports fan knows — which means that, among all the people in the Ryogoku Kokugikan that day, Konishiki is one of the very few who would have understood its application to Chiyonofuji's piss-poor performance. It is perhaps the most damning word in sports. Spoken aloud to an opponent, or expressed in a gesture, it is the gauntlet that guarantees extracurricular fisticuffs. Addressed to a game official after a disputed call, it means automatic expulsion.

What happened to Chiyonofuji?

Bluntly put, he choked.

Chiyonofuji was a *rikishi* who survived with his body but won with his mind. A choke is the offspring of a flaccid mind, a sign that apprehension has conquered the human will. At some time, it happens to every athlete — to every human being, for that matter. In sports, it is always on naked display, and it's always impolitic to point it out.

That day, in Chiyonofuji's defeat, the choke was on. The choke was the turning point, and it came before the match began. In fact, that match probably turned six months before in Kyushu, when Chiyonofuji discovered that Konishiki could take Chiyo's very best, and whip him.

When I explained the choke to my wife, Junko, she tried to render it as *nigate ishiki* — which can be translated as a "premonition of defeat," or "I got a bad feeling about that son of a bitch," or simply a "tough matchup." *Nigate ishiki* is a feeling that applies, for instance, whenever basketball opponents enter the horrifying uproar of the Dean E. Smith Center at the University of North Carolina. In the same vein, Nate Thurmond always gave Wilt Chamberlain fits: *nigate ishiki*. Pedro Martinez couldn't seem to get Derek Jeter out in the clutch; the Packers got scorched time and again by the insufferable Randy Moss. *Nigate ishiki*.

But that's not choking. These classic confrontations might have been jinxed for the losing side. They were discouraging matchups, but in none of them was there even a hint of pre-emptive surrender. On the contrary, Martinez probably worked harder against Jeter than against any other opponent in the American League. Asahifuji, in sumo, always had trouble with Akinoshima — which is why, in the tournaments he defeated Akinoshima, he usually won the championship. *Nigate ishiki* is the nameless dread that simultaneously spawns self-doubt and inspires stern determination, redoubling both with every disappointment.

The choke is different. It is the public display of self-doubt. It means that you don't, in your gut, believe you belong on the same mat with the other guy. You're not ready. You've thought, and worried, and talked yourself out of the game.

In sumo, the choke, and all its lesser psychological variations, play a central role — very likely more than in any other sport. More goes on before the game, in sumo, than in most other sports, and sumo is far less forgiving to the athlete whose head isn't in the game from the word *"jikan."*

In a sport related to sumo, amateur wrestling, the shortest match I ever saw was 12 seconds long. That's just about twice the average duration of a sumo match. Most wrestling matches last their full six or nine minutes — long enough for a good wrestler to recover from a private funk or a slow start. Adrenaline can save most athletes from choking at the start. Sumo provides no such indulgence. If you're not all there at the split second the other guy jumps into your face, you're roadkill.

The psychological burden of sumo is also greater because of the Sumo Association's diabolical scheduling system. There is no other sport in which the competitor has more than 24 hours — every day for 15 days — to anticipate a match that will last, in most cases, less than ten seconds. The imbalance between anticipation and action is torturous.

The Locker Room

Shinko, the restauranteur who retired in 1985, was a middling *rikishi*. He was the underdog much of the time, so he
learned better than most those feelings of anxiety and inferi-
ority — *nigate ishiki* — that undermine the athlete and incu-
bate the choke.

In each *basho*, Shinko explained, before the day's matches,
the *rikishi* report to the arena several hours early. In the first
half of their preparations, wrestlers talk, especially to their
tsukebito, the apprentice wrestlers from their own stables
who serve as their grooms. These willing lackeys praise the
sekitori, strategize with them about the day's match, rub their
backs, bring their tea and help dress them for the ring-entering ceremony. Just about every *rikishi*'s routine varies. But
almost everyone, in the midst of the daily buildup, pauses to
ponder the schedule — for tomorrow.

Tomorrow's schedule. Before every match, each *rikishi* has
two opponents on his mind. Just as he's about to step onto
the *dohyo* against today's foe — about whom he's been thinking for 24 hours — the Sumo Association posts the name of
the opponent he will have to wrestle 24 hours hence.

"As soon as you read the schedule, the younger wrestlers
start talking about how to win the next day's match," said
Shinko. "Sometimes you say to yourself, 'Oh, I can't beat
him. There's no way.' But that can work in your favor, to
keep from getting too tense."

Another former *rikishi*, Koji Kitao, who competed as Futahaguro, said, "Everything starts from when you know whom
you'll be wrestling in your next match. Immediately, you start
thinking about the weak points of tomorrow's opponent."

Yes, said Kitao Formerly Futahaguro, you can't help but
tear your attention away from now and focus on tomorrow.

"You have to think, remember all the different patterns
that all the *rikishi* have," he said. "It's like a puzzle — and

the puzzle is toughest when your next match is one of the younger wrestlers, a new guy. You don't know what their tendencies are, and they can ambush you."

The next morning, after brooding all night over this shifting puzzle and before a new puzzle is revealed by the scheduling fiends, each *rikishi* plunges into a last-minute practice session. "You have time to prepare," said Kitao/Futahaguro. "You use the young guys, who impersonate your opponent for that day. You do it again and again, until you've found the grip you think will work and your body memorizes the movements you've practiced. From then until you're in the locker room, your mind keeps returning to the other guy's weaknesses…"

For each athlete, in essence, every *basho* is an unbroken spiral of solitary mind games. But, regardless of the games — or more accurately, because of them — said Shinko, the tension grows, without relief, for 15 days.

"The sitting, the waiting," added Kitao/Futahaguro, speaking of the *basho*. "That's when you build up this huge load of tension."

And because of the timing of the schedule announcement, the pressure and distractions are always worst in the locker room just before the match. In the last minutes before wrestling against, say, great big Miyabiyama, a *rikishi* suddenly finds himself contemplating the tendencies of someone entirely different, like cat-quick Harumafuji — whom he won't face 'til tomorrow. Every fan knows that "looking ahead" like this can screw up a jock's concentration, even if he isn't prone to choke.

An example: Back to the Natsu Basho, 1990. Kirishima — one of my favorite *rikishi*, ever — was riding incredibly high. He was on a roll that went back 16 months — when he began a relentless comeback from a 1-14 record in the first *basho* of 1989. In eight subsequent *basho*, Kirishima's record was

76-49, with seven victories over *yokozuna*. He had accomplished the extraordinary feat of improving in eight straight tournaments. He had been promoted to *ozeki* after wrestling through 91 *basho* in the lower ranks (one of the longest overtures in sumo history) and he was 8-0 going into Day 9. For the second straight *basho*, he was in the race for the title.

Kirishima's eighth win the day before had clinched *kachikoshi*, the second most coveted objective — after the *yusho* (tournament title) — in sumo. *Kachikoshi* is the magic "8," a majority of victories in the 15-day ordeal; it insures the wrestler against demotion to a lower rank. There are few de-motivators in sport as potent as *kachikoshi*. And Kirishima had it.

This wasn't just wasn't your everyday garden-variety *kachikoshi*, either. Kirishima had needed it — and needed it decisively — in his first *basho* as *ozeki*, to prove that his 16-month ascent was no fluke. It was vindication for himself and for his *oyakata* (head coach), Izutsu. Kirishima's majority-clinching victory the day before was also his first real chance in more than a year to lie back and contemplate his success. He was at the top of his game, the toast of Tokyo, and he had an easy match — against Oginohana, an overmatched rookie who had eked out only two victories in eight days. A pushover.

As he prepared for his victory over Oginohana, Kirishima received the Day 10 schedule. A day after Oginohana, he was slated against *ozeki* Asahifuji — who was always tough, but especially tough in this *basho*. Irresistibly, Kirishima looked ahead, and blew the *yusho*.

On the *dohyo* that day, Kirishima's gait was subtly different. His eyes wandered. He hesitated at *tachiai* (the face-off) and ended up too high as Oginohana plowed into him. While Kirishima was looking forward to Asahifuji, the rookie kicked his ass. And of course, the next day, dwelling on that careless defeat, Kirishima was easy pickings for Asahifuji. After his 8-0 start, Kirishima went 1-6. He didn't choke, but almost as bad — he cracked.

The psychological pressure of sumo has few comparisons. Perhaps the closest parallel was the pre-1991 Super Bowl, which required the players to slog through two weeks of anticipation, preparation, and hype before they finally got to play the game. That's a ratio of 336 hours of anxiety to 60 minutes of football. In sumo, through 15 days of competition, the ratio of anxiety to actual wrestling is 360 hours to 90 seconds.

Because they can't really see this unparalleled imbalance between sitting around and throwing punches, most fans don't understand the mental fortitude required in sumo. Chiyonofuji was a brilliant *rikishi* because his powers of concentration were extraordinary. It is a measure of the pressure that sumo exerts on the mind that even Chiyonofuji, said to be the iceman of sumo, could psych himself out of a match as totally as he did in that Natsu Basho defeat at the hands of Konishiki.

Aprons and Ads
In the midst of the pre-match tension, the *rikishi* do, however, get one break. They all get dressed up in their aprons and…

Aprons? Guys in aprons? Like Dagwood Bumstead doing the dishes?

Well, there's a reason for this.

Advertising.

Each apron, *kesho-mawashi* or "sumo skirt," is different. The pretty picture on the front is unique, and embroidered just above the fringe is the name of a sponsor who paid for it. "East Hokkaido Sumo Boosters," "Shimonoseki Rotary Club," "Chiba City Tool & Die" — that sort of thing. Kind of like the outfield fences in the Carolina League. The *rikishi* don't have much say in the design of their own sumo skirts, since they're not paying for them. The skirts themselves are slightly more tasteful than a display of oil paintings on black velvet in a K-Mart parking lot, but not as artistically sublime as your average mural of Mt. Fuji in a Tokyo public bath. If your husband, for instance, brought home an only-slightly-soiled sumo skirt, bragging about how he got it cheap and it was actually worn by Kaio in his next-to-last *basho*, and he started insisting that it should be hung in a prominent place, you'd have to humor him — for the sake of the family's reputation. "It's really beautiful, dear, and I'd love it right above the davenport, but that wouldn't be fair to you."

"Huh? Why not?"

"Well, sweetheart, you're hardly ever in the living room. It would be much better to hang it in the garage — right over your workbench. To inspire you as you, er... create."

Sumo skirts — some sillier than others (Tochiozan's apron depicted a dog dressed up as a sumo wrestler, Wakanosato disported himself with a drowning dragon, and Toyozakura, for some reason, displayed a Canadian motif, a loon surrounded by maple leaves) — have never been, as far as I know, criticized on the basis of "artistic impression," for three reasons: 1) Nobody ever criticizes anything in Japan, 2) someone's mom worked her fingers to the bone sewing that incredible thing, and 3) sumo wrestlers have always worn sumo skirts. It's traditional!

Anyhow, in the midst of sweating over today's opponent and fretting about tomorrow's match, all the *rikishi* break into two groups, East and West (a meaningless differentiation), march single-file up to the *dohyo*, do one slow dignified lap around the *tawara*, raise their arms, do a little curtsey with their sumo skirts, and march on out again.

And nobody giggles.

The *yokozuna* each have an individual ring-entering routine. It's more elaborate, with leg-stomping, hand-clapping, arm-lifting, and a kind of macho Japanese version of the "mashed potato" — but it all comes down to pomp and circumstance signifying nothing. This is sumo's *Kyrie eleison*, beloved of the culture vultures, but a good time for the sports fan to slip outside for a cigarette and a whiz.

The Meditations of the Beast

Once the *rikishi* get backstage and shed their sumo skirts, the locker room changes dramatically. Nobody says a word. Absolute silence.

"No one talks," said Shinko. "If I needed a drink, or a back rub, the younger wrestlers would have to see it in my eyes. Or sense it. And they did. I always got what I needed."

Eerie and mystical, huh?

For the student of culture unfamiliar with the universal tendency of overbearing higher-ups to expect subordinates to "read my mind," this unspoken understanding among the *rikishi* and their lackeys is uniquely Japanese, and the locker-room atmosphere conveys a transcendental Zen-like mystery. One can only conclude that it is from this preternatural silence that the *rikishi* must draw their strength.

For the sports fan, however, it means one thing: more tension. Here, after all, is your jock — your sumo jock. He's probably a junior high school dropout with an IQ that puts him in the same range as Boo Radley and Darryl Dawkins. Already, he's not too mentally stable, or he would have stayed in school and learned a trade. In a few minutes, he's going out in front of several thousand people to fight a guy who almost broke his neck two months ago. And he just found out that in 24 hours he's going up against a wrestler whose personal motto is: "Brain damage isn't everything. It's the only thing."

What you have here is a worried, scared, emotionally immature stud-muffin who needs to be talked to, jollied up, reassured, stroked, praised, and encouraged. He needs one of the guys to chuck him upside the chin and say, "Go get 'em, Moose!" Or, "Win this one for the Gipper." Or, "This is your day, bro! That muhfuh be hist'ry, dog." Any of those things that jocks grunt to each other. It would be nice — words of encouragement. But tradition intrudes. Instead, all of a sudden, it's church.

Ssssh.

But let's not feel too sorry. Although it seems pretty mean to put these kids in the deep freeze at such a critical juncture, they get used to it. Some even like it.

Kitao/Futahaguro, for example, offered some insight into why, in 1986, at the age of 22, he became one of the youngest — and craziest — *rikishi* ever promoted to *yokozuna* (only to be expelled from sumo after a violent episode two years later). "You can't break the tension," he said, "but you can learn to enjoy it. You get yourself aroused. You know whether your opponent that day is tough, so you build up hatred. If he's not so tough, you're still impatient for the match, building up confidence, looking forward to the kill. When you're really tense, people say you have to be calm, but at the same time, you have to turn yourself into a beast."

As they morph into beast mode, there are ways for *rikishi* to keep busy, to shorten the time and ease some of the pressure. They all have to change *mawashi*, swab down their bods and get their hair done. And they warm up, some of them — like the Sweathog — vigorously. They dance and scowl and hyperventilate, lounge and scratch, flex and fester. Some even doze off. Naked men in church, waiting, thinking, oxidizing.

The silent society of the sumo locker room gets an athlete strangely prepared for the battle. In one sense, because he is watched and petted by his gang of pudgy acolytes, he is the center of a social whirl, a prince on a silk chaise. But in the unnatural quiet, he is also an outcast, alone with his thoughts and haunted by the infinity of simple, sudden mistakes that can ruin a sumo match — and his day — with no chance for recovery.

The taut tranquility of the locker room is unique. What a difference — and probably a relief — when the *rikishi* steps from the wings and strides, slightly bowlegged and chafing all the way, down the *hanamichi* to the *dohyo*! The arena is noisy and it smells slightly of rice, beer and *yakitori*. The fans are festive and other wrestlers are already on the *dohyo*, pawing and snorting and glaring carnivorously at each other's throats. The *rikishi* is like a toreador who visits the chapel in the last moment before facing the bull, only to find himself pushed incongruously into an immense saloon where drunks commune with wild animals.

The casual fan is oblivious to the tension, the endless waiting and recriminating that dominates sumo's backstage. The fan gets only the result; bread and circus. The thinking fan, however, understands the pressure that must build in so much delay, in so perverse a silence; he shifts to the edge of his seat, sees behind the ample flesh of the two combatants the ratcheting of bruised nerves; and such a fan tenses also, for the inevitable. Explosion.

The explosion is called *tachiai*

But wait. No. Not quite yet.

There are still a few inches left on the fuse.

CHAPTER 5

THE SUMOTORI RAG
Pose-striking, Time-killing and the Eight Forms of Screwing Around

Let's flash back a while and drop into Shibuya, perhaps Tokyo's most fashionable consumer circus. Not long ago, not far from Shibuya Station, as you wove your way patiently through the neighborhood's plankton of post-pubescent trendiness, you encountered a sort of hill, paved in brick and guarded at each end by shops called Loft and Ticket Saison. Once, at the top of the hill, a saloon called the Wave Bar strategically installed several uncomfortable benches and a patch of foliage. The Wave Bar has since disappeared, but this doesn't matter, because in Shibuya, Harajuku, Shinjuku, Shinbashi — all over town — watering holes just like it are an eternal element of the Tokyo milieu. In each of them, some of Tokyo's most self-conscious lounge lizards stand vigil for tardy companions.

Her, for instance.

Her ensemble fairly shimmers. It bespeaks the toniest labels available in the city's antiseptic boutiques. Her make-up and hair are mock-Parisienne — a face of bone china, black eyes like the sunken stare of an infant refugee, a scarlet wound for a mouth, a helmet of auburn hair that's been scalpeled just above her neo-Braque earrings. The bag, from Hermes or Coach, slouches against her thigh, half of which is impeccably nude. The other leg dangles above and supports her arms.

Her whitened limbs, tense in their studied repose, are the window of her demeanor — and her demeanor is her message. She leans forward, one hand a lifeless claw. In the other hand, she conducts a thin cigarette, a graceful flow that visits her lips then returns to the tableau of her blood-daubed talons. She leans her head back to exhale smoke, in a thin stream that — incongruously — brings to mind a factory whistle at lunchtime. Her leaden eyelids overstate her ennui just enough (shades of Theda Bara) to ensure that the hayseeds in the balcony don't miss the drift. It's barely possible to catch the flicker of her pupils as she glimpses to see if anyone (please, someone!) notices. To stare at her affords rich gratification, because in return you can feel the electric rush she gets from attention.

She is a living cameo of that singular Tokyo type: the virgin vamp.

And him?

He has spread-eagled his calfskin legs outward, and pass-ers-by must step high that they don't nick one of his hand-tooled Buck Owens boots and hit the bricks face-first. The jacket is also leather — mauve, cut to the waist and fastened there, but open above to display the shirt and tie — pastels coordinated, by rote, with the other components. The hair is a raven coiffure, sustained by mousse, that defies gravity, centrifugal force, and gale-force winds (but might be flam-mable). It cants outward, spikes upward, glistens weirdly in the presence of neon, and turns his silhouette into something resembling the carcass of a mangled arthropod.

Again, though, you must observe his angle of repose. He has spread his hands wide behind, so that his body forms, roughly, a bent "X." The inevitable Marlboro smolders be-tween two fingers, and he stabs it at his mouth in regular, surly thrusts. His lip curls, Bogart-style, with each painful drag. He doesn't exhale, exactly, but lets the smoke seep be-tween his parted lips and wreathe his face. As he waits, his restless gaze scans, pauses, examines, scans again. Here is Joe Cool, awaiting his main squeeze but alert just in case, ready to improvise if a more interesting prospect crosses his path.

At the right hour of a Friday night, the countless Wave Bars of Tokyo exhibit a steady relay of poseurs, in a panoply of costumes, in an array of roles that would inspire Brecht — each of them laboriously, theatrically aloof.

The tableau always crumbles, when the date — or very often, the group —arrives, turning erstwhile Brads and Ange-linas back into antic Japanese adolescents. Watching the vigil, at the Wave Bar, or at Almond in Roppongi, or in front of the San-Ai Building in Ginza, is like being caught in a mass screen test — because Japan, especially Tokyo, is the world capital of pose-striking. No group of young people on earth — not in Paris or South Beach — is quite so stylish, so slavish in adherence to the written instructions dispensed in the fashion magazines. No population Does and Doesn't so religiously its *Glamour* "Do's and Don't's," nor is so aware of the proper physical attitude necessary to exhibit the costly threads that serve as the uniforms of each peer group.

Pose-striking in Japan, whether intentional or instinctual, expresses both ego and group absorption. Even though one does not — wisely — reject attachment to some group, there is consolation in choosing one's subgroup, deciding in which little repertory company you prefer to play your role. Pose-striking is, simultaneously, the escape from the group to which one must belong, and the signature of the group to which one wants to belong. It defines one's identity, in equal measure, in a kabuki cast or a motorcycle gang. The point, at bottom, is not to be an "original," as it might be in the West, but to be an archetype.

The Importance of the Overture

Sumo wrestlers, of course, live by the pose. From the moment the *rikishi* leaves the silent sweatbox of the locker room and strides down the aisle toward the *dohyo*, he joins a slow-motion tango of pose-striking. In his three to five minutes before *tachiai*, he portrays himself — with all eyes on him and no hand controlling him — not as he is, but in his version of how an ideal warrior ought to be. He strives to symbolize the essence of sumo, the archetype of his posse. The prematch performance of the *rikishi*, his personal overture, is an eloquent set of poses, because it is both contrived and unconscious, because the *rikishi* springs from one of the most rigid, disciplined, and hypnotic subcultures in a rigid, disciplined, and hypnotized nation.

For every sumo match, for every *rikishi*, every movement in the overture is ostensibly the same. Every *rikishi* who makes it to the big time is an honor graduate of the Hollyhock & Calabash Academy of Terpsichory. Except, ah, you can't force every little thing. These are jocks — big dumb, immature, sheltered guys with swollen egos — and you have to give them all some room to get ready, each according to his own drummer. The Sumotori Rag has, thankfully, a thousand variations.

The differences, however, aren't readily apparent. To the Western eye, these overtures — every cockamamie match! — seem endless, pointless, interesting a few times but eventually tedious (even if you insist that you just love Japanese rituals)...

... Unless you know the *rikishi*.

You can't cancel the Sumotori Rag. You cannot fast-forward to the action, because if you did, the match would be a premature anticlimax. You would shrink the *rikishi* to indistinguishable blobs and reduce the drama to little more than noises from the pigsty. The overture is where, in all the apparently senseless wandering and stomping, clapping and scowling, posing and dicking around, you find the personality of the *rikishi*, the imp beneath the archetype, the boy beneath the blubber.

Here's how it happens.

The *rikishi* steps forth from the proscenium and waddles down the aisle several matches before his own. The crowd is inches away on both sides, and when the *rikishi* sits down beside one of the five ring judges to await his match, he is literally part of the audience. Sumo has no dugouts, bullpens, player's box, or foul territory. However, the *rikishi* is comfy, because he sits on a ridiculously plump cushion — his very own personal pillow — that has been set in place ahead of his arrival by one of the elves from his *sumobeya*. As Fatsoyama awaits his match, he poses. His legs are crossed. His arms are either (a) crossed belligerently and nestled on the bulge of his belly or (b) planted on his knees. Unless one of the behemoths fighting up on the *dohyo* threatens to land on him, he holds that pose until he is called. Sometimes he is so engrossed in that pose that he doesn't — or can't — move out of the way in time. Once, Fujinoshin froze so stoically in his ringside pose that he himself became the landing strip for a flying *rikishi*. While his pose-striking may have been commendable, having to default the rest of the *basho* with a broken ankle was ludicrous.

Normally, the *rikishi* only moves when the ref (*gyoji*) hollers for him. The ref himself is a genius of pose-striking. Any ref who can't deck himself out and stiffen his back like a tourist-shop *geisha* doll never moves up from the minor leagues. The ref's costume (traditional, of course) is… well, some outfits defy description. Suffice to say that if Liberace and Salvador Dali had gotten together to design sleepwear for the Phashionable Pharisee, their inspiration would have probably fallen short of the pink, lavender, chartreuse and magenta frippery in which your typical sumo ref minces about the *dohyo*.

To bestir the *rikishi* from ringside, the ref holds out his indispensable "war fan" (*goombai*). He passes it over each *rikishi* as he announces the wrestlers' (a) names, (b) *sumobeya*, and (c) home prefectures — in a bone-jangling squall that would put him into the Hog-Calling Finals, at 6-5 for the title, at any county fair in Arkansas. The ref's pose, complete with the Oscar de la Renta peignoir, is medieval, florid, silly, and superb. It presents a luscious contrast to the *rikishi*'s pallid nudity. Also, the refs ecclesiastical solemnity, underscored by his nail-on-the-blackboard ring announcement, is a sharp reminder that most sumo fans still aren't sure whether this is High Mass or a Tijuana cockfight.

Finally, the *rikishi* clamber up the steps and onto the *dohyo*. They begin their overture. From the first movements, everything is scripted. Officially, there are six distinct steps in the Sumotori Rag, after each of which the *rikishi* return to their corners and pick up a handful of salt, which they toss before themselves (purifying the ground Shintoistically) as they step back onto the *dohyo*. The official movements, in their usual order, are:

1) The entrance ritual. Back to back, they face each other.

2) The spitting, screaming ritual. While the *rikishi* drink holy *chikara-mizu*, spit it out into the dirt, and then wipe their mouths with the sacred napkin, the ref screams their names.

3) The stomping ritual, in which they face each other, clap their hands, lift each leg in turn and stomp the *dohyo*. They do this twice, once from a distance, once at the center of the *dohyo*.

4) The shuffling ritual, in which they paw the sand with their feet.

5) The squatting ritual, which they perform three, four or five times — depending on rank. They squat and check each other out, lean forward and touch their fists to the sand, then return to their squat, stand and go back to the corner. This ritual offers many opportunities for ad-libbing.

6) Finally, *tachiai*.

"Kokoro" and KITSH

Needless to say, these basic steps are only the skeleton of the rich and varied screwing around that precedes the match. Sumo nerds aver that this period (as short as a minute, as long as six minutes) of the Sumotori Rag is one of the most "uniquely Japanese" of all sumo's features. This assertion is harmless and romantic, and simplistic enough to carry a measure of truth. It's especially attractive for those who cherish sumo mainly because it evokes that ineffable throbbing within Japanese culture which the natives call *"kokoro."* This is a word that, of course, they insist is untranslatable but which seems nicely covered by the word "soul."

The truly distinctive feature, actually, in the pre-*tachiai* overture is that it epitomizes the Japanese talent for expressing individuality while falling in with one's group. It is the canticle of the Pose.

By the same token, pre-*tachiai* screwing around is readily familiar to any observant sports fan. For instance, go to a few track meets and watch the sprinters shaking their legs, or go to a football game and check out the linemen running into each other's helmets and pounding shoulder pads, or go to a baseball game and watch as all the players carry on their own tiresome rituals of chewing, spitting, cleat-tapping, juggling the resin bag, adjusting their caps, enjoying the Velcro in their batting gloves, and hitching up their gonads.

No difference. It all comes under the rubric of Killing Time 'til Something Happens (KITSH). The beauty of sumo is that the match itself contains no KITSH whatsoever. Compare soccer, if you will — the world's most popular game — in which far too many games end in scoreless ties, so that the 90 minutes of regulation play, and a half-hour of "extra time," serve mainly as prelude to the shameful tie-breaker shootout that finally decides the game.

Most of American football consists of KITSH — huddles and communiqués from the sidelines. Too much basketball is wasted on timeouts, free throws, guys lying on the floor with sprained ankles, and undergraduate volunteers wiping sweat off the floor after the guys with the sprains get carried away. And don't forget baseball, in which the stretch position is a microcosm of the each game's entire three hours of suspense, and/or sleep (depending on your point of view).

In sumo, at least, KITSH has an honored role. It's part of the game and nobody ever talks about ways to reduce the screwing around and speed up the action. The prescribed rituals — as in other sports — serve the jocks as an energy release and a kind of self-hypnosis. For each *rikishi*, pre-*tachiai* pose-striking is an unconscious routine. "If I noticed what I was doing, if I noticed something different," said former *sekitori* Shinko, "I knew I was in trouble."

Kitao/Futahaguro echoed Shinko's explanation. "Once you're on the *dohyo*, you think of nothing," he said. "You empty your mind. You operate only on your built-up confidence, and you forget the battle plan. Your body has to remember, automatically, what to do. If you start thinking now, you're dead meat."

This self-hypnosis is the reason, I suspect, why a *rikishi* is not ready for the big time until he has devised his very own Rag. It's a groove you have to find before you can comfortably walk beneath a spotlight with your clothes off, in front of 11,000 people (not to mention a national TV audience) and charge head-first into a 350-pound psychotic cretin with hands like cinder blocks.

The KITSH Pecking Order

KITSH in sumo, thus justified, has its standard rituals. But within these movements, the *rikishi* extemporize subtly, artistically, infinitely. Always in Japan, within the group forms, there are private forms of screwing around. It is in these personal poses and flourishes that each *rikishi* offers his message to the world; these subtleties signify the encroachment of *tachiai* and the texture of the impending clash. It is here that the fan refines his appreciation of sumo's overtures, of sumo itself.

Screwing around before the match is a privilege a *riki-shi* must earn. The higher your rank, the more KITSH you get. The lowest-level *jonokuchi* matches are little more than wham-bam-thank-you-ma'am, with the wrestlers hustled on and off the *dohyo* at little more than 60 seconds a pop. In the lower ranks, referees wear simpler nighties and go barefoot, and the wrestlers don't get a saltbox to play with. They wear brown hand-me-down *mawashi* and they don't qualify for hairdressing privileges. Instead of 15 matches in a *basho*, the scrubs only get seven matches to strut their stuff.

A novice nun, or a first-year seminarian, would understand the life of an apprentice *rikishi*. Life sucks, and then you pray.

It is in the preliminary matches that the fan learns to appreciate the aristocratic elegance and leisurely melodrama that attends the longer, loftier matches.

In the two upper divisions, which come complete with bright belts, saltboxes, flunkies, and a personal washcloth for every *rikishi*, the differences in rank are defined by the duration of KITSH. In the second division — *juryo* — matches, each wrestler gets about three minutes to shuffle, flex, and scratch his nuts. I've timed the matches, and recorded a KITSH range between 2:50 and 3:25.

In the lower levels of the upper, *makuuchi*, division, from the bottom *maegashira* all the way up to *sekiwake* (the third highest rank), *rikishi* are permitted minimum KITSH of 3:20, and nobody asks questions if they take as long as 3:50. Among the two top ranks, *ozeki* and *yokozuna*, screwing around is performance art. This is where delay takes on shades and permutations that would win an admiring nod from its greatest connoisseur, C. Northcote "Parkinson's Law" Parkinson. The fastest *ozeki/yokozuna* match in this century might have gotten off in three minutes and fifty seconds. Four minutes is really fast, and most *ozeki/ yokozuna* clashes offer around five minutes of KITSH.

The all-time master of screwing around before the match, however — no contest — was Konishiki, the Hawaiian Hippo. Chiyonofuji, for example, was an efficient, no-nonsense screwer-around, who normally got to *tachiai* in 4:40. But when he wrestled Konishiki — who always sets the pace — the time dragged on to around 5:50. Konishiki is the only *rikishi* to break the six-minute Sumotori Rag. His strategy was apparent and effective. When you weigh 580 pounds, it's a wise policy to make your opponent look as long as possible at those 580 great whopping, swollen, bulging, bursting, drooping, shivering, crushing, monstrous, hostile pounds, and think about them before smashing head-first into the pile and trying to get ahold of it.

Konishiki won many of his matches by just sitting there. His pose was a bludgeon. He seemed to grow before your eyes.

Eight Ways to Screw Around

Konishiki's talent for KITSH ran the proverbial gamut. Few *rikishi* use, as well as he did, the eight basic forms of screwing around: stomping, squatting, sand-shuffling, salt-pitching, finger-licking, staring, self-abuse, and armpit-wiping. Some of these techniques are part of the standard overture set forth by the Sumo Association, some are expansions and variations, and some are unauthorized. To help you to distinguish these nuances, here is some KITSH Lore.

1) STOMPING. The *rikishi* are all required, as they start the Rag, to lift each leg in turn and stomp it on the ground. This is called *shiko*.

   Shiko dates back at least to the 17th century, and it's part of a buck-and-wing that was originally meant to show that the *rikishi* is one tough sumbitch even with his clothes off and no concealed weapons. The modern mystique that surrounds sumo stomping, however, is far more curious.

Every time we discuss sumo, Junko's pal, Hitomi, reminds me that *shiko* is one of the greatest exercises in the world. It bestows robust health and demonstrates a level of agility that would dwarf (if that's possible) a Chinese gymnast. I always nod indulgently, because Hitomi is a true believer in *shiko*. Like millions of others, she's been won over by propagandists who proselytize the restorative magic of sumo stomping. It beats the hell out of tai chi, yoga, dancercise, even wheat-germ tea!

I've learned that it lies neither in the power nor province of one agnostic *gaijin* to uproot this faith. The reason for the Japanese faith in this rather ungainly leg-lifting act, I think, is that *shiko* is the rebuttal to those skeptics who insist that sumo isn't a real sport because the players are all fat, out-of-breath and chronically dyspeptic.

"A lot you know," retorts the true believer. "These guys may not be built like Michelangelo's David, but answer me this: Could Michelangelo's David do *shiko*?"

A pretty devastating rejoinder... except, well, yeah, if he wasn't a statue, David could do *shiko*. Easy.

I can do *shiko*. My octogenarian mother-in-law can do it. Yamamotoyama, f'Chrissake — 560 pounds of dangerous, unsightly fat — he does it every day. It's a simple exercise. It doesn't require any sort of conditioning. It takes about ten minutes to learn how to do it as niftily as a 20-year sumo veteran. It's not aerobic, not anaerobic, not even much of a strain until you hit about 15 reps. And sumo wrestlers don't do reps. Reps ain't dignified.

There is some evidence to support the assertion that sumo stomping does indicate a certain flexibility around the hips and groin, but this probably derives not so much from *shiko* as from the standard Japanese toilet stance — which requires a deep, deep knee-bend over a hole in the floor, and also accounts for Japan's incredibly high incidence of hemorrhoids.

The actual, honest beauty of sumo stomping, and the reason I love it despite its uselessness, is that it looks so good. It's a wonderful pose, and I think the world would be a happier, healthier, sillier place if everybody — before they head for the bar and start talking property values — would face off for a congenial session of leg-lifting and foot-stomping.

Naturally, each *rikishi* has his own *shiko*. The young, athletic *rikishi* tend to emphasize elevation and a powerful finish. The whales prefer to stay low and affect a worldly disdain. Kaio, who was still wrestling beyond 1,700 matches at age 37, was barely getting his *shiko* feet off the ground toward the end of his career. It wasn't that he couldn't do it anymore; he just couldn't be bothered.

2) SQUATTING. Squatting is the soul of the Sumotori Rag. At the highest levels, each *rikishi* in each match has to squat at least eight times. During the squatting ritual, each squat is actually a double-squat — because both wrestlers lean forward into a four-point stance, returning to the squat before standing again.

Because the squat is the most complicated form of KITSH in sumo, it invites creativity. It was in his squat that Konishiki extended his matches. He descended slowly, lingered majestically and rose deliberately. While deep in his squat, he assumed a pose that became his signature. On his right knee his right paw, on his left knee his left elbow — so that Konishiki canted

that awesome brown bod slightly to the left. He looked
— yes! Rakish.

Others have since adopted this pose, the Hawaiian
Tilt, but no one else ever did it with such intimidating
panache. My favorite variation, in recent years, was developed by a middling (but lovable) *maegashira* named
Tochitsukasa. He starts out in the standard squat,
but you notice right away how deep he sinks. His ass
almost brushes the floor. Then he leans into the four-
point stance, squats back, and for a wonderful moment,
you think maybe Tochitsukasa is stuck. He can't stand
all that weight up again! He rocks back and forth like a
Land Rover axle-deep in mud. In the meantime, he puts
up his pudgy little dukes, elbows inside his knees.

Of course, he isn't stuck! This is theater. The rocking
accelerates, his fists tighten, his face assumes a menac-
ing scowl, and then, thrusting his forearms forward
once more and slapping the outside of his knees, his
last hip swivel brings him upright again. He stalks back
to his corner. The fans go wild.

A later advocate of the Tochitsukasa Rock was Harumafuji, a nimble Mongolian who would dip so close
to the dirt on his last squat that he suggested Pope John
Paul II kneeling down to kiss a tarmac.

The Goldfish (Ozutsu) used to do a variation called
the "duck landing." In this bit of KITSH, his squat is
tense, and as he rises, his elbows are outside his knees,
his short arms almost straight, and his fists aimed at
the floor — just about the way a duck spreads its wings
down as it's about to hit the pond.

Aminishiki and old-timer Kaio, both afflicted
throughout their careers with balky knees, often used
their squatting to swing both knees in and out, suggest-
ing that they might suddenly break into the Charleston.

And so it goes. A squat, to the untrained eye, is only a squat. By the same token, the fair-weather fan couldn't tell the difference between Juan Marichal's leg-kick and Bill Lee's eephus.

3) SAND-SHUFFLING. Before the first complete squat-and-face-off, the two *rikishi* resemble a couple of baseball hitters, kicking the dirt around the batter's box. They watch their feet, roll their shoulders, clutch their belts, and try to look casually dangerous. Some make semicircles in the sand, some draw lines, some barely disturb the dirt — just look at it with an air of pensiveness. But this always: Only when they get into the squat do they deign to acknowledge one another.

Thereafter, all the sand-shuffling occurs in their strolls to the saltbox and back. The variations are infinite. Asashoryu, the frightening *yokozuna*, mastered the "robot walk," a stiff-legged gait that suggested a pent-up, psychopathic fury, barely contained. The Sweathog (Fujinoshin) had a habit of dragging his toes on the sand as he rose from the squat and turned toward the saltbox. Konishiki's most delicate habit was to rid himself of sand by tapping each foot on the opposite calf.

Toyonoshima worked the sand, over and over, in arcs so wide that you thought of a dog circling the rug mysteriously before plopping down to rest. Takamisakari, who was always fanatically focused on the battle, never messed with the sand at all — a remarkable trait, because sand is a seduction for bare feet. It radiates warmth or cold up your legs; it offers purchase but gives treacherously under pressure. It tempts the feet to dance, to slip and slide, to shuffle and kick. It seems, in a sense, ominously alive — like cavorting on the back of a sleeping ogre.

4) SALT-PITCHING. After they attend funerals and before
   they re-enter their houses, Japanese people exercise
   a Shinto belief in salt as a symbol of purification by
   sprinkling it on their doorsteps. The salt prevents the
   contagion of death from clinging to them within their
   homes. Thus, salt in the sumo ring poetically kills
   germs, whitens the path of the *rikishi*, and banishes the
   specter of past defeats.

   I doubt that any *rikishi* considers this ancient sorcery
as he marches forth and back in a day of sumo. The
only fans who think this way are the *gaijin* rubes that
are still bogged down in Cultural Appreciation.

   Salt-pitching is the most picturesque moment in the
Sumotori Rag. Check through any sumo guide or peri-
odical. Half the portraits of *rikishi* depict them spreading purification before them. The guides never offer any
text, though, about methods of salt-pitching — an unfortunate omission because this is the instant when all
the fans momentarily pause, rest their chopsticks, freeze
the beer glass on their lips, and peer at the *dohyo*.

   Then two portions of salt mingle in the air, the
rikishi step forth, the ref twirls his *goombai*, the fans
burp, the *rikishi* face off... the moment passes. But it
always comes around again, strange and fascinating
and flavorful.

   There are three basic deliveries for salt-pitching, the
underhand, the sidearm and the flip. Lately, the flip
seems most popular, but fashion is notoriously fickle.
The sidearm delivery, for instance, enjoyed a prolonged
vogue because Chiyonofuji — the most influential
stylist of recent times — brought it from the third-base
side. His most exalted successor was Asashoryu, whose
sidearm delivery started above his shoulder.

No two *rikishi* ever pitched salt exactly alike, because variations occur in such areas as wrist-action (an inward twist, an outward twist, no twist at all), volume and elevation of salt, and follow-through.

Hokutoumi, for instance, threw underhand, with an inward twist, moderate volume, elevation slightly above eye level, and a moderate follow-through. He was the classic conservative salt pitcher — appropriate to his lofty station. The power of Hokutoumi's salt routine lay in his face, where an air of hostility suggested that he was spreading not salt, but a mixture of broken glass and the ground-up bones of his victims.

There was once a middling *rikishi* named Kushimaumi (or "Stretch") who entered the *makuuchi* lists with a refined salt delivery, learned from four years of stellar intercollegiate sumo. He was a sidearmer, didn't throw a lot of salt and got no elevation (sidearmers rarely do). But an early release and a sweeping follow-through created a distinctive motion. In almost every aspect of the Sumotori Rag, Stretch was one of the prettiest stylists of his time. He moved like three or four Fred Astaires (apparently after having eaten Ginger Rogers for lunch).

One of the 21st century's foreign *rikishi*, Baruto (Fred Thompson) had a very conventional salt-toss, except for one endearing quirk. After he'd let it go, he stood there on the *tawara* for an appreciative moment, watching his salt arc upward and array itself on the sand — as though reading portent in its pattern of distribution.

Tamakairiki, who had a forgettable career, was memorable because he affected the rare overhand delivery, dashing the salt at his feet in a hard spray.

Kimurayama always cast his salt disdainfully to the side. Konishiki was a dribbler, as were, in later years, Asasekiryu and Tochiozan.

No discussion of salt-pitching, however, is adequate without a description of Mitoizumi's routine. It was from his salt-pitching extravagance that he earned our affectionate nickname, "The Asshole." In all but his final pitch, Mitoizumi's delivery was less than desultory. He picked up barely a pinch of salt, then flipped it carelessly aside, with no wrist-English.

All this diffidence was — as everyone in the arena knew — a tease. Mitoizumi came out for his final pitch like Evel Knievel hitting the wall of fire. He would typically empty the entire saltbox into his paw, spin toward the *dohyo*, swing back his pitching arm and launch the whole four-pound handful, ten meters into the air, in a slo-pitch softball underhand that created a cloudburst of salt that seasoned spectators as far as five rows deep in the box seats. Mitoizumi's act trampled every standard of athletic forbearance and daily rankled the Sumo Association. He received, in return, a joyful round of oohs, ahs, and giggles from the middle-aged ladies in the audience, very few of whom have ever had an orgasm or seen Wayne Newton Live.

Occasionally, this juvenile routine even helped the Asshole. Any *rikishi* who watched, and reacted to Mitoizumi's dopey display was just distracted enough to be easy pickings at *tachiai*. I've seen better wrestlers lose solely because they paused to roll their eyes at the sight of Mitoizumi's descending saltstorm. Such breaks in concentration were the method in the Asshole's madness.

5) FINGER-LICKING. Compared to squatting and salt-throwing, finger-licking is a minor feature of the Sumotori Rag. Some *rikishi* lick salt from their fingers for good luck. Most don't bother. Sumo wrestlers who finger-lick are like the white basketball players at Holy Cross who make the sign of the cross at the free-throw line.

Usually, *rikishi* try to do their finger-licking as quickly and daintily as possible (except maniacs like Mitoizumi and Takamisakari, who would hit themselves in the face and lick their palms like a beagle in a Beggin' Strips commercial). Walking up to *tachiai* with a sudden overdose of salt (and the accompanying urge to spit it out and get a drink of water) is the sort of distraction that cancels the salt's dubious felicity.

6) STARING. Looking daggers at your opponent is probably the most outright entertaining step in the Sumotori Rag — which is, of course, why it invites the censure of the old farts in the Sumo Association (who all used to do it themselves).

History's most prominent anti-staring decree came just prior to the May Basho of 1990, when Futagoyama, Old Fart Number One (head of the Sumo Association), announced that Konishiki's trademark staring contests were *hin ga nai* ("Tacky, tacky, tacky!"). Futagoyama's ire was duly leaked to the weekly press — so that the public would know that Konishiki's wrist had been slapped. Konishiki, for his part, knew that his chances for promotion to *yokozuna* rested not just on his performance on the *dohyo*, but on his willingness to cramp his crowd-pleasing style by bowing to the generalissimo. It was as if the NFL commissioner had

banned touchdown spikes, or David Stern had ordered
Michael Jordan to stop wearing Bermuda shorts and
sticking out his tongue.

Konishiki complied, robbing sumo of a wonderful
moment. However, the stare that had gotten Konishiki
into all that trouble was classic. He would linger in
each of his pre-*tachiai* squats, Mauna Keanly inert
in his Hawaiian Tilt, glaring at his foe and waiting,
forcing the other guy — always — to look away first.
Every fan knew what was going on. Guys have been
working on their stares since Turok, Son of Stone took
on Alley Oop for dibs on Raquel Welch. Konishiki's
glower — later resurrected by "Hinganai" himself,
Asashoryu — was the same staring contest that has
preceded every playground scuffle since the invention
of recess. It is the same chin-to-chin sneer that drives
fight fans to frenzy just before the main event. It is Jack
Palance, in *Shane*, looking down from the loading dock
into Elisha Cook's rabbit eyes, and waiting — waiting
for the poor dumb sodbuster to make the first move
and seal his bloody fate.

Konishiki reserved his best stare for important
matches. His strategy was to prolong the Sumotori
Rag, alter the other *rikishi*'s rhythm and divert energy
from the actual fighting to the preliminary showing
off. Tochinowaka, another epic starer, was almost
mesmerized by Konishiki. Even Hokutoumi — whose
Charles Manson glower was the only stare more hor-
rible than Konishiki's — betrayed a hint of trepida-
tion when he brushed eyeballs with Konishiki. A few
rikishi, Chiyonofuji among them, solved the problem
by refusing to engage Konishiki in the Great Stare. This
was the exception, though, because among jocks any

challenge so overt is irresistible. To back off is to aban-
don the pose that places you among the brotherhood of
manly men.

Among those who disagreed with Futagoyama's staring ban was Shinko, a devout follower of almost all of
sumo's rules, but also a fan of Konishiki and a connoisseur of pizzazz. "Every *rikishi* has to express his own
style," said Shinko. "Konishiki was just getting ready
in his own way. Besides, the fans loved it."

All this controversy aside, the Old Fart's ban was
a passing ripple. Staring returned, because staring
is more intrinsic to modern sumo than squatting or
chankonabe. When done well by two *rikishi* with a
flair for the glare, it's a crescendo that starts with a
glance, proceeds to a look, advances to a scowl and
ascends in the last face-off to a glacial glower of vaude-
villian loathing. It is beautiful, demented, histrionic and
— at best — it seems to go on forever and ever. It is the
height of The Pose. The great staring contests prompt
spontaneous applause and nervous laughter, simultaneously and contagiously, among the 11,000 fans in the
Ryogoku Kokugikan. At home, they inspire the couch
potato to put down his beer, sit up straight and call his
mate to share the moment, because this is it! Here's the
match everybody'll be talking about tomorrow!

7) SELF-ABUSE. As the countdown nears its end, *rikishi*
   will start hitting themselves on the face and thighs,
   slapping their ass and thumping their *mawashi*. The
   last thirty seconds before *tachiai* sounds vaguely like
   rutting season among bighorn rams in the High Sierra.
   But the secretion reaching critical mass at this moment
   is not testosterone but adrenaline.

In team sports, you can always count on your teammates to high-five, low-five and elbow-bang you to a
fare-thee-well, rub your shoulders, tousle your hair,
bash your helmet, abuse your pads and rub your ass
'til it's rosy-red — at which point your adrenaline is
high enough to send you through a concrete wall without pain.

Sumo, however, is one of the loneliest sports in the
world. Even the guys on your side — the pudgy *tsukebito* who hover behind you, carry your pillow and wait
in the wings with your bathrobe — are forbidden from
laying comradely hands on you. In sumo, if you don't
abuse yourself into a wild-eyed, slobbering frenzy, ain't
nobody gonna do it for ya.

Kaio, who had one of the simplest Sumotori Rags,
was nonetheless an epic self-slapper. In any given
match, he might hit himself more than 40 times, usually from the waist down. Tamanoshima was almost as
prolific. Of course, no one ever smacked his own face
harder than Mitoizumi.

But recently, the foremost flagellator — heir to the
Asshole — was Mad Dog. Throughout the Sumotori
Rag, Takamisakari whaled away at his decorator-col-
ored *mawashi* and pummeled himself on the ass. Just
before *tachiai*, he whacked himself in the lymph glands,
struck himself on the shoulders and chest, pumped his
arms nearly out of their sockets and strode onto the
dohyo with a resounding belt-thump and an answering
roar from the crowd.

Sometimes it all works, sometimes it doesn't, but
who cares? What a show! Hit yourself again, big guy!

8) ARMPIT-WIPING. Guys like Mad Dog and the Asshole
   are frantic and fun, but for all that screwing around,
   this sort of Sumotori Rag is inefficient. It fails often,
   because these guys work harder at The Pose than at
   the job.

   By comparison, Chiyonofuji's Rag was almost invisible. His pose enhanced his art. He prepared himself
   with unwavering consistency, and a cold-blooded
   economy of energy. Nothing altered, nothing wasted. It
   was Chiyonofuji whom I always watched most intently
   through the Rag. I always knew, in his matches, when
   tachiai was nigh — because of the pink washcloth.

   Each *rikishi* brings a washcloth *(oshibori)* to his
   match. It's kept by the ringside flunky, who offers it to
   him after the last face-off before *tachiai*. Most (Hokutoumi, the Sweathog, Hakuho) accepted it; some
   (Asahifuji, Harumafuji) always went *oshibori*-free.
   Those who use it, swab themselves off manfully — con-
   centrating on the face, the chest, lastly of course, the
   pits (except for Kimurayama who, inexplicably, went
   pits-first, then washed his face). Hokutoumi's washcloth routine was especially distinctive. He shrugged
   his shoulders and looked searchingly into the washcloth before immersing his face — like a contestant in a
   life-or-death apple-bob. More recently, Yamamotoyama
   developed a distinctive washcloth routine by pausing
   — a moment of zen? — and staring pensively into the
   distance while nestling his *oshibori* in the cleft between
   his vast Dolly Parton breasts.

   For the fan, the important aspect of armpit-wiping
   is that it signals *tachiai*. When Chiyo takes the pink
   washcloth from the fat kid in the corner and swabs
   himself off, the Rag is over. Put down your newspaper.
   It's time to boogie.

Casual fans tend not to appreciate the Sumotori Rag, because they don't understand that sumo is largely psychological. Concentration wins matches — more than muscle, more than finesse, more than memorizing all the polysyllabic *kimarite* that identify every throw. A great *rikishi* spends those five minutes before the match tightening his focus to the point where he wouldn't recognize his own mother if she handed him a baby-blue *oshibori*, pinched his cheek and said, "Kick butt, sonny!"

Screwing around: If you love it, you're a fan. If you don't, you're a seat number.

CHAPTER 6

TACHIAI
Hookers, Bulldozers, Boxers, Stranglers, Matadors and Low-down Yankee Liars

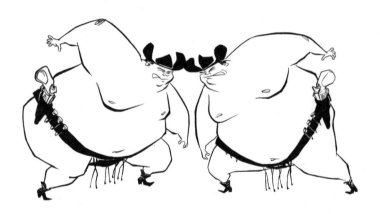

"You're a low-down Yankee liar."

"Prove it."

Thus, Elisha Cook as the hot-tempered farmer challenges Jack Palance, the hired gun, in *Shane*. The next few seconds provide one of film history's most poignant moments of suspense. Cook, angry, terrified, and spoiling for a fight, goes for his gun, only to hear — he doesn't even *see* — Palance's lightning draw. Cook is still looking at his holster, like a bad basketball player watching his own dribble, while Palance's six-shooter is leveled at his heart. He waits, frozen.

In director George Stevens' heartbreaking parody of all the thousands of movie gunfights ever filmed, Cook lifts his Colt slowly, hopelessly, still averting his gaze from the killer's dead eyes. Palance ends the torture abruptly. One shot flings the overmatched farmer dead, into the wagon-tracked mud.

Later in the movie, Alan Ladd (Shane), of course, reverses the drama, facing Palance in Grafton's Saloon and waiting him out. He forces Palance to draw first and blasts him... into the pickle barrel and Kingdom Come.

Great, stirring stuff — now a relic of the Old West and vintage movies. Except in Japan! For sumo is the last refuge of the "quick draw." Sumo re-enacts the tension of the classic Western showdown every day of every *basho* — 200 times a day and 3,000 times every tournament (give or take a few matches). How so? Because every *tachiai* — the moment that two *rikishi* burst from their last squat into a clash of muscle, flab, dirt and palm-oil pomade — has more in common with a Wild West gunfight than any face-off in any other modern professional sport. Sumo, unlike every other popular sport, requires its competitors to start themselves — like Cook and Palance waiting each other out beneath the brooding Teton skies. There's no whistle, no starting gun, no tip-off, nobody to drop the puck, and no goddamn astigmatic ump to holler "Play ball."

There's a ref, of course, resplendent in his lavender taffeta frock and flourishing his shiny *goombai*, but all he says is "On your mark... get set... "

The "go" goes to the jocks. As the tension builds, they squat, they glare, they sweat, and they wait. They "breathe together." Their hands — in Elisha Cook slow-motion — descend toward the sand. Ideally, the drop of the hands occurs in synchrony, and when both *rikishi* brush the *dohyo* with two — not one! Two — hands, they lunge at each other simultaneously.

Ideally.

Sure.

In 79 percent of all sumo matches, according to a highly reliable independent study done by me, one *rikishi* draws first. He disdains the "ideal" and tries to get the jump on his opponent. The old boys in the Sumo Association try to enforce the illusion that every *tachiai* is — or at least ought to be — dead even. They should shut up.

Jumpers and Receivers

When I understood, after a year or so of watching sumo, the intent of *tachiai* as defined by sumo ideologues, compared to the reality of *tachiai* — one guy grabbing a split-second edge on the other — I wondered if it mattered either way. I supposed, at first — one always supposes — that the guy with the jump (the Jumper) gains a tiny, but crucial advantage over the guy who starts late (the Receiver).

Evidence from other sports, however, argues against this supposition. Carl Lewis, for instance — possibly the best Olympic sprinter ever — was a notoriously slow starter. He said he derived extra motivation from his tardy starts, because they allowed him to see the field of runners in front of him. He knew what he had to do, how hard he had to push, and how far before he caught up.

Theoretically, the evidence provided by Elisha Cook, Alan Ladd, Jack Palance, James Arness, Gary Cooper, Quick Draw McGraw, and many others, support the Lewis proposition, that the Receiver — goaded by desperation — has the real edge over the Jumper.

But maybe Carl Lewis was just alibiing his lone athletic deficiency. And really, Marv, how can you trust gunfight data, when the only documentation you have comes from Hollywood scriptwriters who ultimately have to kill the Bad Guy and reinforce the one absolute code of the Western movie: Good Guys never draw first?

Wait, wait! There's proof.

Receivers beat Jumpers. It's true. We even have data…

Sort of.

OK, so I don't have it on me. So maybe it's apocryphal. I still believe it.

Besides, it's fun.

You see, when I was a kid, I read this article about Neils Bohr, the Nobel Prize physicist, the one who helped conceptualize the atom bomb. Remember?

Well, Bohr, it seems, was nuts about Western movies. He watched hundreds of Westerns. Eventually, the same question occurred to Neils Bohr that strikes everyone as they watch their umpty-ninth shootout. Is it just a Hollywood convention that the (usually Bad) guy who draws first tends to lose, or are such results a true depiction of physical, scientific reality? Neils Bohr wanted to know. He was, after all, a scientist. He did not sickly o'er in the presence of an unsolved conundrum.

But how to solve it?

He couldn't restore the Wild West, and he lived in an era prior to the time-travel breakthroughs of Michael J. Fox and Christopher Lloyd, so Neils Bohr did the next best thing. He ordered everyone working in his nuclear physics lab (in Denmark, by the way) to strap toy six-guns onto their hips. He told them that, every time they met in the corridor, they should slap leather and draw, blast away at each other and then record the results.

The results, at least according to this possibly apocryphal and certainly unverifiable tale I read when I was a child — which, incidentally, turned me into a Neils Bohr fan for life

— strongly supported the surprising conclusion that (all other factors being equal [which they never are]) a Receiver will consistently beat a Jumper. Bohr's subsequent hypothesis was that, in seeing the Jumper go for his gun, the Receiver receives a stimulus — a mental message that screams "HURRY!" — and an accompanying rush of adrenaline that compensates for his instant of hesitation and sends the Jumper, that low-down Yankee liar, to Boot Hill.

Bohr's Constant vs. The Human Factor

Tachiai is the same — the only modern parallel to the now-defunct Wild West gunfight. Only through sumo can we even remotely relive those thrilling days of yesteryear — AND — duplicate Neils Bohr's groundbreaking research in gunslingin'.

Which I've done.

I studied 17 days of sumo, in two typical *basho*, running videotape backward and forward in slow-motion 'til I was cross-eyed. I studied 443 *tachiai*, in the *juryo* and *makuuchi* divisions. Of this total, 117 *tachiai* — 26 percent — were either dead even or were not relevant to the outcome of the match.

In the remaining 326 *tachiai*, one *rikishi* got the jump, sometimes infinitesimal but discernible. The Jumpers won 134 matches (41 percent), the Receivers won 192 (59 percent). Of the 17 days I studied, Receivers won a majority of matches over Jumpers 15 times, with one victory for the Jumpers and one day tied.

Ergo? Bohr's Constant applies to sumo. The guy who draws first — in roughly six cases out of ten — bites the dust.

My results supported my expectations, but they also undermined them. Several purely human factors mitigate against this largely mechanical analysis.

For instance, the truly second-rate *rikishi* who gains an advantage in *tachiai* is likely to waste it immediately with his next dumb move.

Second, the significance of *tachiai* decreases with the length of the match. In any match that runs beyond 30 seconds — which is a marathon! — the fruits of *tachiai* cease to be a factor.

Moreover, there are some wrestlers, regardless of the above odds, who build successful *makuuchi* careers as Jumpers. Among sumo's most intimidating Jumpers were *yokozuna* Hokutoumi, *ozeki* Konishiki, and Terao — who was slashingly quick and wildly inconsistent. When matched against a great Jumper, the other wrestler is often compelled to become a Jumper himself. This means he's trying to out-jump the master, which increases the advantage for the more experienced Jumper.

The success of several very highly ranked Jumpers also demonstrates the effectiveness of a really great jump. In any contact sport, when you catch the other guy totally flatfooted, you are almost unbeatable. One of the matches in my statistical sample was a classic all-Jumper showdown between Hokutoumi and Terao. Terao blitzed Hokutoumi by — literally — stealing *tachiai*. Terao was up and in Hokutoumi's face while Hokutoumi was still getting up from his squat. Terao cheated, yes, but the ref didn't call it. On the same day in the same tournament, but with a different ref, Owakamatsu pulled a similar heist on Tamaryu. Tamaryu was beaten so badly that he thought Owakamatsu had false-started and he didn't even fight back.

So, y'see, once in a blue moon, a Jumper can steal a match. Terao might have been the best *tachiai*-jacker in sumo history. Receivers, on the other hand (like Alan Ladd and the Lone Ranger), never steal. They rely instead, and wisely, on Bohr's Constant — which means that you don't mess with the percentages. Receivers, over the long haul, still have the edge.

There's a good reason for this, and its embodiment is, again, in the best *rikishi* of his generation, Chiyonofuji. Chiyo was a Receiver, one of the greats. Comparisons to Don Hutson, Jerry Rice, Yogi Berra. When he jumped — and he did sometimes — Chiyonofuji broke form. He abandoned the patience and precision that placed him in a class by himself. Chiyonofuji, as a Jumper, was merely average, and very beatable.

But when he waited...

Chiyonofuji read his opponent as the other guy was just rising from his squat. Chiyo met the charge with his right shoulder low and his right arm stiff against his chest. The left hand would dart at the other wrestler's belt. If the left missed the belt, Chiyo was unruffled, because his position was solid. The right shoulder was still low, the left hand still poised for attack. At this point, who got the jump on whom is irrelevant, because the wrestlers are erect and active, facing each other in mid-*dohyo*. Chiyonofuji, because he was always the better wrestler, was under control. I watched him bounce off an opponent as many as five times, in that unique crouch, before finally getting his grip and reeling in, tightening up and flattening the poor slob.

Receivers tend, like Chiyonofuji, to be superior wrestlers. All wrestling is, at bottom, a balance of move and countermove. It is the transformation of a good defensive posture into a strong offensive thrust. Jumping at *tachiai* can be a devastating offensive ploy, but unless it is immediately and decisively successful, it tends to leave the *rikishi* in a defensive position so tenuous that he must scramble to recover.

For instance, I remember a high school wrestler from Milwaukee named Hector Cruz. Hector had only one functional hand. The other was a shrivelled-up birth defect. Theoretically, every one of Cruz' opponents needed only to attack Cruz on the side of the crippled hand. Which they did — which, of course, is exactly where Cruz wanted them to go. Cruz had built his entire defensive posture around the protection of that obvious physical weakness. All of his offensive moves, therefore, grew from that defensive preoccupation. If you attacked Hector's bad hand, he was waiting for you. You were toast.

Hector Cruz (he was a Receiver because his body forced him to be) won the state championship that year because his opponents usually misjudged him at the start of the match — and went downhill from there.

"Fast Is Good, Heavy Is Better"

In sumo — each match little more than six seconds — the start is even more critical. In sumo, the start is almost always the finish. The quality of *tachiai* determines victory or defeat at least two-thirds of the time (probably more). If nothing else, my statistics emphasize the intuitive physics of Bohr's Constant. Countermoves prevail over pre-emptive attacks just about 60 percent of the time.

Disregarding statistics, the texture of a sumo match expresses this tendency even more clearly. You can usually spot the underdog because he's the one who looks nervous. (An exception to this rule was the Mongolian *rikishi*, Harumafuji — formerly Ama — who always looked like a white mouse in a snakepit.) Typically, the favorite exudes confidence, even arrogance. While the underdog coils for a lightning attack, his legs bunching, his shoulders leaning across the white line, the favored *rikishi* settles comfortably into a vigilant crouch. His tension is in his eyes — watching, studying, and anticipating. Since he has reviewed his opponent's tendencies and limitations, he usually receives the attack he expects. There's no reason to hurry. Indeed, if he did hurry, he'd be wasting the skill and experience that gives him — even before *tachiai* — the upper hand. For the *rikishi* who brings to the match a touch of athletic genius, six seconds is an eternity.

So, "Go ahead," his eyes say. "Make my day."

Former *rikishi* Shinko amends this recipe for a good *tachiai*. "Fast is all right, but heavy is better," said Shinko. A very fast charge at *tachiai* tends to extend the upper part of the *rikishi*'s body out in front of him. Since *rikishi* — blessed as they are with bellies bigger than beer kegs — tend to be top-heavy, this lightning thrust can backfire into a fatal imbalance, especially when the other *rikishi* doesn't cooperate. If your opponent doesn't match your dive, lean on you with equal and opposite force, essentially holding you up, you can end up facedown in the dirt in nine-tenths of a second. Many matches end this way.

I thought it a clever tactic for a lighter *rikishi* to move laterally at *tachiai* against a bigger opponent, trying to sidestep the monster. But Shinko said no, for the same reason: balance. Even if a *rikishi* is heavily outweighed, "He has to go straight in — head-to-head," like Jim Braddock plunging into Max Baer's deadly wheelhouse in *Cinderella Man*.

There's a measure of machismo in this outlook, but it also makes sense as strategy. For a boxer like Braddock, a basic coaching tenet is "stick and move." The word order is instructive. In sumo — even more than in boxing — you have to make solid contact. Smash that sucker, stop him in his tracks, and then — if you must — start dancing. Stick again, move again. Mobility without contact, in a circle only 15 feet across, is simply a postponement of the inevitable.

Ideally, said Shinko, the *rikishi* comes in low and quick, with his head up. His weight is centered on his hips and thighs. His feet are spread and moving forward in short, balanced steps. This is a "heavy" *tachiai*.

As indicated, however, by the success of several reckless Jumpers, there are *rikishi* who do just fine with a *tachiai* that's all light and goofy. Athletic skill, body type, emotional stability, the identity of the opponent — all these elements alter a *rikishi*'s style of *tachiai*, and serve, now and then, to upset the percentages. No *rikishi* clings invariably to a single approach. He couldn't survive if he were so predictable. But in any given match, the two *rikishi* fall into one of five categories.

The Five Styles of *Tachiai*
Dividing them into groups, you've got your hookers, your bulldozers, your boxers, your stranglers and your matadors.

The HOOKER is the classic sumo wrestler. He extends his strong hand (Chiyonofuji's dangerous left, or Harumafuji's right) as he bursts from his squat, reaching out to hook his opponent's *mawashi* with his fingers. *Rikishi* fall short of many other athletes in areas like abdominal muscle-tone, but they have perhaps the strongest hands in the sports world — because of all the clawing and clinging necessary for the perfect, unbreakable belt-grip.

A hooker who, on the first grab from *tachiai*, gets his grip is most of the way to winning the match.

The BULLDOZER is a *rikishi* who depends on exceptional body mass and a powerful launch. He puts his head down, rather than up, fires forward (often off-balance), plants his paws in the other guy's gut, then rips and flails like a crazed Cape buffalo tipping over a tourist bus. When all this body English meshes, the bulldozer is simply unstoppable and the only defense is to get the hell out of his way. If you can. Bulldozers are pretty quick. Hesitate, and you're on your heels until you're off the *dohyo*.

My favorite bulldozer ever was a Samoan named Nankairyu, who had shoulders like an ox and legs like a bridge abutment. When he launched his full charge and hit an opponent head-on, they both ended up in the fifth row, and it was up to the ring judges to decide who landed first. Unfortunately, Nankairyu was predictable. Other *rikishi* regularly anticipated his lunatic rush and countered it with increasing effectiveness. Unable to master any other techniques, Nankairyu hung up his cup and went back to Samoa — breaking my heart but probably pleasing his mom. (Sumo nerds also note that Nankairyu had an array of poignant personal problems, but who cares? This is a sumo wrestler, not Holden Caulfield.)

BOXERS explode from *tachiai* with two methods of attack, called *tsuppari* and *hataki* both can be translated, simply, as "hitting," or open-handed boxing. They batter the other *rikishi*'s chest, shoulders, head and face with a furious flurry of blows, some of them violent enough to draw blood and all of them richly entertaining. Boxers force their opponents to box back. When they work, *tsuppari/hataki* attacks precede two possible results. The preferred result is that the boxing assault — as many as 25 blows in less than five seconds — so overwhelms the victim that he staggers backward across the *tawara*. If that doesn't work, the boxer strives to knock his opponent momentarily off balance, so that he can grab something — head, arm, shoulder, belt, nostril — that will give him leverage.

Tsuppari and *hataki* are savage, simple, wonderful to watch and — when effective — withering. The problem is that boxing robs both *rikishi* equally of their balance. The attacker is just as likely as the receiver to find himself cartwheeling off the *dohyo* and landing in somebody's 3,000-yen *obento*. Nevertheless, because boxing is a mainstay for lightweight underdogs to fend off Hippos, bulldozers and other pituitary mutants, it will remain forever a fundamental element of sumo.

A STRANGLER is a boxer who doesn't bother to hit the other guy. He rises from his squat, extends one hand, clamps it on the other guy's throat, and pushes the poor bastard's larynx into the bleachers. The unfailing characteristics of stranglers are (a) real good upper body strength, and (b) a grip like a vise. Hokutoumi, for instance, could give a few pointers to Albert DeSalvo. He was one of few *rikishi* who could virtually lead an opponent off the *dohyo* by his throat.

The disadvantage to this stranglehold (called *nodowa*) is that, with a powerful swipe, an opponent can break the grip and simultaneously tip the strangler off-balance. If the receiver then seizes that instant of imbalance, the strangler becomes easy pickings.

Finally, everybody in sumo at one time or another plays MATADOR. All you have to do is pretend you're about to smash into the other guy with all your might. Then, instead, you jump aside, let the other guy go flying by, and watch him crash and burn on the sand. Maybe, just for good measure, you give him a little shove, a little whack upside the head as he goes by. The only thing missing in this scene is a red cape.

The matador move works, at times, against any unwary *rikishi*, but it's especially effective (and funny) against chronic bulldozers. Nankairyu gave up sumo mainly because everyone started playing matador against him. In some matches, he looked like a Keystone Kop in a Hal Roach comedy — charging pell-mell to smash open a door only to see it swing open at the last second.

The matador move, however, is used sparingly — for two reasons. The first is that the Sumo Association tends to frown on matadors. According to the prevailing mythology, the true *rikishi* is a Spartan stoic who smashes headlong into obstacles and scrambles his brains with reckless valor. The matador move is too clever and evasive — you can win without even touching the other guy — to enjoy favor among sumo's scramble-brained traditionalists.

Using the matador move is a sure way to displease the old farts in the Sumo Association. A prime example of this was Harumafuji's first championship, in the May 2009 basho, when he went 15-1, beat both *yokozuna* (Hakuho in a Day 15 wrestle-off) and — by my count — scored 175 points. But the next week, when the old farts convened to consider promoting Harumafuji from *ozeki* to *yokozuna*, the kid got the big "No way!" The reason was that he was accused of *henka* on Day 11 of the basho, against Kisenosato. In dodgeball terminology, this means he ducked rather than dove, sidestepping Kisenosato's bull rush and snatching a cheap victory. This one Muhammed Ali moment — even though Harumafuji later said he actually blundered into the move — was sufficient to quash his hopes for promotion.

The best reason not to overdo the matador maneuver, however, is that it can backfire against a good Receiver. A seasoned Receiver can twist suddenly toward the would-be matador while he's still perched perilously on his elusive tippy-toes and, hence, completely vulnerable. In this embarrassing eventuality — technically known as the Old Switcheroo — there's no defense. For instance, I never saw Chiyonofuji, the Nureyev of the Old Switcheroo, beaten by a matador. The rest of the guys gave up even trying it against him.

Sumo's guardians frown on the matador dodge for the same reason they fumed at Konishiki's staredowns. It's gamesmanship. The Sumo Association prefers the comforting fiction that sumo is unsoiled by guile, deceit, and base trickery. However, as we see, the entire prelude to the match is electric with gamesmanship — and much more amusing because of it.

To Live and Die at *Tachiai*

Tachiai is the climax of the battle of wits. Even though, logically, the advantage lies with those who react rather than with those who leap, there is a deep seated temptation to fool the ref, sneak a huge jump and steal a cheap victory in the grueling midst of a the fifteen-day tournament. That's why the Sumotori Rag enjoys such infinite variety and all the pose-striking unfolds with such mirthless gravity. That's why *rikishi* mind-game 'til the very last seconds before the charge.

That's why sumo's final squat, just before *tachiai*, is a magic moment in sports. The wrestlers creak into position, tug at their belts, paw the dust, stare blankly at the ground, fussily arrange the useless fringe *(sagari)* that hangs from the front of their *mawashi*, and watch each other intently as one hand, and then the other, stretches down, touches the sand and gradually, exquisitely, precipitates the crash.

Some *rikishi* add features to this drama. Mitoizumi (the Asshole), for instance, habitually called off the charge, insisting that he wasn't ready — forcing the ref to relax his *goombai* and re-set the squat. Inevitably, Mitoizumi's opponents started to counter this gimmick by deliberately false-starting, barging into the Asshole before he could pull his "I'm not ready" routine.

False starts are a common device, and they're often intentional — as intimidation or as a tension release. When they happen, the ring judges look distressed. If one *basho* features too many false starts, the old farts punish all the *rikishi* like schoolboys by convening an all-day *tachiai* seminar. They publicly complain that this new generation of *rikishi* can't do *tachiai* like they did in the old days when they had to walk three miles uphill in the snow to get to sumo practice. This is all horseshit, but it injects into the gamesmanship of *tachiai* an odor of the forbidden that enhances its enjoyment.

When a *rikishi* false-starts accidentally, though, it often tips the balance of gamesmanship hopelessly against him. The one advantage that the two opponents share — as they mirror each other through the Sumotori Rag and the last squat — is mystery. They don't know, for sure, what the other guy's gonna try. This mystery is especially deep among old wrestlers, who get cagier as their talent collapses into sawdust and cholesterol.

A false start can shatter the mystery — exposing a *rikishi*'s plan before he can execute it. If this first gambit is revealed in a false start, Lardass has perhaps five seconds to make a new plan and apply to it the full force of his will — which is almost impossible (especially considering the dim intellect of your average jock).

Even if a *rikishi* has preserved the mystery of his strategy, he is exposed at the very instant of *tachiai*. Whatever he is going to do is done, in the blink of an eye. All of sumo's intricate plotting is concentrated in that split second. There are a thousand moves and countermoves in sumo — as there are in every other wrestling sport. But the difference is that in sumo, every subsequent action lives or dies at *tachiai*. If Move No. 1 fails, you may never get to Move No. 2.

Stonewall (Elisha Cook, Jr.) and Jack Wilson (Jack Palance) — and Nankairyu, the Samoan cannonball — ended up learning the hard way the first principle of gunslinging, and sumo: If you fumble the draw, ain't nobody shifty enough to duck the bullet.

CHAPTER 7

THE FISTFIGHT
at the Malamute Saloon
and Other Japanese
Cultural Treasures

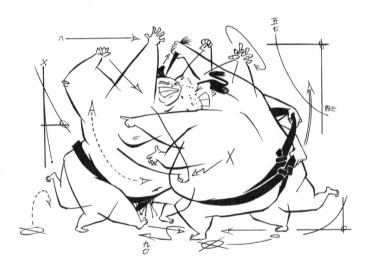

Now, I wouldn't want to suggest that, after *tachiai*, the rest of the sumo match is just a matter of mopping up — although this actually proves true in many cases. Once a *rikishi* has gained even a tenuous advantage at *tachiai*, it is his to squander, and it is his opponent's to overcome. Herein, then, lies the drama of sumo, the heart of the matter.

The fight is the thing.

And here is sumo's heart-warming simplicity — because all a fan has to know is that one guy is trying to push the other guy into the dirt or off the dance floor. Touch the ground with anything but your feet, set one little piggie over the straw ridge, and you lose. Time to go.

Perhaps more important, however, to all you tourists and culture vultures out there, is that those sweaty, grunting, thunderous few seconds between *tachiai* and the decision contain sumo's visual splendor and disturbing (or — if you're inclined that way — alluring) sensuality. Here is sumo's great jiggling mass of flesh, the almost sexual sprawl of naked men — bobbling breasts; moist, protuberant lips; pudgy hands grasping, groping, feeling, seeking purchase on the sweat-slicked body of another; pulsating buttocks; neon codpieces; thighs like Star Jones...

In a word: Culture!

This is the moment in sumo that drives observers — from the novice to the jaded commentator — to dizzy heights of socio-anthropological insight and raptures of overstatement. It's hard to keep your cool while watching Onokuni jump on top of Kyokudozan and squish him like a cockroach. The verbal crapola that emerges in the heat of a day's sumo, especially after a few rousing matches, is almost unparalleled in sports, and it tends to distort the fan's perception of sumo as fun and games.

The Expert

For instance, one day in the mercifully distant past, NHK's guest commentator was an American I'll mercifully refer to as Fred. Fred's apparent qualifications for commenting authoritatively on sumo's intricacies stemmed from his hobby as a sumo photographer. He was also teaching courses (none of them sumo) at a Japanese university. Like many *gaijin* in Japan, Fred's genuine talents were difficult to judge because he had been pressed into service by his eager Japanese hosts to pontificate in a dazzling variety of fields, not because he knew whereof he spoke but because he was fluent in the local lingo.

I manfully maintained an open mind about Fred's sumo wherewithal until he exposed himself with the following statement:

"You can't understand Japanese culture unless you understand sumo."

Oh, puh-lease!

This breathtaking simplification — a common feat among *gaijin* spokespeople in Japan — inevitably won murmurs of xenophobic approval from the NHK flacks who man the mikes. It served, after all, to reinforce the official sumo propaganda package. The NHK boys egged Fred on to further banalities while I pondered variations on this always popular "You can't understand... unless..." formula. The one that struck the truest note to me was one that has occurred to me often as I watched the matches on NHK: "You can't really understand sumo (ergo, Japanese culture) unless you understand basketball."

A wild conjecture! Red Auerbach as a repository of Oriental mystery?

It can't be true, but there's a point. Anyone versed in the fundamentals of many sports will quickly grasp the mind and method that govern *rikishi* during the apparently frantic burst of clutching and pounding that follows *tachiai*. After watching closely just a handful of matches, the observant fan will grasp that this classic, visceral clash contains nothing really mysterious. In sumo's face-off, there is, indeed, more of man-to-man coverage than socio-anthropology. Here — as any observer of NBA paint combat, or NFL trench warfare, knows — the best way to grasp what's happening in these desperate seconds is to watch the monsters' hands and feet.

Hands, Feet and Angles

Sumo is a wrestling sport, which means that — most of the time — skill, balance and intellect will beat sheer size and brute force. To see how this happens, how Akinoshima — a veritable nymph at 1.76 m (5'9") and 135 kg (297 pounds) — compiled a 9-2 record versus Konishiki — 1.87 m (6'2") and 264 kg (580 pounds) — the educated fan tears his eyes away from those amber waves of flab and looks for Akinoshima's hands.

Chances are those meathooks are frantically hammering at Konishiki's arms. And Konishiki's hands are lunging toward Akinoshima's throat, for the stranglehold that Konishiki can use to frogwalk the smaller man off the *dohyo*. Unless Konishiki can get the grip he wants, his enormous size is a dangerous burden, teetering on hips and knees which — regardless of how awesome they look — are too small to move him safely in the feints and circles that Akinoshima prefers. Akinoshima slaps, claws and yanks at Konishiki's immense arms, battling to force the giant, just once, to sway unsteadily. If this occurs, Konishiki must relent in his assault and regain his balance, which permits Akinoshima to seize the offense, snapping and punching at Konishiki like a mockingbird harassing a crow.

HANDS, in sumo, dictate offense.

Chiyonofuji, for instance, never lost when he reached in, through a desperate opponent's guard, and hooked a solid belt grip. He was equally dangerous with (a) his left arm on the belt over the other guy's arm *(hidari-uwate,* for you would-be nerds), or (b) his right arm on the belt inside the other guy's arm *(migi-yotsu).* He would attack either side with equal tenacity and sink that grip deeper and deeper as his opponent struggled against it. And then he'd drag his victim down.

As he aged, Chiyonofuji was beaten when he fell into a predictable pattern of going repeatedly for one side. He was also vulnerable when the other guy worked like mad to keep Chiyo's hands off his *mawashi*. Without his grip, Chiyono-fuji was a small man fighting a big guy, and things tended to even out.

The point, above all, is that once you'd watched Chiyo through a dozen matches, you concentrated on his hands, and on his opponent's hands, because you knew that the whole match lay in where they each got — or didn't get — a grip.

After hands comes, no, not feet — we'll get to that — the *MAWASHI*, the belt. It is an irony of sumo that its practitioners are regarded as the nakedest (not counting those naughty ancient Greeks; and I'm leaving out topless lady Jell-O wrestlers, too, OK?) of all grapplers. The tank-top, short-legged, crotch-grabbing jumpsuit worn by amateur wrestlers is intended to simulate nudity, but covers all the erogenous zones, as do the lollipop panties favored by professional wrestlers. Sumo wrestlers look nakeder because their butt-cheeks are out there for all the women of Japan to admire and compare.

However, in a practical sense, the sumo wrestler is less naked than all his fellow grapplers. The key to all sumo technique lies in the *mawashi*, which is wrapped so many times around the *rikishi*'s waist (I'm not sure how many times around, but Doreen knows, and she insists that Lora doesn't) that it sticks out. You can use the belt for leverage. The presence of the *mawashi*, around each *rikishi*'s ample middle, makes sumo the rare wrestling sport in which your opponent is not functionally nude; the only wrestling sport in which you have something other than a body part to grab hold of.

The *mawashi* is the attacker's goal and the defender's weakness. Because the *mawashi* naturally evolved, many moons ago, as a magnet for the sumo wrestler's strength and imagination, it turned sumo inevitably into an above-the-waist (more Greco-Roman than freestyle) wrestling sport.

There is no ban on leg-holds in sumo, but they are almost nonexistent. Some wrestlers attempt leg-holds in desperation, but usually — just as quickly — let go, as though they'd just stuck a hand into something dead and smelly. Leg-holds carry a stigma of cowardliness. They suggest that, jeez, if you gotta trip the other guy to win, maybe you should go into another line of work, like nursing, or hairdressing.

This explains, logically, why the better *rikishi* are deft in belt technique, and why — often apparently in a suicidal impulse — smaller *rikishi* plunge headlong into the bottomless flesh of Hippos. Even if it seems futile in the short term, you won't last in sumo over the long term unless you figure out a way to handle the other guy's *mawashi*.

The standard wisdom in sumo, as belt grips go, is that it's good to get your strongest arm inside the other *rikishi*'s arm. It's even better to get two arms inside. This is called *morozashi*. However; the supposed advantage of *morozashi* is arguable, especially against a tall Hippo. Hippos — Onokuni was a prime example — will often invite short guys to get *morozashi*. "G'head. Take my belt. C'mon, l'il fella!"

So, the little guy goes ahead. He gets his *morozashi*. "Look, Mom! Two hands!" But then, suddenly, Onokuni clamps his enormous arms around the little guy's little arms, in a kind of frontal hammerlock that I call the Crab Grip. Once a Hippo has closed the Crab Grip and pinned the other guy's arms against his sides, he can reel the little guy in at his leisure. If a smaller *rikishi*, however strong and agile he might be, finds himself plastered against a Hippo's much bigger belly, he's a man without arms, without leverage, without a prayer. All he can do is hold on and hope that a sudden aneurysm strikes the Hippo dead.

The Hippo, for his part, executes the second phase of the Crab Grip, known as the Hippo Waddle, in which he simply plods forward, bending over his pathetic opponent, pressing him tighter and tighter to his belly until the poor guy's heels are perched on the *tawara*. Then a few belly-bounces and, alley-oop! The pipsqueak is airborne.

Morozashi can also be ineffective against superb technicians, like Chiyonofuji, whose wrestling repertoire was so vast that he could counter almost any apparent advantage, and dominate a match from a seemingly inferior position. A *rikishi* who got a quick *morozashi* on Chiyonofuji was usually charging into a trap.

FEET, in sumo, dictate defense.

As all that hand jive unfolds, the *rikishi* who forgets to use footwork to his advantage is like a basketball player with Nike-prints on his chest. Good *rikishi* will always keep their weight on the balls of their feet, evenly distributed in a broad stance — the classic defensive pose in basketball. When *rikishi* lock into the familiar stalemate position, heads on each other's shoulders, hands on each other's *mawashi*, they extend their legs back as far as possible from the other *rikishi*, for balance. One foot is slightly forward of the other, thus balancing the *rikishi*'s weight forward and backward, as well as laterally.

The best example for the importance of footwork in sumo was probably Terao, who built a lovably inconsistent record around his superb sense of natural balance — and his Mr. Hyde tendency to completely ignore it at times. Terao's *tachiai* resembled an active firehose without a fireman attached. He roared in, spraying punches in all directions, intent on knocking his usually larger opponent off balance while concealed in a cloud of dust. When he concentrated on keeping his stance wide throughout this blitz, he virtually doubled his size, and sent his disoriented opponent reeling off the *dohyo* — or diving for a spot where Terao was just a second ago. Thump.

On the other hand, Terao lost his concentration as regularly as Fanny Hill sacrificed her virtue. He had a habit of getting his legs together, or even crossing them as he pursued — or fled — his opponent. When that happened, you could usually count to about three before Terao landed — upside-down — in somebody's lap. Terao's flying Tsukaharas into the crowd were one of sumo's all-time pleasures.

More important, Terao's vaults were a classic illustration of why a solid defensive position is fundamental to sumo, or basketball.

ANGLES, in sumo, suggest the advantage. But not always.

Any time a *rikishi* can turn his opponent, he has leverage. He is moving straight ahead against the opponent, while the opponent is applying his strength sideways, inefficiently. The other guy's in trouble.

When two *rikishi* have their shoulders parallel, and on the same vertical plane, they're stalemated, feeling for a better grip, working for position, thinking. If one of them changes the plane of that parallel, so that his shoulders are above — or below — the opponent's shoulders, an advantage emerges again. However, the advantage in this situation — when the *rikishi* remain face-to-face but not shoulder-to-shoulder — isn't determined by angles. Then the difference goes back to the relative position of hands and feet.

Here's how angles play a decisive role. In one long-ago Nagoya Basho, Takamisugi (Butterball, 319 lbs) was wrestling Kyokudozan (Jock, 222 lbs). Both knew that, face-to-face, Takamisugi had the edge, because he was heavier and more likely to buffalo the stronger but smaller *rikishi* off the *dohyo*. When he wrestled, the underweight Kyokudozan always had to counter this threat, so he consistently worked to plant himself at an angle to his opponent's body.

Predictably, Takamisugi fired out fiercely at *tachiai*. He moved Kyokudozan back, almost to the *tawara*. Kyokudozan bounced off Takamisugi and sidestepped, momentarily achieving his angle. But Takamisugi, an old warhorse who knew the danger of pushing an advantage too hard too fast, suspended his charge and turned into Kyokudozan. Splat. Face-to-face. Stalemate. They nuzzled each other's necks for a moment, clinging to each other's *mawashi*. They waited. Loosing his grip on the left and using his speed advantage, Kyokudozan jumped to the right. He pulled hard on his right-hand grip, hoping to unbalance Takamisugi and upend him with an arm-throw. It didn't quite work. Takamisugi was a mite too heavy to just toss around like a beach chair, and — for a whale — he was also pretty quick. But Kyokudozan's move was still much better than Takamisugi's response, because he was able to hold a position with his shoulders at a 45-degree angle to Takamisugi's. He had him. Takamisugi twisted, trying to regain the stalemate and backpedaled to give himself room. But as he did so, his feet closed, his grip lost its conviction. Kyokudozan pressed the advantage, driving into Takamisugi's shoulder — all the way off the *dohyo*.

Hands, feet and angles.

While this was all going on, there was a lot of noise. Screaming, to be exact. Not from the crowd. It was from the referee.

The Guy in the Pajamas

By a rather felicitous tradition, sumo has the most useless referees (*gyoji*) in all of sport. They dress really pretty, and sumo nerds wallow in explanations of the ritual significance of all the doo-dads and thingamagummies referees carry with them. And they carry a lot of thingamagummies. By comparison, Kid Sheleen in full regalia was a sartorial minimalist. Every referee, for instance, has his silk pajamas, of course, and a hat that makes him look like a bellhop balancing a flat-iron on his head, *tabi* (socks) and *zori* (sandals) on his feet, plus his *goombai* and a long silk rope he trips over during matches — and all these come in colors that tell you his rank, his family, his blood type, the year he first got laid — all kinds of good stuff! None of this, of course, means a thing.

OK, it means something. It's every bit as important as the color of the uniforms the Bonham Boogers of the Texas-Oklahoma League wore during road games in 1922. Remember?

In any case, sumo *gyoji* have a lot of work just keeping their ensemble in order and their silk rope out from underfoot. So their workload during the match is light. Mostly, they scream — in a nasal squeal that evokes the pork queue in an Iowa slaughterhouse. The sense of their screaming is distinctly unhelpful. Mainly, they shout, *"Nokotta, nokotta, nokotta, nokotta, nokotta,"* etc. This means, "You're still in, you're still in, you're still in, you're still in, you're still in," etc. If the match lasts more than ten seconds, the ref intercedes on behalf of all the impatient fans out there in TV-Land who want to take another sip of their beer, and he screams, *"Yoi, hakkeyoi!"* ("Hey, move it!") Just the sort of thing you want to hear from an 85-pound septuagenarian geek while you're trying to uproot the Son of the Blob without benefit of a forklift.

Rarely, a referee leaps into the breach for a spasm of crisis management, largely because the world of sumo eschews the use of modern fastening technology — zippers, velcro, etc. *Rikishi* still get their *mawashi* tied manually in the rear. In the heat of a match, a knot occasionally comes undone — at which the referee halts the hulks in mid-tussle, tells them to freeze in position, and then secures the loose ends. Considering the size difference between *rikishi* and ref, this touching scene tends to resemble an ant gift-wrapping a pair of mid-coital June bugs.

It might happen, but in many years of sumo devotion, I've never seen a referee "call" a violation, personal foul, or illegal hold on a *rikishi*. If a ref ever tried such a thing, it would prompt a big meeting in the middle of the *dohyo*, at which the five judges would talk, the referee would speak only when spoken to, and the five judges would then nod and solemnly return to their places, after which the head judge — who holds more Sumo Association clout in his little finger than any referee has stuffed inside his entire ensemble — would gravely announce that the poor dumb ref is full of shit, sorry, folks, next match! And the referee's career would be over.

The Finish
This, then, is the essence of sumo for the eagle-eyed fan.
  Hands.
  Feet.
  Little guys fighting for an angle.
  Big guys hugging and waddling.
  And pesky, impotent referees.

There's one other thing — the end of the match, the winning move. Now, clearly, the winner does not execute his *coup de grace* without properly setting it up, with a good *tachiai*, deft hands and solid footwork. But most sumo nerds, in discussing what happened in any given match, cut right to the chase — which is the naming of the victorious move (or *kimarite*). This is not because they cherish brevity. They just like to toss around ratatat Japanese terms that most fans can't remember.

They like this part 'cause it's culture!

According to the experts, there are dozens of techniques that determine victory in a sumo match. My favorite expert, for instance, insists that there are 4,667 if you include *goombai taberu* (a rare technique that involves forcing the referee's fan down your opponent's throat). The importance is that each "technique" is difficult to pronounce and is distinctly anticlimactic. I mean, after every middle-aged housewife in the audience has stood up, raised her fist and shouted, "Whoa! All right! In yo' face, fatso!" the solemn announcement that Twin Peaks employed *oshidashi* to secure the victory is depressingly tame. Besides, Twin Peaks can't do anything but *oshidashi*!

Above all, who cares? This is 'rasslin', not art history class. Shove 'im again!

Seriously, though, there is enlightenment to be gained from the rudiments of Sumo Climax Nomenclature (SCN). And even if there isn't, it's something you can't avoid if you watch the sumo matches regularly. Once a match is over, the scramble to name the move dominates the NHK broadcast. As soon as one guy wins, someone (I suspect it's the head judge) decides which technique was used. This decision is relayed to NHK, announced by the play-by-play announcer, and flashed on the TV screen. The public address announcer then passes this intelligence on to the crowd. If it all sounds like gibberish, don't worry. The nice thing about SCN is that you, the fan, have a lot of people to take care of it for you. The Sumo Association, the regiment of sumo nerds, and the guys at NHK are all on duty, telling you incessantly who used what stratagem to whup whom.

Nevertheless, discerning a few key phrases from the TV announcer will help keep you on top of the action. Here they are.

1) SOMEBODY-NO-KACHI. *"Kachi"* means "win." When you're not sure who landed outside the ring first in a match between Toyonoshima and Tamanoshima, *"Toyonoshima no kachi,"* tells you that Tamanoshima bit the dust. (Or maybe the other way around. I could never tell these guys apart.)

Additionally, there is a handy visual aid if the TV camera catches it. The referee's proudest task is to point his *goombai* in the direction from which the winner entered the ring. The ref can be overruled by the ring judges occasionally, but most times, the *goombai* denotes the winner. Nice job, ref. Go to your room.

2) YORIKIRI. This is the commonest and most dignified way to win a sumo match, otherwise known as "the missionary position." It's also usually the dullest. When you hear "*yorikiri*," it means the winner was face-to-face with the loser, hugging him rhythmically and straining to push him backward across the *tawara*, often grinding his codpiece into his opponent's groin. Most *rikishi* are trained to fight for a two-hand belt-grip and taught that *yorikiri* is the manliest form of victory, requiring the maximum of strength, flab, and technical virtuosity. I suspect that it's regarded with such esteem because it's easy to teach to dumb jocks. Whether you call it a bear hug, the missionary position, *yorikiri*, or call it late to dinner, it has the charm of brute instinct.

"*Yorikiri*" is usually the technique announced when two incompetent *rikishi* bungle through a chaotic brawl and collapse on top of each other. In the absence of even a vestige of technique, the usual Sumo Association policy is to put the best possible face on the mess: they invoke the missionary position and hope NHK loses the videotape.

The Hippo Waddle, by the way, is the dullest form of *yorikiri*.

3) SOMETHING-DASHI. There are a host of "*dashi*" moves, but most mean that the winner shoved the loser off the *dohyo*, usually hard, usually all over the fans in the front row—who always giggle. *Oshidashi* is the

commonest -*dashi*, and it is bread and butter for boxers and bulldozers. Stranglers like it, too.

Most -*dashi* are violent and unsophisticated, but *tsuridashi* is a notable exception. It is the *piece de resistance* of sumo's strongest and most athletic *rikishi*. It requires that the winner secure a vise-like two-handed belt grip and lift — literally carrying the other guy off the *dohyo*, as the victim kicks his legs helplessly. *Tsuridashi*, which puts dangerous pressure on the back, demands enormous strength and perfect timing. Chiyonofuji was a master of this move, but late in his career, he was surpassed in this technique by Kirishima, a new *ozeki* who changed his previously mediocre career through a diligent program of unauthorized weight-training.

Among the wave of foreign *rikishi* who entered sumo in the 2000's, Baruto (Fred Thompson) — partly because he towered over most opponents — distinguished himself as the deftest *tsuridashi* practitioner among his peers.

4) SOMETHING-TENAGE. All the -*tenage* (derived from *te*, "arm," and *nageru*, "to throw") are arm throws, with the loser usually landing on his back inside the *dohyo*. Of all sumo moves, these tend to be the most sudden, graceful and athletic. A *rikishi* who works hard to get an "angle" on the other guy is usually working for some sort of -*tenage*. There are many such moves, and they often evolve spontaneously in a match after one or both of the *rikishi* have failed in other moves and find themselves tangled, side-by-side, trying to yank each other to the sand. Any -*tenage* is good entertainment. In the hands of Chiyonofuji, Hakuho, or one of the

other good technicians, it's art.
Definitely more fun than *yorikiri*!

5) UTCHARI deserves special mention because it is sumo's
most stunning move. In amateur wrestling, it would
be called a "reversal." It usually occurs when a small,
strong wrestler has been backed to the *tawara* by
a bigger guy. He has a good belt grip, maybe even
morozashi, but it isn't doing him much good because
he's almost off the *dohyo*. Suddenly, he lifts and turns,
executing what amounts to a twisting *tsuridashi* and
flinging the big palooka off the *dohyo*. Usually, the
big guy drags him down too. But, in a well-executed
utchari, the guy with his back to the wall lifts the other
guy high enough and turns him far enough that he ends
up landing on top of his erstwhile conqueror. It is an
extraordinary move — also hard on your lumbar spine
— that literally turns defeat to victory. Reversals only
work because the winner has a better belt grip. *Utchari*
is all the more dramatic because it usually requires a
smaller *rikishi* to dead-lift a Hippo.

Two of the more astounding examples I've seen were
Kyokudozan (222 lbs) reversing Kushimaumi (407 lbs)
— without even locking his knees first, and Kirishima
(279 pounds) reversing Onokuni (460 pounds).

6) HATAKI KOMI. The Matador (see Chapter 6).

7) MONO-II. In practical terms, this means, "Wait a
minute," and it comes from any one of the five ring
judges (or *shimpan*) who might disagree with the referee's *goombai* in a very close match. Usually, *mono-ii*
are called when both wrestlers tumble off the *dohyo*

together, or hit the dirt almost simultaneously. When a ring judge, who usually happens to be one of the ten biggest wheels in the Sumo Association, raises his hand for *mono-ii*, all the judges gather on the *dohyo* with the referee, who is required to keep his trap shut unless called upon.

The ring judges then consider a number of factors before deciding who really won. These include:
(a) Which wrestler actually touched down first? The ring judges are allowed to check video replays through an audio linkup with the TV truck. They don't look at the video, you understand. They listen to it.
(b) Which wrestler was making a more positive offensive move as the both of them crashed in a cloud of dust?
(c) Which wrestler comes from a more powerful *sumo-beya*, and whether the Sumo Association wants to promote the interests of that stable.

The ring judges discuss only (a) and (b) above. The other, (c), is simply a tacit consideration that tends to outweigh (a) and (b).

Because of these conflicting considerations, the results of *mono-ii* are often surprising to the observant fan. Crews of ring judges rotate, and these *shimpan* — even within the same crew — apply no consistent pattern to their decisions. In some cases when a decision seems impossibly close and *mono-ii* strikes the observer as appropriate, the ring judges sit motionless, possibly asleep. This means that both *rikishi* are relatively unimportant and don't merit special attention from the muckymucks around the *dohyo*.

After *mono-ii*, one of three results might be announced by the head judge — usually in an incomprehensible mumble

Previous page The *piece de resistance* of sumo is *tsuridashi*—literally carrying your helpless opponent off the *dohyo*. Here, Asashoryu humiliates his fellow Mongol, Hakuho.

Top *Yokozuna* start each day's sumo with the ring-entering ritual, or *dohyoiri*, which mostly involves foot-stomping, hand-clapping and sand-shuffling.

Bottom The Sumo Stomp, or *"shiko,"* sumo's foremost form of exercise. The world would be a happier, healthier, sillier place if everyone faced off for a congenial session of leg-lifting and foot-stomping.

Top The guy in the pajamas is the *gyoji*, the least authoritative ref in all of sports. The lacquered ping-pong paddle he's holding is a *goombai*, or "war fan."
Bottom My favorite photo of Konishiki, doing the Hawaiian Tilt and staring daggers at his relatively puny opponent.

Top "Bruce, we have to stop meeting like this." Sudden, intimate contact is inevitable in sumo, occasionally resulting in battered faces and actual bloodshed. In this case, Tochiazuma renews his acquaintance with Chiyotaikai.

Bottom "Back off, Mad Dog!" One of the best ways to keep the other fat guy from grabbing your *mawashi* (belt) is to execute a stiff-arm to his throat.

Right Greased lightning. Notwithstanding all that blubber, sumo is one of the fastest sports you'll ever watch.

Bottom In sumo, you lose if any part of your body, other than your feet, touches the *dohyo*. Ideally, that part should not be your head.

Previous page All decked
out in their sumo aprons
(*kesho-mawashi*), the
upper-division (*makuuchi*)
rikishi take a bow before
the day's matches begin.
Top "The leapfrog" is not
an authorized sumo move.
In this preliminary match
among young wrestlers,
the *rikishi* in the air has
launched himself prema-
turely, providing a tutorial
on how NOT to do *tachiai*.
Right (Almost) all is fair
in love and sumo. As long
as Musoyama, left, doesn't
actually put out Wakanosato's eye or pull his hairdo,
he's cool with the rules.

Top In football, this is called a "pancake." When both *rikishi* execute their favorite arm-throw simultaneously, the result can be a crowd-pleasing crash like this, involving Roho (on top) and Kotooshu. Bottom *Tachiai,* the moment of truth. Note that *yokozuna* Asashoryu (left) is the Receiver in this face-off, meeting his opponent's charge and already plotting a countermove. Receivers beat Jumpers in a clear majority of matches.

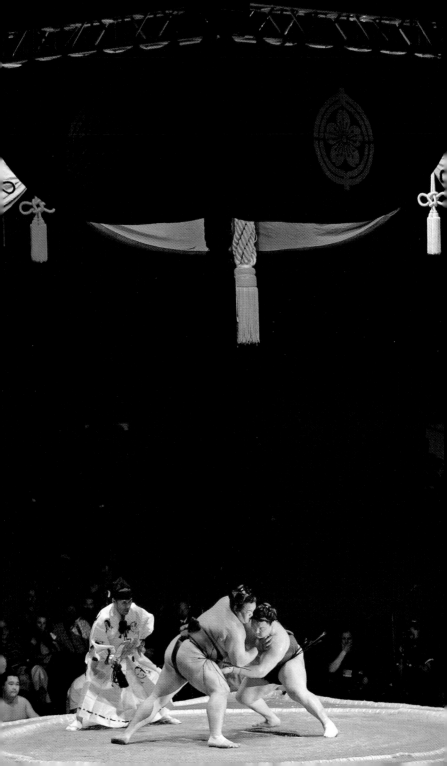

Left The key element in a perfectly executed sumo throw is timing. Here, Hakuho, who maintained his own balance 'til he felt a vulnerable shift in Harumafuji's position, turns 278 pounds casually upside-down.
Bottom Rolling in the dirt, especially at practice, is a fact of sumo life. When it happens in front of 6,000 fans—as it did in this match for Baruto—and you don't have your pants on, it's hard to make a dignified exit.

Previous page The *dohyo*, in symbolic recognition of Japan's agrarian past, consists of soil and rice bales.
Left Asashoryu and Kisenosato in a picturesque sumo tableau.

Top Oops!" One little tippy-toe over the edge (*tawara*) and you're done for the day.

Bottom Kotooshu (underneath Harumafuji here) is an aggressive *rikishi* who takes risks to win, but occasionally ends up in an embarrassing—but entertaining—position.

Right The strain of battle shows vividly on the faces of both the winner (Kaio) and loser (Musoyama) in this match.

Top The joy of sumo. Asashoryu, the first Mongolian *yokozuna*, celebrates one of his last *yusho*, in January, 2009. **Left** The dilemma of sumo. If this little boy aspires to become a professional athlete, he will probably choose almost any sport other than sumo. For most young people in Japan, the ancient traditions of sumo life present few attractions.

over a microphone he keeps in his lap. Possibility No. 1 is that the judges endorse the ref's *goombai*. Possibility No. 2 is a decision reversal, which goes into the ref's record as a black mark. Possibility No. 3 is that nobody could tell who really won, so the two *rikishi* have to wrestle again.

Rematches (or *torinaoshi*) after *mono-ii* sometimes indicate real indecision (and real fairness) on the part of the ring judges. Sometimes, they are shrewd political moves that prevent the backlash that might come after a decision that offends a powerful *sumobeya*. In any case, the fan makes out, because you get to see an extra match.

Extra Terms
As I've already explained, the above terminology is more than the fun-loving fan needs to know. I add two additional terms that help me classify a match not by its conclusion but by the way it unfolds while the two guys are still up and slugging. These are:

1) The Wild Boar Hunt," which describes what happens when a small, agile *rikishi* scurries around the *dohyo*, poking and dodging in a desperate effort to unbalance a Hippo. Konishiki, Onokuni, and Yamamotoyama were involved in more than their share of Wild Boar Hunts, always playing the boar. Terao was easily the most prolific and entertaining boar hunter.

   The boar, by the way, usually wins anyway.

2) "Fistfight at the Malamute Saloon." Credit for the elevation of this wonderful variation really belongs to a young wrestler named Takatoriki, whose *hataki* (face-smacking) attacks throughout the 1990's displayed an almost incomparable verve. Ideally, in a Fistfight at the Malamute Saloon, some chippy punk like Takatoriki

will start trouble by really whacking the other guy
hard, with one of those blows to the ear that make
your head ring and your sinuses drain. This gets the
other guy mad. As a rule, *rikishi* don't lose their tem-
per, but Takatoriki was annoying enough to negate this
rule. The little bastard made just about everybody want
to hit him back, real hard. So they did. Of course, he
then returned the favor, even harder.

In a match like this, pretty soon, neither *rikishi*
seems remotely interested in grabbing a belt and winning the match. They just want to pound the crap out
of each other. Meanwhile, the referee stands by helpless, just like the bartender at the Malamute Saloon.
In a really good barfight like this, the two *rikishi* start
bleeding from the mouth, nose, eyebrows, possibly
even staining the ref's pajamas. The ring judges scowl
disapprovingly. And the fans go wild. Eventually, Takatoriki, who knew what he was doing when he started
the fistfight, puts a move on the other guy and wins.

Other *rikishi*, like Itai, Kotonishiki, Kaio, and Mad
Dog, have been known to start Fistfights at the Malamute Saloon, but the quintessential sumo incarnation
of Dangerous Dan McGrew was Takatoriki, God
bless him.

I hope the point I've made, in this description of sumo's action during the match, demonstrates that sumo — although
it serves nicely as a View Master slide of Japanese culture —
might better be seen as a game, a sport, a fistfight, a basketball
clinic, or any one of a hundred other comparable pastimes.

Perhaps more important is the fact that you don't have to
"understand" sumo — as Fred the *gaijin* insisted while under
the spell of a live microphone — to enjoy it, or even appreciate it. I loved basketball, for instance, before I even remotely

understood it. I screamed and cheered and even got thrown out of the Tomah (Wisconsin) High School gym once when I was nine years old, for losing my cool in the bleachers. All this happened before I knew there was such a thing as a fundamental defensive position, before I knew the definition of goaltending, before I had ever heard of the pick-and-roll.

I just liked watching these great tall heroes from my own hometown battling the villains from enemy hamlets. I was like my son, Aaron, who saw his first sumo matches one day in Tokyo when he was fifteen. He didn't know *okurihiki-otoshi* from *okuritsuriotoshi* (and neither do I), but he knew a good fight when he saw one. And he had fun, especially when Takatoriki undertook to break another guy's eardrum, and when Konishiki crushed Kotofuji like a jackboot descending on a cigar butt.

Fred and I — and the eternal legion of sumo nerds — all agree that the terminology and nuances create, in your average know-it-all, a proprietary interest in a sport. The little things fuel our addiction and breed our points of view. We argue with deep conviction and anoint our petty knowledge of esoterica by insisting that its importance is not in the sports arena but in the tabernacle of culture.

High priests, after all, get more respect than gallery gods.

But the monkey wrench in all this posturing is that sumo is still two fat guys in the dirt, slugging each other. And if they didn't do that, and if one of the fat guys didn't win and the other one didn't lose, there wouldn't be any "culture" to understand, at least not from sumo. We might as well be taking adult-ed at the museum, peering at vases and puttering with *origami*.

CHAPTER 8

THE RIPSNORTER
in Nagoya

A sumo *basho* is designed as a crescendo. If everything proceeds according to the Sumo Association's program, the importance of the matches, the tension, the excitement build steadily from Day 1 through Day 15 — with the biggest thrills jammed into the very last match of the last day.

It doesn't always work out this way, partly because the Sumo Association has a knack for choreographing politically correct results and killing suspense. But with six *basho* a year, you get a great finale in sumo a lot more often than you get a nail-biting, down-to-the-wire Super Bowl or a high-scoring, run-and-gun World Cup final. Occasionally, there is an epic match, a perfect fight — what my old weatherbeaten Grandma Annie would call a "ripsnorter." In Nagoya, July 22, 1990, Chiyonofuji and Asahifuji put on a ripsnorter.

Of course, since that match, there have been many that were comparably well-fought and momentous, such as the long series of last-day battles between Takanohana (Little Spoon) and Akebono (The Great Pumpkin), or the more recent all-Mongolia clashes of Asashoryu (Hinganai) and Hakuho (UPS). But few sumo matches, past, present or future, so perfectly pitted two brilliant warriors — each at a critical juncture in his career — in a confrontation of such genuine significance. It was that rare big game that transcended its hype. Long before the *gyoji* lifted his *goombai* over Asahifuji and the Wolf, every fan in Japan knew this one was a classic.

As the moment approached, my wife Junko and I were torn. On the one hand, we both admired Chiyonofuji, for his athletic brilliance, his unconventional style, his class, and his gorgeous buns. On the other hand, we had a soft spot in our hearts for Asahifuji — because he never got the respect he deserved. For three years, in our judgment, he had wrestled at *yokozuna* level without getting the appropriate rank. He kept beating people, but they wouldn't promote him from *ozeki* to *yokozuna*.

So we wanted both of them to win.

The rest of Japan, excluding the village of Kizukuri in Aomori — Asahifuji's hometown — was more clearly in Chiyonofuji's corner. Even in Kizukuri, where about a hundred natives sat grimly on their haunches in the community center to watch the *basho*'s final match on NHK, the commitment to Asahifuji was weirdly restrained. Speaking to an NHK reporter on behalf of the town, the mayor of Kizukuri said Asahifuji was on the brink of being inducted into the village Hall of Fame. All he had to do was win this match and nail down his promotion. What if he lost, though?

The mayor hemmed, the mayor hawed. "Well, we'll see..."

The smaller the Hall of Fame, obviously, the pickier the entrance exam!

Besides the love of the nation, the bookies also favored Chiyo. Everyone knew, after all, that Asahifuji was jinxed in Big Matches.

But things were different this time, weren't they? Asahifuji, for one thing, was leading this tournament. After fourteen days in Nagoya, he was 13-1, his only loss a screw-up against Ryogoku (Trashcan) on Day 3. Chiyonofuji, in second place at 12-2, had also blown his match with Trashcan. (Overall, Ryogoku had had a mediocre *basho*, at 7-8, but he had two new clips for his private highlight film.)

After his loss to Trashcan, Asahifuji managed to regain his concentration, and wasn't seriously threatened again, even against old nemeses Tochinowaka, Konishiki, Akinoshima and Hokutoumi.

Chiyonofuji's Ghosts

But Chiyonofuji lost again, on Day 8, to Kotonishiki, and stirred familiar concerns among both his friends and rivals. More than six months before, the only American sumo coach, Jesse Kuhaulua (who has three other names, by the way... *rikishi* name: Takamiyama; *oyakata* name: Azumazeki; Japanese name: Daigoro Watanabe) had bluntly said that Chiyonofuji was over the hill and he would hang up his codpiece in 1990. Chiyo quickly shut Jesse up by winning the 1990 New Year Basho in January. But the Wolf missed the title in March with a 10-5 record and lost again in May at 13-2. When Kotonishiki overpowered Chiyo on Day 8 in Nagoya, even Chiyo's coach, Kokonoe, began to worry. Kokonoe was pessimistic before Chiyonofuji's Day 10 test against Akinoshima — a stubborn little defensive specialist everybody hated to wrestle. Akinoshima had actually spent one whole day as the unbeaten *basho* leader — before a resounding loss to Asahifuji. Regardless of his *basho* record, Akinoshima was always at his best against the best and he represented — with the possible exception of Konishiki — Chiyo's most fearsome opponent.

Against Chiyonofuji in Nagoya, however, Akinoshima (talented but dumb) was out of his league. Chiyo came into the match with a plan and creamed the kid without breaking a sweat. "He rose like a phoenix," said Kokonoe. "I stopped worrying."

But Junko and I were still worrying. And so, I suspect, was the Sumo Association. Chiyonofuji was sumo's official cover boy — on most editions of the official sumo program. When Japan Airlines produced a TV commercial featuring the 1990 Sumo Tour to Brazil, the guy the producers would put out front was a foregone conclusion. The Wolf. Everybody else in the commercial — including Futagoyama, head of the Sumo Association — brought up the rear.

Although it's easy to forget, Chiyonofuji had not always enjoyed such favor from the Establishment. When he decided to take some of his physical training outside the sacred dungeon of the *sumobeya*, to a fitness center where he lifted weights and sculpted his rippling mass of upper-body muscle, he violated a sumo taboo. Only when he became an idol of millions, the handsomest sumo star of the 20th Century, and the winningest *rikishi* of the '80s, did the Sumo Association declare no-hard-feelings and embrace Chiyonofuji as the symbol of all that is good and pure in the sport.

Chiyo was, indeed, a hard guy to hate. He was good-looking, with a (relatively) small tummy, and that face — smooth, rugged, and kissable enough for one of those "Take it all off"

Noxzema shaving commercials. His physique was, by any athletic standard, impressive. Naked, he could be mistaken for an NFL linebacker, a heavyweight contender, or a large economy-size *Cosmo* centerfold. His athleticism would have made him a star in a dozen other sports, and his charm resulted in thoughtful, modest, humorous interviews. He was everybody's favorite son.

Of course, this means that, coming into the final match in Nagoya, he was under terrific pressure. It wasn't just a matter of fighting, from one loss down, for the *yusho* (tournament championship) against the hottest wrestler in sumo. Chiyonofuji was a haunted man. The worst ghost was his age. He had just turned 35, an age at which even the great *rikishi* have given up hope for championships. He was also haunted by his popularity. Because he was a kind of Japanese national treasure, everyone expected him to keep on winning forever, despite his age and the odds and his size (he was among the smallest men in sumo) and the strength of his younger, hungrier opponents.

Finally, he had to cope with the dozens of ghosts of sumo past, old timers who would not concede Chiyonofuji's greatness unless he became the winningest sumo wrestler of all time. In the March Basho, Chiyo had become the first *rikishi* ever to win a thousand matches, but he still needed two more *yusho* to tie Taiho's 1956-71 record of 32 *basho* championships. While once the march to the *yusho* seemed easy for Chiyonofuji, it now demanded every ounce of his strength and his will. The concentration that used to make him invincible was now prone to the occasional short circuit. A year before, that silly loss to Trashcan would have been unthinkable.

The voices, the ghosts, kept telling Chiyonofuji, from Day 1 through Day 15, that this *basho*, this crescendo, might be his last chance.

Asahifuji's Jinx

The voices, however, were whispering similarly to Asahifuji. According to all of Japan's sumo pundits, this *basho* was Asahifuji's last chance for *tsunatori* (*yokozuna* promotion). He'd won the Summer Basho in May with a 14-1 record, and he had 13 wins this time out. This level of excellence would require the bigwigs to give Asahifuji another chance — his seventh nomination. Six times before, he'd been rejected — for almost every reason under the rising sun, but mainly, they said, because he couldn't win the Big Match, the one at the very end against some fair-haired Kokonoe superstar (Chiyo or Hokutoumi). Asahifuji was the Buffalo Bills, the Washington Generals, the Cubbies — always a bridesmaid, never a bride.

With this record of persistence and futility, you might think Asahifuji was perfect for the role of the Lovable Underdog. The crowds should have been rooting for him affectionately; even the Sumo Association should have had a soft spot for the guy, right?

Forget it. Hardly anybody really cared if Asahifuji made it to the top or dropped dead two feet shy. In his quest for *yokozuna*, he was all alone out there.

Asahifuji's dilemma, like Joe Frazier or Alex Rodriguez, was that he was never a naturally appealing guy. For one thing, like Frank "Ferret-Face" Burns in *M.A.S.H.*, he had no lips. And his head always looked too small for his body. These and other physical oddities meant that — no matter how hard he tried — Asahifuji just couldn't look, well... tough.

Consider, by comparison, Hokutoumi, Chiyonofuji's stablemate — also a *yokozuna*. You got the feeling, looking at Hokutoumi, that sumo was the only thing that had steered him away from a life of incredibly violent crime. Hokutoumi looked, and fought, like the bully who chased you home from second grade and then set fire to your cat. There was a memorable newsreel film, in 1990, of Hokutoumi visiting a little old Japanese lady in Brazil during the sumo goodwill tour. Even as Hokutoumi mugged for the cameras, one saw the pitbull glint in his eye and felt a nameless dread, that Hokutoumi might suddenly revert to his natural state, seize the old lady's head between his paws, and crush it like a muskmelon.

In the same newsreel, there were films of Asahifuji greeting little old Japanese ladies, and each one he met, he looked as though he was apologizing for not sending a Mother's Day card.

"I'm sorry, Grandma... I forgot, Grandma, I'm really sorry... Gosh, Grandma, it just slipped my mind..."

Pathetic.

Asahifuji was cursed with the face of a 297-pound weakling. The fickle public might have forgiven this flaw if Asahifuji had possessed some compensating virtue, like Chiyonofuji's beauty. If Asahifuji had been even slightly blessed in this respect and had developed a more than lukewarm public following, the Sumo Association might also have worked up a little enthusiasm for his promotion. But Asahifuji was one of the most ill-favored *yokozuna* candidates of modern times.

His six rejections for *tsunatori* were unprecedented. And a look at his record shows these rejections were not just unlucky, but unjust.

Over nine *basho* from January 1988 through mid-1989, Asahifuji had won more matches than either Chiyonofuji or Hokutoumi. His winning percentage (.825) was second to Chiyo's (.905), but ahead of Hokutoumi (.804). More important, he had a tougher schedule because, while teammates Chiyonofuji and Hokutoumi never wrestled against one another, Asahifuji had to face both of them in every tournament. In the first three basho of 1989, Asahifuji's record against the Kokonoe duo was 5-2.

For this exceptional performance, Asahifuji was turned down three times in 1989 for promotion to *yokozuna*. The Sumo Association, of course, provided plenty of excuses.

For one thing, they insisted, it wouldn't be appropriate to award a promotion if Asahifuji had not won an outright championship. He'd lost two playoffs against Hokutoumi, but that wasn't good enough. The message here was that the Sumo Association didn't want another Futahaguro embarrassment.

Remember Futahaguro (alias Koji Kitao)?

In 1986, the Sumo Association had promoted Futahaguro, then a young, glamorous *ozeki*, to *yokozuna*, before he ever won a championship. Futahaguro's best finish was a tie for the *yusho*, after which he lost a wrestle-off (something Asahifuji did regularly). As it turned out, Futahaguro never did win a *yusho*. He settled down into the good life of being a pampered star, and in 1988 got into a fight with his coach. Futahaguro was promptly kicked out of sumo, banned for life, and exiled to a clown's career in Japanese professional wrestling, from which his notoriety constantly reminded the Sumo Association of its only *yokozuna* to ever "retire" without once winning a title.

Also, said the Sumo Association in its *yokozuna* refusals, they couldn't promote Asahifuji because he didn't wrestle Chiyonofuji in one *basho* in early 1989 (because Chiyonofuji wasn't there). Two *yusho* in two tries wasn't convincing enough, especially since — until 1989 — Asahifuji's record against Chiyo was 2-24.

Then, for five *basho*, from July, 1989 through March, 1990, the issue of Asahifuji's promotion became moot. He went into a decline that seemed to seal his status permanently at *ozeki*. Part of this regression stemmed, I think, from mental fatigue. The pressure of maintaining so high a level of performance for eighteen months, plus the repeated disappointments, finally caught up to Asahifuji. His body sagged, his mind cracked, and his guts went sour. In mid-1989, Asahifuji suffered a flare up of his chronic illness, pancreatitis — an occupational hazard caused by the rich, fat-laden diet that all *rikishi* devour. Despite relentless pain, however, Asahifuji kept wrestling, through records of 8-7, 9-6, 8-7, 9-6, and 8-7.

To keep going, Asahifuji and his wife Junko formulated a diet of mushy food that would sustain Asahifuji's weight while soothing his delicate tummy. Wherever he traveled, he took along special pots and utensils for cooking this mush. By all rights, however, Asahifuji should have been finished — because he could not have the one thing he needed most: rest.

The sumo world has yet to discover the concept of sports medicine, or to discover the fact that "playing with pain" — if carried too far — can ruin, or even kill, athletes. Sumo embodies the conviction that Vince Lombardi immortalized when he said. "Nobody is hurt. Hurt is in the mind. If you can walk, you can run."

Or limp out onto the *dohyo* and slug it out against the Pudding that Ate Chicago! An injured or ailing *rikishi* is not expected to "grin and bear it." He is encouraged to "scowl and aggravate it," a fact that made Asahifuji's return to form in 1990 all the more surprising.

In May, 1990, Asahifuji won the Summer Basho. He was 14-1. He beat everyone except Chiyonofuji (13-2). Now, having won two career *yusho*, Asahifuji was up again for promotion. His rejection in May, however, was no surprise. The excuses were familiar. His previous *basho* (8-7) was mediocre, and — even though he won the May *yusho* — he did so without beating his nemesis, Chiyonofuji.

There was a new excuse, too. The Sumo Association had recently begun expressing its reluctance to promote anyone to *yokozuna* unless they had won two — count 'em, two — *yusho* in a row. This was a tricky wrinkle, because it had been seventeen years since any *rikishi* had charged quite so triumphantly into the *yokozuna* ranks. According to the *Asahi Shimbun*, that was a guy named Kotozakura, who'd gone 9-6, 14-1 and 14-1, with two straight championships, in 1973. None of Asahifuji's contemporaries, not Onokuni, Hokutoumi, Chiyonofuji, or the notorious Futahaguro, had won back-to-back *yusho* before they got elevated.

Another complaint emerged from several highly placed detractors in the Sumo Association. It was often said that Asahifuji's sumo style was "weak." The explanation of this charge is that Asahifuji's strength always lay in his defensive skill. He absorbed his opponent's charge, positioned himself well, and usually initiated his winning move after an offensive foray by the opponent. Asahifuji won with reflexes, agility and cunning. This is hardly a description of "weak" sumo, but it was enough to saddle him with the charge that his game was not "complete." The same charge, of course, applied even more emphatically to Hokutoumi and Onokuni, whose offensive skills were resoundingly two-dimensional. Among Asahifuji's contemporaries in the upper ranks, only Chiyonofuji was a real virtuoso of offense. An objective ranking of "strong" sumo, made in spring, 1990, would have put Asahifuji solidly in second place.

Sumo is not an objective sport. The handwriting was on the wall in dense red ink. The big boys were hardballing Asahifuji. But why?

The Sumo Association's objections went deeper than Asahifuji's unlovely face and "weak" style. A big drawback was that Asahifuji did not wrestle out of a powerful *sumobeya*. His *oyakata*, Oshima, was an excellent coach, admired by most in the sumo world. But Oshima wasn't a power broker in the Sumo Association. In the world's most incestuous sports organization, Asahifuji got no points for being well-connected.

Even worse, Asahifuji lost points with his uncooperative attitude toward *yaochozumo*, Japanese for "arranged matches" — in other words, "taking a dive." In sumo, every *rikishi* — in order to create or repay debts — tanks a match from time to time. But Asahifuji was not an enthusiastic participant in this tradition. He might, for instance, have greased his promotion in 1990 — regardless of his record — if he hadn't made Hokutoumi work so hard in those two 1989 wrestle-offs.

By playing it straight over the years, Asahifuji had made life complicated for his "betters," especially the boys from the Kokonoe stable (Hokutoumi and Chiyonofuji) — which, for most of the 1980s, was sumo's flagship, its glamour factory.

This, at bottom, was why the final match of the Nagoya Basho, 1990, was a ripsnorter in the making. It was a grudge match between two wrestlers, and two *sumobeya*, who didn't like each other and didn't make deals with each other, and didn't let the Sumo Association make deals for 'em. This meant — and all the smart fans knew it — that this match was the genuine article.

And you couldn't pick a favorite. Once upon a time, Chiyonifuji had dominated Asahifuji completely. But in the last eight *basho*, Chiyo's edge was only 5-3. Asahifuji was catching up.

Everyone knew that this match pitted the Establishment vs. the Party-Crasher. The Sumo Association didn't really want Asahifuji in the Club. If he was going to make it, he had to barge in, take on the Club champ, and then make sure he was the only one still on his feet when the dust settled.

In Nagoya, technically, Asahifuji had two cracks at the Champ — because he had a one-match lead. "I knew that if I lost," said Asahifuji, "I had another chance (in a wrestle-off)."

Think again, ferret-face!

The Sumo Association was watching Asahifuji for the slightest misstep. If he lost to Chiyonofuji and then won the wrestle-off, he was only 1-2 in two basho against the Sumo God, and 6-30 for his career.

Not good enough, chump.

At that moment, the clearest fact of life for Asahifuji (or for any aspiring *rikishi*) was that the price of glory in sumo was to beat — or suck up to — Chiyonofuji. All roads to promotion led, literally, through the Wolf.

The magic that radiated from that ripsnorter in Nagoya was that the fans knew Chiyonofuji had the Establishment on his side, and he didn't need them. He had defied the Club himself once, and he was a genius in his sport. He didn't need anybody's help to whip Asahifuji.

Meanwhile, Asahifuji finally had his body, his mind and his talent at a point where he was Chiyonofuji's equal. No one else could touch his record of 27-2 in the last two tournaments. He, too, was OK all by himself. He could beat the Champ.

Together, these were the two finest, most determined, most desperate *rikishi* to face off for all the marbles in years.

The Match

I leaned toward the TV.

Chiyonofuji, after the last crouch, had indulged himself in a little staring and pose-striking with Asahifuji — unusual for him. Asahifuji's lipless mouth turned into a pencil line between his little nose and his little chin. He pounded his belt.

After a long (5 minutes, 30 seconds) Sumotori Rag, they step out for *tachiai*. The head ref, Shonosuke Kimura (actually, all head refs are Shonosuke Kimura; this one's real name was Sokichi Kumagai), holds up his *goombai* and tells the boys to go when they feel the urge...

Chiyonofuji's urge comes first...

If anything typified Chiyonofuji's anxiety at growing older, it was the fact that in 1990, many times, he didn't wait at *tachiai*, to measure his opponent and react.

This time, Chiyo gets a huge jump. His left hand lunges and slaps Asahifuji's face while Asahifuji is still rising from his crouch...

But Asahifuji, whose eyes never waver from Chiyonofuji, gets the reward of waiting. His left hand, outside Chiyonofuji's right arm, finds a solid belt grip. His right hand sneaks inside Chiyo's dangerous left. As they meet, Chiyonofuji's feet are too far forward, literally under his chin and too close together. Asahifuji's feet are in balance, behind him and spread. His *tachiai* is "heavy," and — for a few precious seconds — Chiyonofuji is light...

Chiyo feels it. He stretches his right hand inside to Asahifuji's belt. But as he does, Asahifuji pulls hard with his left hand. This moves Asahifuji momentarily beside Chiyo, and Chiyonofuji then has to adjust, shifting his right hand to the middle of Asahifuji's belt, right under his navel. It's a deep belt grip, but hard to use...

Asahifuji attacks again, swings to the left, tightening his left hand. Chiyo counters, clutching Asahifuji's left arm as they spin together. Asahifuji broadens his stance, holds his balance. He coils his legs now, ready to drive into Chiyonofuji...

Chiyo senses the coming charge. He pushes back and tries to brace himself. But Asahifuji still has him turned, pressing Chiyo's right shoulder...

Chiyo now has to do something. Asahifuji is pushing him around, closing his grip and shrinking the *dohyo*...

Move, now!

Chiyo moves, reeling in Asahifuji with his right hand, suddenly jerking his 300-pound opponent like a Muppet.

As he pulls, Chiyonofuji straightens up, drawing his feet under him, stretching for Asahifuji's belt with his left...

Now the fans see what Chiyo is doing. Summoning his power. The sound they create is one of breath drawn hungrily into 10,000 throats...

Not yet, kids.

Asahifuji, whose agility is a match for Chiyonofuji and whose reactions are his mainstay, feels Chiyo pulling him tight, and he moves, too. He drives, twists left, grabbing Chiyonofuji's *mawashi* with his right hand inside. A moment of struggle, belly-to-belly, and they're stalemated...

"I pulled him into my body," said Chiyonofuji after the match. "That was a mistake."

But not a fatal mistake. It's just that Chiyo, outmaneuvered by Asahifuji, was now holding onto a mess. His right hand had slipped to the left. Asahifuji's *mawashi* climbed up his body as Chiyo pulled on it. Now Chiyo had a clumsy belt grip. Instead of holding Asahifuji by the waist, he was tugging at his chest.

Chiyo's left-outside grip was also high, but a little tighter than his right hand. He had to keep that left grip; it was his strong side — now, his only anchor. Asahifuji, on the other hand, now had a left-outside belt grip that was deep and dangerous.

Chiyo can't risk waiting. He makes the first of several powerful upper-body twists, pulling at Asahifuji's belt with his left hand while rocking to the right...

Under Chiyo's violent pressure Asahifuji can't keep the right-hand grip. He has to let go. He rocks onto one leg — his first moment off-balance. He clings with his left hand. He counters, gets his feet back. Asahifuji tightens his left-hand grip, all the way behind Chiyonofuji's back. He lowers his shoulder into Chiyonofuji's chest...

Asahifuji drives. Chiyo strains to stop him. Chiyo backpedals, his feet shuffling toward the ridge...

Chiyo turns, another flash of power — Asahifuji powerless in Chiyonofuji's arms for one split second — escaping to the left...

This was the first critical moment, because Asahifuji's grip and balance were good enough to beat almost any other human being. Against Chiyonofuji, Asahifuji gained, at most, 24 inches of space on the *dohyo*.

Chiyonofuji seizes the offense. A left arm throw, *uwatenage,* shakes Asahifuji but fails. Asahifuji reacts. He leans on Chiyo's right side. Chiyo retreats, feeling the sand under his feet, slipping...

He feels the ridge, plants his feet. The crowd murmurs, terrified, thrilled. Asahifuji hugs Chiyonofuji, adjusts that deep left hand hold on Chiyo's *mawashi*. He's ready...

The quick kill! *Yorikiri!*

No!

Asahifuji hurried too much. He isn't set, and Chiyonofuji, somehow, feels it. Asahifuji wants to drive from the right, but his right foot is in the bucket, too far back...

You can't beat Chiyonofuji with only your shoulders, dipshit! Where are your legs?!

Instinct saves Chiyonofuji. He feels Asahifuji's mistake. He darts to the left, his feet now on the *tawara*...

Chase him, Asahifuji!

Asahifuji is still finding his feet. Chiyonofuji attacks, tries *uwatenage* again — the same leaning, twisting, crushing left arm. It doesn't work, but Asahifuji's grip relents. His right hand slips again, off Chiyo's belt. Asahifuji is one-handed again, at least momentarily...

The chase continues with Chiyo sliding left, Asahifuji hanging on, each of them one-handed. For a second, Asahifuji is vulnerable, his feet under his chin. But Chiyo doesn't feel it, doesn't drive. The instant passes...

A moment at stalemate, then Asahifuji mounts his second offensive. He gets his right hand grip back inside Chiyo's left arm. He braces. Lifts. Turns. Pushes!...

No good. Chiyonofuji is too solid. He balances, straightens, and saps Asahifuji's power. But as he does, Asahifuji is ready. He was waiting for Chiyo's strength, so he could redirect it. Asahifuji shifts again...

Suddenly, he takes his left hand away from the belt, and plunges it inside Chiyonofuji's right arm. Chiyo, recovering his balance, can't counterpunch. He can't stop it...

Asahifuji is there. Two hands inside...

Morozashi! The death grip.

Asahifuji wanted to end it right then. "I had *morozashi*," said Asahifuji later. "I remember thinking, 'Now all I have to do is push.'"

He squeezes Chiyonofuji's belt. Push! Chiyonofuji is struggling. His arms are outside and high, holding onto Asahifuji's slippery *mawashi* like a first-time lover trying to pull off his girlfriend's brassiere over her head...

Chiyonofuji's feet touch the ridge again. Asahifuji is pushing, shifting his hands behind Chiyo's back, his feet clawing at the sand, groping for a position one millimeter higher, just high enough to topple Chiyo backwards...

Come on!

Chiyo bends against Asahifuji's body, like a bamboo rod, forestalling what seems inevitable. He can't get out...

Jesus Christ, he's out! Look at that!

Leaning only on one shoulder and his right leg, Chiyo simply bulldozes Asahifuji back while gliding to his right. One step. Two steps. Chiyo is off the ridge. Suddenly, Asahifuji's death grip turns out to be just another manly hug...

The crisis past, they trade arm throws, and fail. Asahifuji fights back to *morozashi*. Chiyonofuji has overpowered Asahifuji with his shoulders repeatedly, but through it all, Asahifuji has never surrendered the deep hold he got at *tachiai*. He hangs on. He must. He doesn't want to face Chiyonofuji, empty-handed, on an open *dohyo*. Not again. Not this time. Not with so much on the line...

The match has passed 20 seconds. The crowd is alternately hushed and shrieking. On one side of the *dohyo*, Hokutoumi — just beaten by Konishiki — watches Chiyo and gnaws his lip...

Feeling Asahifuji tighten *morozashi* again, Chiyonofuji moves faster. He turns hard, leaning on his left arm, straining to snap Asahifuji's hold. He's on one leg again...

Asahifuji feels weakness. He attacks, drives Chiyo to the *tawara*. The bamboo rod bends again. Chiyo is cornered, but again, Asahifuji's move is too fast. Asahifuji's right hand is loose for, how long? — half a second...

It's enough!

Chiyo escapes again. A burst of movement to his left, those shoulders and arms forcing Asahifuji unwillingly back, two effortless strides and they are in the middle of the dohyo, head to head...

Well, goddamn!

Start all over again.

Shonosuke Kimura, the distinguished ref, hovers near, his mouth gaping stupidly...

Asahifuji tries pushing again, but fails. He gets beside Chiyo, but Chiyo twists him back to stalemate. Then, lightning. Chiyonofuji commits...

This is it.

He yanks Asahifuji to his left side; he plants his left leg between Asahifuji's legs...

Chiyonofuji starts to pull. . .

Asahifuji is above him, his *morozashi* still intact, wrapped python-like around Chiyonofuji's waist. They crouch, glued together, heaving with fatigue...

Chiyonofuji's chin is 18 scant inches from the sand. Asahifuji's head, beside his, is almost as close...

Chiyo's plan is obvious. He's stronger. This is his best move. *Uwatenage*. Left hand on top, with a death-grip on the other guy's *mawashi*. His feet are wide; he is lower and his balance, if this move works, will survive any pressure Asahifuji can apply from above...

If it works...

No, it will work. He can do it!

Chiyonofuji has been on the defensive for 27 seconds, but now he's home. He's got his hold. He can beat this lipless upstart!...

Trouble is: the lipless upstart can do it, too! Chiyo might have his beloved *uwatenage* all set up, but he still has to break Asahifuji's *morozashi*. Otherwise, he can't move Asahifuji an inch. A *morozashi* this deep on Chiyo is a once-in-a-lifetime advantage. All Asahifuji has to do is keep leaning on him. Continue to press him down. Crush him to the sand!...

When I first watched it, this moment seemed to last for minutes. The two *rikishi* frozen together, bent over each other, their heads invisible, every sinew in their backs and arms stretched and naked. Only once in a thousand matches does so much desperation radiate so equally from two *rikishi* as gifted as these. Hold it there! Stay there for an hour! This is too good to end.

There was only one difference. Chiyonofuji, who was underneath except for that one dominant hand, had no options. Asahifuji, somehow, realized he had one.

He let go.

He gave up *morozashi*, pulled his left hand out from the knot of flesh and slapped it onto the back of Chiyonofuji's neck.

With that daring maneuver, Asahifuji committed. He leaned on Chiyo's neck as hard as his left arm could lean, and he threw the rest of himself at Chiyonofuji. If Chiyo could hold his feet, and twist Asahifuji quickly enough, he could throw Asahifuji beneath his body, and land on top.

They begin to fall, together. Toward Chiyo's right. Chiyo pulls, twists at Asahifuji's back. Asahifuji leans...

They fall...

"I thought I'd lost," said Asahifuji. "I thought my knee touched the *dohyo* first."

It wasn't that close. Asahifuji's last desperate push closed Chiyonofuji's stance like an accordion. Asahifuji's knees were still spread above the sand, stiff and unsoiled as the Wolf lay curled on the *tawara*.

No one could challenge the result. Chiyo was down. Sand on his back. Beaten. Asahifuji stood, looking first to Chiyonofuji, seeming to search for an answer in his eyes. Was he offering to help him up? Was he trying to show the respect due a worthy opponent?

He probably was, but such gestures are disdained among the Spartans of sumo. Your only comrades are in your own stable. So Chiyonofuji rose alone, stalked back to his corner and made a sullen exit.

Asahifuji, bewildered ("Didn't my knee touch first?"), crouched for the blessing from Shonosuke Kimura, and received his victory — like a schoolboy shocked by praise from the principal.

"I couldn't think of anything," he said. "I was empty, drained."

Two powerful sumo officials, Futagoyama and Kokonoe, couldn't think of much either. Asked about the match, and Asahifuji's now unavoidable promotion, they dodged the issue with faint praise.

"It was a great sumo match." said Futagoyama, President of the Sumo Association.

"Good sumo," said Kokonoe.

The mayor of Kizukuri, at least, knew a historic moment when he saw one. "The kid's in the Hall of Fame," he said. "Definitely!"

Chiyonofuji had somehow lost his grace for a moment. He slumped in the passage, on the way to the locker room. "I'm so tired. To get so close, and then to lose…"

They asked him about Asahifuji's impending *tsunatori*. Chiyonofuji said he didn't care what happened to Asahifuji, one way or the other.

"That's somebody else's affair. It has nothing to do with me."

Of course, it had everything to do with him — and this was both his greatness and his burden. He had become an immortal in the midst of his own trials. As long as he wrestled, Chiyonofuji was — for every other *rikishi* — the ultimate gut check, the final exam. The rite of passage.

Three days later, Asahifuji was promoted.

CHAPTER 9

AFTERWARD
"Keep Up Appearances Whatever You Do"

Fat invites ridicule.

No physical anomaly wallows so deep in the mire of our antipathy. "The glutton," said Saadia Gaon in the 10th century, "is like a dog that is never satiated, he becomes disgusting to everyone and, being subject to diarrhea, his body becomes like a sieve... "

Gross, huh?

"Obesity," said Joseph O. Kern II in the 20th century "is really widespread."

Tall people we call Stretch, or Slim, or Stringbean — more a matter of acknowledgment than disparagement. Thin people we envy.

And short people? Well, we're not easy on them, but we give 'em a break because they're cute. We might call a short person Shorty, or Squirt, Shrimp, Midge, Halfpint, PeeWee, even Dink. But not "pigface," "sweathog" or "tub of shit." We seem to store up our vulgarity for the obese.

Sumo, alone among all the sports in the world, cultivates fat. The fatter in sumo, it seems, the better. Hippos, enormous and crowd-pleasing, advance swiftly up the ranks. This is a delicate precept, however, because it so flagrantly flouts the twin virtues of slimness and beauty that represent the modern ideal. Even in Japan, memories of postwar privation are finally fading; healthy fat is losing its cachet. The sunken-cheeked ideal, in the past decade or so, has established itself as aggressively in Tokyo as in New York, Paris, or Venice Beach. Pitted thus against such formidable social mores, sumo teeters perpetually on the brink of burlesque, a wobbling parody of itself. Every *rikishi*, potentially, is a baggy-pants minstrel bereft his baggy pants.

With ridicule inherent in the very shape and nature of its athletes, the Sumo Association guards very jealously the dignity of its sport. This is no easy job.

At the end of every match, there occurs a crisis in dignity, when Fatsoyama triumphs over Lardass, and both of them — usually — end up wallowing in the sand, struggling like tipped-over turtles to right themselves and find their feet. This oft-repeated scene could turn ludicrous, especially if one of them decides to act up. A triumphant shimmy here, a petulant jiggle there, and suddenly the two noble athletes look like Fatty Arbuckle and Oliver Hardy fighting over a cookie in a Turkish bath.

The Sumo Association's solution is to return to, and enforce, the Code of the Manly Pose. In the aftermath of the match, *rikishi* follow ritual. They depict the ideal, and they do it in sedate slow motion. They are watched carefully for deviance. Forbidden above all is emotion, because emotion spawns movement — and movement, among fat men, is amusing.

Whether victorious or defeated, the *rikishi* is stoic and virile. Occasionally, a guy like Takamisakari (Mad Dog) — who tended to lose his momentum and suffer sudden, ridiculous reversals — would vent his frustration by screwing up his little moonface and tossing a handful of sand at the *dohyo*. This is OK, because it is outwardly sincere, self-directed and — best of all — brief. If Mad Dog made this a habit, however, he would have to visit the principal's office.

Winners, on the other hand, receive no indulgence. If Asahifuji, for example, had raised a fist and roared with joy after beating Chiyonofuji in Nagoya, he would have instantly placed himself on the verge of expulsion — rather than promotion. Emotionally, sumo is a police state.

"After beating a *yokozuna*," said Shinko, "you want to jump up and shout. But you have to hold in all that feeling. You're not allowed to show anything."

The Membrane of Sportsmanship

On the other hand — and this is why I admire this mandatory stoicism — sumo is uncluttered by the amateur theatrics that have begun to accompany even the smallest milestones in every meaningless contest in other sports, and which degenerate almost instantly into unintentional self-mockery.

I refer to sack dances, touchdown boogies, finger-pointing, flag-draping, backboard-climbing, pigpiles, high-fives, low-fives, split-level fives, slam dunks over the crossbar, taunting, various forms of mime, fist-shaking, and hugging everybody in sight after another lousy hockey goal, another crummy home run, another measly run-of-the-mill last-second free throw.

I exclude those gestures of brotherly communication between teammates that signal approval or thanks — a touch, a pat, a pointed finger, a smiled or a clenched hand, or just a knowing glance. There's a difference between a taunt and a tribute, between showing off and giving notice.

If you're a fan, you know what I mean. And if you're a fan, you share my ambivalence about the divas and ham actors who've come to populate professional sports, who feel compelled to amend every simple act of athletic grace with a commercial message about *me*. When my own team has the upper hand, I secretly relish the jeer, the sneer, the swagger, the finger that humiliates a beaten foe. But when my side is trailing, or when I have no stake either way, I'm embarrassed by the wretched excess of these juvenile theatrics. And I'm haunted by an old moral dictum about not kicking a man while he's down. I remember the simplicity of a Jim Brown touchdown, a Henry Aaron home run, a slicing Steve Nash drive to the hoop. No mustard, no fluff, no grandstanding — just execution.

I think most of us — veteran fans — prefer the understated in our athletic heroes, probably because we know that beyond what they do on the field, they don't have much to say. They don't live our lives; they don't know our problems. They are a fortunate, pampered, child-like elite, and so we admire them most when they are strong and silent. John Wayne, not Jerry Lewis. Jerry Rice, not Terrell Owens. And consider how much more we liked Muhammad Ali after he developed a speech impediment!

I often wish we could do something to restore that simplicity and grace, that appreciation for the thing itself without caps and italics. I wish this primarily because sack dances and chocolate thunder are dangerous to the civility of sport. They stretch the thin membrane of sportsmanship, and bring athletes a little closer to the savage that throbs beneath the skin.

The Sumo Association, I think, is keenly sensitive to the fact that the first sumo wrestling was no competition at all — merely a form of human bearbaiting. They wonder how easily it could return to that pass if their jocks began to jiggle and jeer.

It has struck me often that the vogue for flouting the fallen foe subjects sports, unwisely, to the vicissitudes of fashion. It isn't tough enough for a strong-armed hillbilly from Dogpatch to pass basket-weaving and nostril hygiene 101 at Panhandle Tech plus learn an entire 200-page playbook and remember the color of his team's jerseys. Nowadays, he has to remember this year's handshake, and whether the trendy touchdown dance this season is closer to a funky chicken or a foxtrot. How can you respect your quarterback if he's still doing last year's finger-flick?

What I've always noted, in the midst of the touchdown boogie, is the aloneness of the performer. For that moment, he divorces himself from the team, from all the athletes on the field, and he celebrates himself. "Hey, look at me! Lookit what I did!… Look on my six points, ye mighty, and despair!"

In celebrating himself, he reveals too much of himself. He stands a little too naked. His display depicts not strength but weakness, his dependence on a team that worked together to fashion this small private triumph, his fear of letting the act speak for itself, his fear of letting this shining achievement pass too quickly perhaps never to occur again. He intimates his mortality; he reveals the wailing child within the man's body.

"We work," said sportswriter Jimmy Cannon, "in the toy department."

We have seen so many of these prancing displays, these chest-thumping solos, that we no longer trust them. The showoff turns our empathy to contempt. Maradona, for instance, in the 1990 World Cup Final, joined in his team's effort to stall the game into a 120-minute scoreless tie, in hopes of winning a penalty shootout. It was a travesty that failed. But the crowning shame on this abortion was Maradona, wailing at referees, lamenting his team's well-deserved defeat, and gushing with crocodile tears.

Tears for a homeland where he never played pro soccer — because they couldn't pay him enough.

Nobody likes a showoff, and almost everyone — in his heart — wants to see the son of a bitch get beat.

I've noticed that, even while the modern athlete appears not to understand this truth, our popular art reinforces it. In *The Karate Kid,* director John Avildsen created instant antipathy for hero Daniel's enemies, the Cobra Kai karate jocks, by depicting them as swaggering bullies. And we knew they were bullies, because they swaggered! In the climactic karate tournament, the contrast is nearly overdone. The Cobra Kai dance and strut on the mat, bob and weave, threaten their opponents and, even after they've won, pounce on their opponents, and rain them with insults. Daniel, on the other hand, fights with cool, cautious concentration, from a still and balanced defensive position, repeatedly scoring points on Cobra Kai villains while they shuck and jive.

And the moment after Daniel wins his unlikely victory, Avildsen applied an almost unnoticed but thoughtful directorial touch. While the crowd goes wild and Daniel's supporters rush to the mat to celebrate and hug — and jeer the evil Cobra Kai, Daniel, his concentration unbroken, returns to his defensive position, holds his balance. Even in certain victory, he is disciplined, silent, and humble.

Then, to emphasize the stoic, the quiet, the simple beauty of a man's victory on the playing field, Avildsen cuts away from the mob scene, to Mr. Miyagi, the old *sensei*. Miyagi stands apart from the madness, and he nods. His only emotion is the glint of a tear.

Perfect.

The Rite of Withdrawal

Somehow, sometime, sumo's elders accepted the beauty of understatement, and figured out that it goes double for the morbidly obese. The idea of fat guys, stripped down to g-strings and doing touchdown boogies over other fat guys is pretty risky — because it could turn the whole sport into a fabric of vendettas and intentional injuries. But the bigger danger is sheer silliness. It's Chris Farley dancing topless on "Saturday Night Live."

Sumo wrestlers, typically, are neither mature nor well-educated. Many are recruited straight out of junior high school and immersed immediately into a cloistered sumo world that doesn't encourage a lot of emotional and intellectual growth. Even at the age of 30 or older, Fatsoyama is very likely an immense infant, impulsive, demonstrative and unpredictable. None of this frailty is allowed to show, however, at the end of a sumo match. At that moment, win or lose, Fatsoyama is expected to follow rigid guidelines for his exit from the *dohyo*. If he has lost, he gets to his feet as humbly and quickly as possible and moves to his side of the *dohyo*. He waits for the winner to face him. Then, a short bow. Then, Fatsoyama steps off the *dohyo*; he takes several steps down the aisle, turns, and bows again to everybody in general.

Decorum then requires that he turn on his heel and march impassively down the aisle and into the runway that leads to the locker room. Only when he passes that barrier is any emotion permitted. Then, he can shake his head in disappointment, curse at one of the elves from his *sumobeya*, toss his fringe in disgust, or kick a water cooler.

If Fatsoyama is the winner, he proceeds, with all due gravity, to his side of the *dohyo* and matches the loser's bow. Then, his feelings swelling deliciously beneath his cool exterior, he crouches. The ref (fresh off another round of virtuoso screaming) squats to face Fatsoyama, to whom he offers an envelope containing his "reward" for victory. Each match has a number of sponsors (like Tokyo Disneyland, McDonald's, Kenji's Bar & Grill, etc.) who contribute cash to a winner-take-all pot. The money goes into envelopes and one of the *tsukebito* holds these until the match is over. Then the elf passes the loot to the ref and the ref pays the winner. Tacky, you say? Tackier than Randy Moss hiring Drew Rosenhaus and whining for a contract extension? Come on. Besides, sumo money is a religious thing — Shinto, remember?

Anyway, Fatsoyama must patiently complete the charade before he gets paid. He's expected to make three distinct chopping movements with his hand — this has some sort of ritual significance — before grabbing the dough. The three chops are usually done with a kind of macho carelessness — as though the victory, and the prize, mean nothing.

"All in a day's work, ref. I'm outa here."

Well, not quite. Next, Fatsoyama, still maintaining that stony, Spartan gaze (although sucking wind and sweating like a bay steer), stops at the corner of the *dohyo*, behind the salt box and the water bucket.

Now, perhaps, he feels the temptation to rub a bruised elbow, straighten his mussed hair, or brush sand from his bod.

He stifles the urge.

Real men don't freshen up.

If, however, his *mawashi* has been yanked up to his nipples, he has permission to tuck it back under his bellybutton. The Sumo Association approves this much public grooming because the specter of laughter lurks in the off-kilter Day-Glo *mawashi*. It looks silly.

While the flunky in the corner folds Fatsoyama's fringe and his prize money into a neat package, Fatso takes a drink of *chikara-mizu*. He spits it out. He fills the water scoop again. The second scoop is for the next wrestler. After the obligatory stomping and clapping, the next wrestler comes over. Fatsoyama gives him the scoop and bows. The other guy drinks and spits. The flunky gives Fatso a tiny napkin, which he promptly hands to the other guy, who dabs his mouth.

That's it. Fatsoyama is done for the day. He moves up the aisle a step or two, turns, bows, and strides manfully toward the locker room. As he proceeds up the aisle, little ladies and old men scurry to intercept him, patting him giddily on the shoulders as he passes. True to the code, Fatso accepts these caresses without joy or discomfort. Water off a duck's back.

"A man's gotta do what a man's gotta do..."

Finally, the runway. Elves surround Fatsoyama. Finally, he can be Himself. He grins merrily, slaps hands with one, two, three elves. What, is that a giggle? Is he actually skipping?

It doesn't matter. Nobody can see him now. The rules have protected him from his own exuberance. Forced to march in a narrow groove — even in defiance of his nature — Fatsoyama preserves the dignity of sumo and all his fellow whales. By following the rules, Fatso partakes (although imperfectly) of that ironic, endearing grace that heavy men exude when they conquer the absurdity of their shape. As often as we laugh cruelly at Tweedledum and Tweedledee and all their roly-poly peers, we respond with incongruous esteem to those fat men whose suavity transcends their obesity.

In the presence (or memory) of certain swollen eminences, we simply do not laugh. Sidney Greenstreet, Orson Welles, Charles Laughton, Peter Ustinov. Babe Ruth! John Madden, Honoré de Balzac, Nikita Khrushchev. Kate Smith, Pavarotti, Aretha, Queen Latifah. The piano Fatses: Waller & Domino. Colonel Sanders. G.K. Chesterton and Alfred Hitchcock.

Konishiki!

The ultimate portrait of the impeccable, intimidating fat man was Jackie Gleason, portraying Minnesota Fats in *The Hustler.* When Fast Eddy called him "fat man" with a voice of contempt, it came to the ear with the resonance of awe. This is the respect the Sumo Association seeks relentlessly to impose on an unwilling public. It shrouds its giants in exceeding gravity, dresses them in the classic simplicity of a bygone, romantic time: *yukata,* the simple robe; *obi,* the plain belt; *geta,* the wooden shoes of the rice farmer. When they wrestle (barefoot), the only garment, the *mawashi,* is a *fundoshi* — medieval underwear.

And it all works.

The aftermath, the ritual of withdrawal, in sumo, is timeless and funereal. We see *rikishi* not as individual combatants, with style and personality, calm or excitable, loud or reticent. They are, in the Sumo Association's prescription, elements in a procession, concealed behind a mask of deportment.

"Keep up appearances," said Pecksniff, "whatever you do."

If you let them act according to their own devices, they would, alas, act like children. Playful children. Flabby children. Embarrassing children.

Of course, there are breaks in this solid front. According to the rules, for instance, it is bad form to offer one's hand to a beaten opponent. As a Real Man, one must disdain the fallen warrior and leave him to lift himself by his own bootstraps like another Real Man (even though he doesn't have any boots and he's rolling on the ground like a beached porpoise). Now and then, however, an impulse of unbridled compassion seizes a *rikishi.* He reaches out to help the loser. And once in a blue moon, without considering his dignity, his machismo, or the good of the Association, the loser accepts that kindness and they pass that most forbidden of sentiments in sumo — fellowship toward athletes from another club.

Even more often, there are acts of sportsmanship — both good and bad — that are a little more subtle. After a *rikishi* has been driven across the ridge in defeat, his back to the audience, and his momentum uncontrollable, he is obviously vulnerable. The winner can choose to send him flying — perhaps to injury — with an extra nudge. Or he can save him by simply planting his feet and holding on. Asashoryu (Hinganai), who always seemed to have a chip on his shoulder, usually chooses the former — heaving his opponent into the audience and then glowering at the tangle of bodies he had created. Slightly more often, however, a *rikishi* will relent and hold on, saving a beaten foe from the fall. The Sumo Association overlooks both gestures.

In the January basho of 2009, I saw a gesture I never thought I'd see in sumo. Mongolian *rikishi* Tokitenku (The Temporal Universe) beat his Japanese opponent Homasho and then, as they passed each other on the *dohyo,* Tokitenku gave Homasho a brotherly pat on the ass. It was a moment rarer than a day in spring and more creative than a thousand touchdown dances.

And Tokitenku probably ended up in the principal's office!

The Interview

The place where post-match etiquette faces its most serious challenge, and — ironically — enjoys its brightest spotlight, is in the inimitable NHK sumo interview. These occur only after the mighty have fallen, when a lesser wrestler defeats a giant. Everyone who beats a *yokozuna* (except another *yokozuna*) gets interviewed, and almost everyone who ever beat Konishiki got interviewed. These interviews, if they were entirely free-wheeling and candid, would certainly provide the Sumo Association with ample opportunity for embarrassment. However, they are conducted by NHK "sportscasters," who have two overwhelming priorities. The first is to advance and glorify the Sumo Association. The second is to ingratiate themselves with the *rikishi*. Both purposes are served by asking questions that would not fluster an orangutan.

In fact, the ideal sumo interview reminds the viewer of an interview with a lesser primate. In recent times, the ideal interview subject was Akinoshima — who, I always hoped, is not nearly as tragically stupid as he seemed when interviewed after wrestling. If he actually were that dim, he would belong in an institution somewhere, wearing a bib at every meal and playing with his toes.

But we'll get to Akinoshima momentarily. First, one must understand that to "interview" a sumo wrestler is essentially a contradiction in principles — because this guy, by administrative fiat, is supposed to be the strong silent (verging on catatonic) type.

However, since an outright gag rule would peg the Sumo Association as obstructionist, most *rikishi* have learned an interview style that gives the average listener a renewed appreciation for silence. The end of a sumo interview is always a relief.

The characteristics of a truly accomplished sumo interviewee include the following techniques:

A deep, rasping, breathy voice. Picture a throat cancer victim attempting to place an obscene phone call.

Breathing into the mike, deafeningly. Even when a *rikishi* has mastered the Voice of the Cancer Victim, some of what he says might still be intelligible if one listens carefully. Apparently to prevent this possibility, NHK never puts one of those sponge-rubber baffles onto its microphones. This allows interviewees to smother, with an ear-rending gasp, every monosyllable they utter. The world's record for gasping thunderously into a mike during a sumo interview belongs to the unchallenged master, Kotogaume, who did it 33 times in one 60-second interview. Not a word he said could even be guessed at.

Face-wiping. Even after a one-second "matador," your typical *rikishi* interviewee will arrive at an NHK interview gushing with sweat, hoarse with exhaustion and gasping like a chain smoker in the Boston Marathon. So he brings his towel along. This allows him to cover his face fifteen or twenty times in the course of the interview, placing the towel over his mouth with every answer — usually just after woofing into the microphone.

- Stupid questions, stupid answers. Roughly 90 percent of all questions asked to athletes by TV interviewers in Japan begin with the phrase, "How did you feel?... " This is an approach much approved by virtually everyone in the sports world, from commissioners to athletes to the water boy, because it's always something your proverbial orangutan could handle with a one-word response.

- No vowels. One sign of true manliness in Japan, besides speaking in a guttural rumble that makes Don Corleone, by comparison, sound like Minnie Mouse, is to eschew vowels. Japan's foremost vowel droppers are sumo wrestlers. And since vowel sounds do exist in Japanese, the virtually unintelligible responses gurgled forth in a sumo interview become a linguistic conundrum more appropriate to anthropologists than sports fans. Let's drop in, for instance, on Akinoshima, as he's interviewed after yet another stirring defeat of Konishiki. His eyes are glassy, his body drenched with sweat, his mouth slack. One wonders if he's alive, until the microphone inches closer to his face and picks up the telltale roar of his breath.

Akinoshima wipes his face, apparently to no effect. Rivulets spurt from every pore.

The interviewer cringes to Akinoshima's right, barely visible on the edge of the TV screen. There is something in the constriction of his voice that tells us he's smiling as he tries to talk. A Japanese sportscaster who can't grin and talk simultaneously never makes it to the big time. He begins:

NHK: "Akinoshima, that was a wonderful match. One of the great moments in sumo history. I was personally moved and overwhelmed by the drama of such great sumo. Congratulations. What can I say? You were wonderful! What a future you have! I hope I have children who grow up to be just like you and that they have identical children and that their children are also just like you. Now, excuse me, big guy, but I must ask you something, please, and I hope I'm not prying, because if I am, I'm terribly sorry. I'll ask a different question. Or I'll just go away. What I want to know, please, if you don't mind, is: How did you feel before the match?"

AKINOSHIMA: (Gasping into the mike as he wipes his face.) "Rr." [Translation: "Rr."]

NHK: "Oh, I forgot to say—how could it have slipped my mind? What a blunder. I'm really sorry, I hope you'll forgive me—I forgot to congratulate not only you, but your brilliant *oyakata*, Fujishima-*sensei*, who prepared you so flawlessly for this wonderful effort. Listen, can you tell me what Fujishima-*sensei* told you before today's match?"

AKINOSHIMA: *(Wipe. Gasp. Roar. A long, thoughtful pause. Several woofs.)* "Wsrmsht."
["I can't remember."]

NHK: "Really? Well, how did you feel as he was passing these instructions along?"

AKINOSHIMA: *(Gasp. Roar. Wipe.)* "Wsrmsht'."

["I don't remember that, either."]

NHK: "Fascinating! Great! Well, then, how did you feel at the moment that Konishiki got *migi-yotsu* and started driving you off the *dohyo*. That was a pretty scary moment, wasn't it?"

AKINOSHIMA: *(Wipe. Gasp.)* "S' ds' ne."

["Yup."]

NHK: "And then, you must have felt better when he tripped on his own feet and started to fall, huh?"

AKINOSHIMA: *(Silence, save for the rhythmic roaring of the mike, the sound of sweat trickling gently 'twixt valleys of flab.)*

NHK: "Well, of course. Then, when he actually fell, aided by that brilliant move you made, by getting out of his way, then, tell me, what were your feelings at that triumphant moment? Were you glad? Did you think it was over?"

AKINOSHIMA: "Rr."

NHK: "Well, Akinoshima, as usual, we are amazed not only by your sumo, but by your eloquence off the *dohyo*. Before you leave, if I may indulge you with one more probing question, please, excuse my intrusion, but I'm sure your fans want to know — now think about this one — How do you feel about tomorrow's match?"

AKINOSHIMA: *(Gasp. Roar. Trickle. Wipe.)* "Gmbrms."

["Gonna try hard."]

NHK: "What a trouper. Well, we wish you the very best of the very best luck and we hope you do your best. And congratulations again, and we will all be grateful, for a long time, that you troubled to come back

here and grace us with this unforgettable interview.
Thank you, big guy, thank you. Sorry to have bothered
you. Thanks for coming. Sorry. Thanks. Sorry. Thanks
again. Sorry."

AKINOSHIMA: *(Wipe. Gasp. Roar. A desultory bow.
Gasp. Woof.)* "Rgto gzms." ["Thanks."]

As wretched as most sumo interviews are, there are notable
exceptions, especially when the *rikishi* involved is too happy
to follow the rules. During the best *basho* of his career, for
example, Wakasegawa (Paddington) got his first interview
ever, and he was full of engaging, voluble insights on himself and his matches. Many ex-*gakusei-zumo* (former collegiate *rikishi*) speak thoughtfully and articulately. Chiyonofuji
(who might be the smartest man in Japan who never went to
high school) was also unconventional. He spoke in a normal,
slightly high and boyish voice, joked with the interviewer,
and had a gracious talent for turning the typical stupid questions into revealing answers.

After retirement, his guest shots during NHK's sumo
broadcast reinforced the positive impression he made when
interviewed after matches. The same was true of Mainoumi
(Mighty Mouse).

These exceptions prove the wisdom of the rule. The Sumo
Association's vow of near-silence is a stroke of genius, because it fosters sumo's finest virtue — its wordless, instinctual
simplicity. Sumo athletes are drilled to a level of insensibility
that makes it difficult for them to say what they did — even
in the first moment afterwards — or how they did it.

There is eloquence in allowing the deed to speak for itself.
There is wisdom in restraining the doer from embellishing the
deed with word or action. There is class in preventing him
from gloating, explaining or moralizing in retrospect.

The great *rikishi* and the great gunfighter are kindred.

You remember what happened after Shane snuffed all the outlaws? No shouting, right? No flourish. No swagger. The deed is done, there is nothing to say. Alan Ladd pauses only a moment to consider Jack Palance's corpse. His face reveals nothing; we might read his regard as we wish.

The little boy, Joey (Brandon DeWilde) — who is a dramatic device installed by director George Stevens to elicit Shane's thoughts — does the post-gunfight interview and squeezes from Alan Ladd enough moral lessons to pack a small missal: "Thou shalt not kill"... "Honor thy father and mother"... "Do your thing and keep your mouth shut"... Original sin and predestination ("A man has to be what he is, Joey.")... Gun control... Social security. All this in 73 words. Shane also manages to articulate sumo's attitude toward injuries: Bleed quietly and avoid medical help.

No need to ask any more questions. Shane's silence is his soliloquy. Having gently shed the intrusive Joey, Shane slips away. Like a weary *rikishi* shlepping toward the locker room, he rides off — morally ambiguous and deaf to the child's adulation — into the unknown.

CHAPTER 10

THE BASHO BEAT
"Give that rhythm every-thing you've got"

If the individual match, which I've belabored in the previous six chapters, is sumo's microcosm, then the *basho* is its Big Picture. It is the universe that integrates all the little fights and makes sense of them.

In a *basho*'s schedule lies the flow of sumo — its rhythm, its ordeal. The Sumo Association's subtlest achievement is its refinement of the fifteen-day struggle. The schedule is a work of intellect and balance, a philosophical fabric that has few parallels in sport. It is, moreover, a kind of monastic trial in which most everything is foreordained, in which even the surprises are preceded by their shadows. Once a fan has sensed the flow of the *basho*, he can feel the unexpected coming, in the moments before it unfolds.

Although seemingly a crescendo, the *basho* is more accurately a loose composition, within which improvisation induces infinite variety — a kind of soft-spoken jazz played by fat men. Within the composition, the schedule dances up and down the scale of *rikishi* and through a range of outcomes. This is the melody. The bass line, thumping steadily beneath these flowing notes, is the hierarchy, the rankings of *rikishi* that determine who wrestles whom, and when.

To perceive the sense of the *basho*'s rhythm, you have to understand its strange purpose. The individual *rikishi* does not necessarily pursue the same goal from match-to-match, and he must be perpetually sensitive to the "higher goals" sought — through him — by his *sumobeya* and for the sumo world at large.

For a *rikishi* in a match — most of the time — winning is the objective. Beat the other guy. However, most *rikishi* learn that the institution of sumo is not well-served by practitioners who harbor a single-minded and impolite passion for victory after victory. *Rikishi* learn that, over the course of a *basho*, winning isn't everything, or the only thing. In many cases, it's not even something. The real objective, for all but an elite handful of *rikishi* in sumo's top division, is not to win first prize — or even contend for it. What most of the guys are shooting for is *kachikoshi*.

Kachikoshi is eight wins and seven losses, one match above .500. In most sports, this — a winning percentage of .533 — denotes mediocrity and spurs the earnest jock to work harder and get better. For the overwhelming majority of sumo wrestlers, it is the definition of success. As long as a *rikishi* makes *kachikoshi*, he is assured of creeping upward in the ranks.

In all things sumo, moderation.

The opposite of *kachikoshi* is *makekoshi,* (7-8 or worse) — which isn't good, nor is it exactly a catastrophe. Usually, *makekoshi* gets a *rikishi* demoted to a level where his opponents aren't quite so tough, and so his next *kachikoshi* comes easier. Once he's got Victory No. 8 in a *basho*, a *rikishi* can relax, maybe help out a few other guys with their *kachikoshi*. In sumo, *kachikoshi* is Miller Time. If winning a few more matches looks a little too strenuous, or the prospect of success seems too scary, nobody faults a guy for slacking off. In sumo, 8-7 is just about the same as 11-4 — and much more sociable.

In practical terms, this means that, among the forty-odd *rikishi* in the first — *makuuchi* — division in any given *basho*, there are only three, perhaps four, occasionally five, genuine contenders for the *yusho*. The other three dozen are all aiming at the same golden mean: *kachikoshi*.

To dream the possible dream, to duck the unbeatable foe...

Banzuke: Confucian Confusion

Of course, the Sumo Association does not precede each *basho* by publishing a list of "real contenders" and obligatory also-rans. Their rankings, printed before each *basho* in a beautiful hand-lettered poster called the *banzuke*, follow a formula that dates at least to the seventeenth century. Below the top two ranks of *yokozuna* and *ozeki*, a *rikishi*'s status can really fluctuate according to his previous *basho* record.

After *kachikoshi*, he goes up; *makekoshi*, he goes down.

Yokozuna are officially immune from demotion (although if they stink up the joint repeatedly, they have to retire). *Ozeki* can only be demoted after two straight *makekoshi*.

Remember the ranks for *rikishi* in *makuuchi*? From top to bottom, they are *yokozuna* (the pinnacle), *ozeki, sekiwake, komusubi* and *maegashira*.

It's customary to refer to this hierarchy of ranks in sumo as "Confucian," because it was Confucius' idea that civilization properly forms itself into an interlocking hierarchy of social stations, with people at each level owing obligations to, and receiving indulgence from, those above and those below, a construct often described as "filial piety." "Confucian" is one of the standard buzzwords Westerners use to explain almost everything that happens in Japan. This especially applies to lists. The *banzuke* is a list; ergo, it's Confucian, *ne?*

Actually, sumo rankings aren't Confucian. They're Darwinist. This is because, in day-to-day life, *rikishi* don't put much stock in filial piety. They live on a one-way street. The kids in the lower ranks kiss ass, and the guys up above kick it. The mechanism that determines this pecking order is performance — how well you did in the last *basho* and how far you got promoted. Occasionally, a really virtuoso bootlicker can cling to his bed and board in the *sumobeya* despite a lousy record as a wrestler. But sooner or later, he has to make *kachikoshi*, or look for another line of work.

If you look at your average *banzuke*, even if you can't read the Japanese, it isn't hard to figure out that the upper-ranked wrestlers' names are written real big, and the names shrink as you go down the list. Generally, it's correct to assume that *rikishi* tend to be scheduled against guys whose names are the same size. But you can't count on this. Sumo Association schedulers have both a system and a playful curiosity ("Don't you wonder what would happen if this guy fought that guy?"). A *basho* is full of crossovers, from level to level — which make it possible for lesser wrestlers to test themselves against the studs, and maybe move up.

To make this happen, the Sumo Association applies an un-written code of "practical rankings." For instance, because there are only 10 to 12 *rikishi* in the top four ranks of sumo, a *rikishi* at this level has to wrestle down, among the *mae-gashira*, in as many as six matches per *basho*. Which six guys does he fight? Do those six guys, in turn, have to take on all the *rikishi* on the top?

The answer lies, usually, in where each *rikishi* lands on the *banzuke*. Before a *rikishi* sets eyes on the schedule (which, as you recall, is fixed only two days in advance of each day's wrestling), the *banzuke* gives him a broad notion of how tough his opponents will be in the coming two weeks, and what his expectations ought to be.

One thing he barely thinks about is which "team" he's on. Sometime back in sumo's dim middle ages, the elders divided *rikishi* into "East" and "West" teams — based on where they came from. It's doubtful — in this essentially man-to-man sport — whether anybody ever really had much team spirit for the East Side Purgolders or the West Side Fighting Sand Crabs. But by the 1950's, there wasn't even a remnant of team play. Nowadays, the East/West split is an empty form. However, it is good to know that, for *rikishi* of equal rank on the traditional scale — or instance, *maegashira* No. 7 — the East guy is considered slightly superior to the West guy.

With one exception noted below, however, the thinking fan disregards this East/West business entirely.

The Real Ranks: Upper Echelon

The *banzuke* divides the upper ranks into two groups. At the top are *yokozuna*, and below are the three *sanyaku* ranks: *ozeki, sekiwake,* and *komusubi*. They all wrestle each other, but don't be fooled by mere status. Even in these lofty climes, the objectives of individual *rikishi* vary. Remember, winning isn't everything!

First of all, in terms of sheer quality, the only difference between a *yokozuna* and an *ozeki* is time and politics. Politics kept Asahifuji out of *yokozuna* for years, but in time, they let him join because he kept embarrassing *yokozuna*. Onokuni, although entrenched at *yokozuna* for years, was a panda of a different color. Except for an occasional spasm of good health and enthusiasm, his record was worse than most *ozeki*, and he hardly ever challenged for a *yusho*.

By the same token, for essentially the entire first decade of the millennium, two cagey journeymen, Kaio and Chiyotaikai, were perennial *ozeki*, rarely challenging for the *yusho*. They paced themselves with strategic "injuries" that got them excused from the occasional *basho*, and they always scored *kachikoshi* when they needed it. While younger *rikishi* climbed the ranks and passed them by, they opted for survival.

THE ELITE. In essence, then, *yokozuna* and *ozeki* comprise a single class best referred to simply as the Elite. The Elite breaks down, in a practical sense, into two classes, which can be measured, essentially, according to desire. To wit:

- THE PENNANT RACE comprises only those wrestlers who are seriously competing for the tournament title and are athletically capable of winning it;
- THE GRAVY TRAIN includes those members of the Elite, Kaio and Chiyotaikai being the quintessential examples, who just don't have what it takes to win the championship — victims of the Peter Principle who have reached their level of incompetence and settled in with no further aspirations.

In the 2009 Natsu (May) Basho, for example, I broke the Elite down into four *rikishi* in the Pennant Race — Asashoryu, Hakuho, Kotooshu and Harumafuji, and three *rikishi* on the Gravy Train — Kotomitsuki, Kaio and Chiyotaikai. Results of the basho exemplified this breakdown. The three Gravy Trainers were all 8-7, keeping themselves alive without straining too hard. The Pennant Race four had records of 15-1 (Harumafuji), 14-2 (Hakuho), 12-3 (Asashoryu) and 9-6 (Kotooshu).

Among the Elite in that *basho*, there was a good possibility that at least one Pennant Racer, Kotooshu, might switch over to the Gravy Train within a year.

Below the Elite, two *sanyaku* ranks, *sekiwake* and *komusubi*, present the most brutal schedules in sumo.

THE TIGHTROPE. A *sekiwake* is neither here nor there. He's better than almost all those *maegashira* down below. He's one notch above *komusubi* — otherwise known as the Meatgrinder. His schedule includes everyone in the upper ranks, and he scores the occasional upset among the Elite. But he's generally a *kachikoshi* kinda guy, just trying to stay where he is. He's negotiating a crowded tightrope; there are guys approaching from both ends, eager to push him off.

Rikishi reach the Tightrope and stay there for a while, usually because they have a very effective technique, or some physical feature, that makes them tough to beat. Kotogaume, perhaps sumo's all-time most dangerous Butterball, for instance, was built low to the ground and incredibly dense. He lingered at *sekiwake* for six straight *basho* in 1989-90. Terao, a fanatic battler who was able to overwhelm almost anyone for a period of five seconds, established himself in 1990 as a Tightrope level *rikishi* and spent five *basho* there. In the 2000's, Baruto (Fred Thompson) depended on his height to frustrate opponents and cling to the Tightrope.

When a *sekiwake* like Baruto can't expand his repertoire in response to the intense demands of the Tightrope, gravity will get him by and by — with a stop (possibly even a recovery) in the Meatgrinder on the way down. Kirishima was the rare tightroper who was still learning and growing when he reached *sekiwake*. For him, the Tightrope was a one-*basho* pause on his way to the Elite.

For most, the Tightrope is more likely a place from which to fall. And to fall means into the next lower designation, *komusubi* — not a pleasant fate. I refer to this detention cell for rising and falling *rikishi* instructively as...

THE MEATGRINDER. The Sumo Association uses the Meatgrinder for three distinct and practical purposes:

To punish *maegashira* wrestlers who have succeeded excessively in matches at the lower levels, perhaps by racking up a 10-5 or 11-4 record from some lowly rung like *maegashira* No. 8. The average number of wins per *basho* for *komusubi* is 6.5. The Meatgrinder is the schedule-master's way of saying, "OK, smartass, you think you're hot stuff? We have a few large gentlemen we'd like you to meet."

As an entrance exam for rising stars, to see if they're ready for prime time. When a promising wrestler has been seasoned in the *maegashira* ranks for a while, and he has a good previous *basho*, and there's an opening at *komusubi* (there's almost always an opening at *komusubi*), they put him in the Meatgrinder. There isn't much difference, in this respect, between a test and punishment — except in terms of expectations. It's a punishment when the Sumo Association knows a *rikishi* will get creamed in the Meatgrinder. It's an exam when the *rikishi* has a chance to survive. Even if he doesn't make *kachikoshi*, the Meatgrinder is the rising star's chance to upset an *ozeki* or *yokozuna*, and impress some people. If he can do that, he'll be back for a second chance.

For instance, in January, 1989, Kirishima — then 29 years old and essentially aimless in his sumo career, despite a lot of talent — made the Meatgrinder. In succession, on the first five days, he wrestled a veritable Murderer's Row of champions who eventually accounted for a total of 46 *yusho* in their careers. He started with Onokuni (*yokozuna*), then faced Hokutenyu (*ozeki*), Konishiki (*ozeki*), Chiyonofuji (*yokozuna*), and Hokutoumi (*yokozuna*). He lost every match and fell apart at the seams, putting on sumo's sorriest performance of the year. His 1-14 record wasn't as good as it looks on paper. This was the sort of experience that makes a guy look back on his life and wonder where it all went haywire.

From that nadir, however, Kirishima somehow turned his career around. It took him only 'til July '89 to get back to the Meatgrinder, this time going 7-8. That *makekoshi* included a three-day spectacular — at the beginning of the *basho* — when he beat Chiyonofuji, Hokutenyu and Konishiki in succession. By December, Kirishima was back at *komusubi*, where he did something few *rikishi* have ever done. He survived two straight *basho* in the Meatgrinder, with records of 10-5 and 11-4, and he beat the Elite eight times.

The Meatgrinder also serves as a safety net for *sekiwake* on their way down after *makekoshi*. The schedule is little different, but after losing at *sekiwake*, *komusubi* is the falling *rikishi*'s second chance before he gets kicked down among the riffraff.

How tough is the Meatgrinder? It means you have to wrestle every *rikishi* ranked above you before you get a break and fight a few of the guys underneath. This is the sumo version of Hell Week. By the time you get to the lower-ranked wrestlers, your form and self-esteem are so shattered that beating anyone — including your grandmother — is beyond your wildest dreams. The Meatgrinder is as high as most *rikishi* ever go. In almost every case, it's a ticket down.

In 20 *basho* between January 2006 and March 2009, as a sample, the total record for Meatgrinder occupants was 261-301 (.464). Of the 40 *rikishi* in that span who attained *komusubi,* only 17 made *kachikoshi*.

The Real Ranks: Down Below

Guys like Kirishima and Harumafuji are Cinderellas. Sumo mostly consists of ugly stepsisters, otherwise known as *maegashira*.

In traditional Sumo Association terms, *maegashira* are ranked in neat, descending order from *maegashira* No. 1 through *maegashira* No. 15. In fact, this big category just below *komusubi* breaks down into three groups that I separate by difficulty of schedule. These classifications are Cannon Fodder, the Fish Tank, and the Border Patrol. Here's how they break down.

CANNON FODDER. The bullies up-top (*yokozuna* through *komusubi*) all need small fry down below to pick on, especially in the first half of the *basho*. For this job, the Sumo Association picks out seven of the 30-some *rikishi* below the *sanyaku* level. This platoon of cannon fodder includes East *maegashira* No. 1-4 and West *maegashira* No. 1-3.

The West *maegashira* No. 4 has a much softer schedule than his East Side counterpart — showing that there is, yes, one item of significance in this East/West nonsense. However, West *maegashira* No. 4 isn't necessarily out of cannon range, because when a *rikishi* ranked above him — anyone from *yokozuna* to *maegashira* No. 3 — gets hurt and quits the tourney, he's the guy first in line to fill in the gap upstairs. In some tournaments, with a lot of upper-rank withdrawals, the Grim Reaper of scheduling can reach all the way down to *maegashira* No. 5.

THE FISH TANK. My old friend Schuster was a high school wrestler, and during the season, he suffered almost fatally from two anxieties: 1) keeping his weight at 138 pounds, and 2) his next opponent. Schuster's record hovered eternally around *kachikoshi*, so he had a philosophical grasp of his own limitations. He knew which opponents he could never beat in a million tries, and the ones against whom he dared to envision victory. In a way, Schuster was a kind of human benchmark for wrestling competence; when he saw a guy whom he knew that even he could whip, Schuster found it difficult to respect him. He applied to such opponents wrestling's most scornful putdown: "fish."

Schuster, if he had gone on to a sumo career, would be Cannon Fodder, and he would beat most of the *rikishi* below that level. When Junko and I watch sumo now, we tend to use Schuster's terminology. For instance, Junko would say to me, on Day 4, "So, who does Asashoryu got today?"

I look it up in the schedule posted every day by the Sumo Association and see, pitted against the merciless Mongolian, Kakizoe — who bears an uncanny resemblance to Spanky McFarland from the "Our Gang" comedies.

"Spanky," I say.

"Ah," replies Junko. "A fish."

Rolls right off the tongue.

Hence, a group of about twenty *rikishi* just below Cannon Fodder comprises the Fish Tank. Fish have pretty easy schedules, wrestling among themselves and competing mainly to collect their *kachikoshi*.

However, despite its lowly place in the *makuuchi* scheme of things, the Fish Tank is a source of endless fascination for the fan. Here is sumo's melting pot. Here we find old pugs, pushed from the lofty regions of *sanyaku* and destined never to rise again. But you dare not write them off. These are foxy old scrappers; given the soft schedule that is the blessing of the Fish Tank, they can outwit younger wrestlers, take turns picking each other off, and limp to the next *basho*.

Here, too, are the sprouts, fresh up from *juryo* with stars in their eyes, spring in their muscles, and a pink flush on their pudgy little cheeks. The Fish Tank is where they get baptized into the brutal *tachiai* and sneaky tricks of the old barracudas who lurk among the seaweed fronds.

Here also are the yo-yo's, both youngsters and veterans, so-called because they bounce up and down the ranks of the Fish Tank. They score *kachikoshi* in a *basho* and move up a few notches, maybe even within range of the cannons. Then, *makekoshi*, once — even twice — until they're down far enough to feast on fish dumber and weaker than they are. Then, *kachikoshi* and back up again.

One of my favorite yo-yo's, who eventually just slipped out of sight without leaving a mark behind, was a feisty little toad named Koboyama. His only move was a desperate, bowling-ball lunge at *tachiai*. In the twilight of his career, Koboyama was the fish's fish, hopelessly overmatched every time he stepped on the *dohyo*. Most *rikishi* assumed they could beat him in their sleep. And still, Koboyama hung on, getting impossible mileage out of that ridiculous charge. He had a sixth sense for outsmarting greenhorn kids — who would give him one look, smirk, blow their concentration, and lose.

The Fish Tank also provides a resting place for good athletes who fall from grace through injury or inattention. Tochinowaka (Big Al), for instance, was often so busy admiring himself that he left his brains in his jockstrap for two or three consecutive *basho*. When he found himself treading water in the Fish Tank, he finally woke up, hammered a series of shlemiels and started his way back up toward the Meatgrinder.

Almost every *basho*, one fish turns shark and starts devouring other fish so voraciously that suddenly, in the second week of the *basho*, he finds himself listed among the tournament leaders — alongside all those Mongolians and *ozeki*. For instance, in the 2008 Kyushu (November) Basho, Miyabiyama, a Butterball whom we call "Hotcakes" because his ample flab is layered up and down his torso like a large stack at iHOP, entered the tournament in the Fish Tank at maegashira No. 7. He went through his first eleven matches at 9-2, placing him one match down from *yokozuna* Hakuho (10-1) and tied for second with Ama, a *sekiwake* who the next year changed his name to Harumafuji. At this point, conscious of the potential embarrassment of Miyabiyama blundering into the *yusho*, the Sumo Association put him through a two-day Meatgrinder, first against *ozeki* Chiyotaikai and then Ama.

Hotcakes lost both, pretty decisively. Fulfilling the Sumo Association's plan, he finished the last four days of the *basho* at 1-3. The last guy to beat him, on Day 15, was Mad Dog, a lowly No. 14 *maegashira*, who ended the *basho* matching Hotcakes' record of 10-5.

THE BORDER PATROL. The one thing that no *makuuchi* wrestler wants is demotion to *juryo*. The *rikishi* who falls back to the second division invariably finds his comeback much harder than his initial ascension to *makuuchi*. The reasons for this, I think, lie within the Sumo Association and, perhaps more significantly, within the *rikishi*'s mind.

The Sumo Association, like any other showbiz organization, loves new blood. Management wants to feed fresh young moonfaces to the public. So, when all other measures are equal and the Sumo Association has a choice between lifting an old fish or a rookie from *juryo* to *makuuchi*, the committee tends to lean toward the kid. In order to get back to *makuuchi*, after slipping to *juryo*, an old-timer must clearly dominate his younger (stronger, prettier, quicker, eagerer) opponents in *juryo*. He needs knockouts, not split decisions.

The other barrier to comebacks is the mind, a sense of ennui that seems to overwhelm and defeat older *rikishi* who've dropped a division. I've seen competent *rikishi*, perhaps hindered by nagging injuries, fall to *juryo* — where, even hurt, they are superior to most of their opponents. But they don't show it. They crumble in their first *juryo* tournament and flounder for a year or more in the second division. Some make it back, some just putter around in *juryo* for the rest of their careers. And some just continue to plummet, down to *makushita* (the third division), and down and down, until embarrassment nudges them into retirement.

The better alternative, of course, is not to get caught in that dangerous spiral. The *makuuchi* wrestlers who face that threat are the *rikishi* at the bottom of the first division — the Border Patrol. Depending on the number of *rikishi* in the upper ranks, the Border Patrol guys might be numbered anywhere from *maegashira* No. 12 to *maegashira* No. 16. Typically, the Border Patrol includes two young guys just pushed up from *juryo*, and two older *rikishi* who screwed up in the last *basho* and stand at the crossroads of their careers.

I usually don't waste much sympathy on the young up-and-comers. Frequently, their promotion to *makuuchi* is premature. Few people expect them to stick on their first trip to *makuuchi*, and a lot of us want to see the bloated little snots get their ears boxed before being shipped back down to the minors for a little more seasoning. If they're good, they'll learn from their stint in the Border Patrol and return in a few *basho*. If they're not good enough, at least they've had a cup of coffee in the Bigs.

The real drama in the Border Patrol is with the old guys — like Tosanoumi, a 37-year-old *maegashira* No. 15 who bade *makuuchi* a weary farewell, perhaps forever, in March 2008 with a sad 4-11 showing. Watching *beteran* (or "veterans," the TV commentators favorite euphemism for the over-the-hill gang) like Tosanoumi struggle against the ultimate demotion, the caring fan pauses affectionately, aware that these warhorses are making, maybe, their last stand against age and flab and "... the heartache and the thousand natural shocks/ That flesh is heir to...." A lot of us have been there. Tosanoumi is Everyman, running uphill with a 300-pound ape on his back, on behalf of every other man.

"Come on, you old tub! Get the lead out!"

Occasionally, a different sort of old-timer is recruited into the Border Patrol. The Sumo Association (because they're old guys, too, and they know how it feels) occasionally spot a *juryo* journeyman who's been hauling his ass up to the mat every day for twenty years but he's never going to be good enough. He's hurled a lot of innings, but his heater's got no zip. So they send him up to the Show, anyway. Even though the Border Patrol is *makuuchi*'s softest schedule, he ends up getting punched out and sent back. But so what? He's been there. When he retires, he will retire at the highest rank of his career — *maegashira* — and his pension will be a little bigger.

When you're watching a *basho*, enjoy the Pennant Race. But keep an eye on the Border Patrol, where the rhythm and the drama of sumo throbs just as deep, just as hungrily, and a little more poignantly.

The Weight of Concentration

Regardless of where in the pecking order a *rikishi* finds himself, he faces a psychological pressure that's unique among all the sports in the world. Remember that, in 15 days of the tournament, a typical *rikishi* spends only about a minute and a half actually fighting.

Each day, when he steps on the *dohyo*, he bends under the weight of 24, 48, 72 hours of anticipation. He's been wrestling this match in his head for two days. And he knows that whatever he has imagined will be completely different from what really happens — and he's going to have maybe a half-second to recognize reality and deal with it. In 15 days of relentless tension six times a year, the weight of concentration never lightens. And let's remember these aren't exactly the world's sharpest intellects. Even among sumo's brightest, a split second break, a blink of inattention, can destroy a match, lose a *yusho*.

In the 2009 Haru (March) Basho, Asashoryu (Hinganai) entered Day 10 tied for the lead with Hakuho at 9-0 and had won 24 of his last 25 matches. Hinganai's opponent was *ozeki* Harumafuji, the lightest (280 pounds) *rikishi* in *makuuchi* and an opponent he usually handled. It was Asashoryu's habit, as he awaited the *gyoji*'s summons to the *dohyo*, to crouch on his big pillow with eyes of stone. He saw nothing, felt nothing. He was a gargoyle. But this time, as the camera studied him, then jumped to a shot of Harumafuji and returned to Asashoryu, I noticed: Asashoryu stole a glimpse of his opponent. This was not just a tiny, easily dismissed break in concentration, because Harumafuji has unusual powers to fluster his opponent. Harumafuji, before a match — almost any match — sits there looking scared to death. He doesn't look as though he could beat his little sister at pick-up sticks, much less survive a frontal attack by the 340-pound multi-great grandson of Genghis Khan. Harumafuji's pre-match demeanor is either a supremely devious diversion or simply a result of the fact that he has a really nice face. Either way, any opponent looking into Harumafuji's gentle eyes, and noting the weak set of his jaw, can't help but conclude that he possesses all the fighting spirit of a Hostess cupcake.

So, that day, against his better judgment, Hinganai had looked into Harumafuji's dewy eyes and he had seen chocolate pastry with a whipped-cream center. He lost. Harumafuji got a lightning belt-grip and ragdolled Asashoryu off the *dohyo* before he could set his feet. After that one subtle hitch in his *basho* rhythm, Asashoryu fell out of the lead and never really challenged Hakuho for the title.

Lose the beat, lose the game.

Shinko, when I spoke with him, talked about how hard it is to keep the beat, because there is so little actual wrestling and so much waiting. It begins to weigh on a *rikishi* soon after all that first-week adrenaline disperses. Between Days 6 and 10, said Shinko, concentration falters — and Elite *rikishi* start suffering inexplicable upsets to lesser wrestlers.

Good Basho, Bad Basho

One of the issues raised among sumo nerds toward the end of each tournament is whether or not this was a "good *basho*." I thought this a strange question when first I heard it, and I haven't much changed my opinion.

What I didn't see was how all these disparate events, these hundreds of fights among dozens of wrestlers at four or five different levels spread over more than two weeks, could be so blithely categorized. Since then, however, I've derived some sense of what's meant by this "good *basho*." Sumo nerds (who are pretty faithful to the Sumo Association outlook on these subjective points) apparently think a *basho* is "good" if the climax conforms to the Confucian crescendo envisioned by the boys in charge. Ideally, attention in the last days of the *basho* centers on the battle for the *yusho* among *yokozuna* — who, by this time, should have disdainfully tossed aside all of their lesser opponents, which hardly ever happens. But never mind reality. A *basho*, apparently, is diminished if that favorite son of the masses — the underdog — pulls off a surprise and whips the Elite. Management always roots for the Yankees.

The Sumo Association blushes (needlessly) whenever one of its Elite gets ambushed. This is an interesting outlook, which finally gets us down to the Confucian nitty-gritty. Some pigs are more equal than others, and each little piggie — if he were properly respectful — would always roll over for the Empress of Blandings.

But the best-laid plans of mice and livestock gang aft a-gley, and the Sumo Association, bless their hearts, does not enforce the Confucian code at all costs. When a *yokozuna* can't win anymore, or an upstart like Asahifuji beats a brutal schedule and refuses to lose, so be it. Management endorses the Darwinian change, and institutionalizes a new Elite.

However, although sumo's elders can never entirely control the outcome of *basho* and choreograph the changing of the guard, they can at least plant, in the minds of sumo followers, the presumption that a *basho* that follows an unexpected course and exalts a gang of unruly underdogs is a "bad" *basho*, a naughty *basho*, a *basho* after which a dignified adult can only shake his finger at the miscreants, whisper a few words of admonishment and hasten to the next — presumably more decorous — assembly of the faithful.

This stuffy view of "good *basho*/bad *basho*" curiously denies the delicate rhythm that the Sumo Association has so artfully devised. The sumo schedule's thoughtful division into several distinct levels of difficulty and competition is wonderfully effective. Although, logically, only a few *rikishi* can seriously hope for the championship, the Sumo Association's many-tiered schedule unveils an ascending series of small dramas. At a dozen different steps along the way, small championships are won and lost. The rise of a rookie *makuuchi*, undersized and overeager, from the Border Patrol to the Fish Tank can be more stirring and dramatic than the battle for the *yusho* between the same old faces at the top. That story alone — for a real fan — can make this a good *basho*. There is so much happening in a *basho* that you can find fun almost anywhere you look. With forty wrestlers to choose from — just in *makuuchi* — you have forty candidates for Hero and Villain. An infinite array of possibilities — most predictable, some surprising and at least once every *basho*, something totally preposterous.

Good *basho*? Bad *basho*? No such thing — not if you're a real fan, not if you watch all of it, from top to bottom. Every *banzuke* is a different band, every *basho* a different concert. The schedule is always there, steady and subtle, insinuating structure on improvisation — like Ray Brown thrumming the bass in back while the Blossom Dearie sings out front.

CHAPTER 11

TANK THIS ONE
for the Gipper

They cheat, you know — sumo wrestlers.

Not, however, in the same style or with the same motives as most Western sports fans recognize. They do not connive in the tawdry, slinking, money-grubbing style that we associate with the Black Sox of 1919 and the steroid juicers of the turn of the millennium. *Rikishi* cheat — in a way — honorably, and so, with the knowledge — nay, sanction — nay, example — of their sport's administrators.

This is a thorny concept for a foreign fan to grasp — especially one who, like me, spent a seemingly endless period of his newspaper career rooting out petty corruption among the public officials of a small town in New England. For me, it became virtually second nature, at the faintest whiff of fishy goings on, to spring to my feet and shout, "ExCUSE me, Mr. Chairman! I believe there is Conflict of Interest here!"

Like most Americans, I'm hung up on the notion of the "public trust," a doctrine that has spawned a vast brood of commissions, institutions, volunteer ombudsmen, and watch-dog organizations solely dedicated to the exposure and root-ing out of public officials caught in conflict of (or the "appear-ance of conflict of") interest. Never mind that the ones who actually get nailed are usually small-timers and subordinates (like Greg Anderson, Barry Bonds' syringe valet). The system is pervasive. The fear of investigation clings democratically to all officeholders, dogging their heels as they struggle from the hustings to the big time. The threat is genuine, because almost anybody with a little inside information and a copy of the Law can shout "conflict of interest" and raise an unholy, career-threatening stink.

Japan, on the other hand — blessed with perhaps the world's most pampered and docile media — has yet to ac-cept that interests might somehow, sometimes conflict. Japan is a nation in which an individual interrupted in the midst of clawing, grasping, backstabbing, and conniving his blood-stained way to personal advancement, can piously and sin-cerely insist that he is acting in a sort of common interest derived from longstanding traditions. Even as he cheats his friends and screws his neighbor, he is, in fact, a piece of living history, enjoying privileges bestowed by community consen-sus established long before he was born. If nobody knows exactly how this sort of selfish behavior can contribute to a common good, the only possible answer is that Japan con-tains some mysteries that present-day mortals can neither truly understand nor retrieve from an inscrutable past.

For example, ever since I've been observing Japanese politics, I've noticed its tendency to experience periodic "scandals" that range from massive embezzlement to naked nepotism, sexual shenanigans, kidnapping and murder, during which all the alleged villains check themselves into hospitals. These scandals — often implicating leaders of the ruling party and highly-placed government ministry officials — achieve a fairly spectacular 15 minutes of fame. This media fanfare earns coverage and plaudits, for the "openness" of the Japanese political system, from the international press. Back home, however, the general feeling among Japanese is not so much that the malefactors in this scandal should be ashamed of themselves, but that everyone is ashamed that something like this got into the tabloids and made all of us look bad.

A government investigation nevertheless duly ensues. By and by, several low-ranking scapegoats (none of whom, by some miracle, were influential in the party) are fingered, arraigned, and sent to a brain-numbingly technical trial that's likely to drag on for a decade. Several innocent but magnanimous big shots resign symbolically (from their hospital beds) to take responsibility for their subordinates' tragic waywardness. The mainstream Japanese media — who depend on the party and government ministries for access (and hence for their comfortable salaries and chauffeured limousines) — follow up by quietly relaxing their curiosity about the scandal and setting about the task of rehabilitating the reputation of political heavyweights who had been (unjustly, as it turns out) accused.

In the end, a shortlived "conflict" of interest, which seemingly exposed the misdeeds of selfish and exploitive individuals in high places, resolves into a mere misunderstanding. The scandal was not so great after all, because — in an ethical system that has well-served a simple, honest nation of farm-

ers and fishermen for centuries — a small misstep tends to be
blown far out of proportion by the headline-hungry jackals
of the yellow press. The inevitable outcome of every such
"scandal" is the restoration of a status quo that reinforces a
common interest in the absence of conflicting interests.

Sumo works the same way — except better. The collusion
that permeates and literally governs the sumo world is more
deeply intertwined, and more obvious — once you realize it's
there — than in almost any other institution in Japan. And
it's silly to call any of sumo's interlocking relationships and
quid-pro-quos a "conflict of interest" because the system perceives no conflict. The system, as always, is in harmony.

Little Spoon, Tamaryu and the Politics of Mono-ii

If, for instance, the Sumo Association were to recognize such
an idea as "conflict of interest," it would have to disqualify
many of its ring judges. The ring judges are *oyakata* — coaches — and they sit in judgment on their own wrestlers. I was
pretty slow to perceive the apparent incestuousness of the
judging system until the emergence in 1989 of the most popular brother act in sumo history. Takanohana Formerly Takahanada (Little Spoon) in 1989 became the youngest *rikishi*, at
seventeen, to gain promotion to *juryo* (the second division).
A few *basho* later, both he and his older brother, Wakanohana Formerly Wakahanada (Big Spoon), were in *juryo*. And
in a few months, Little Spoon, who was lean, long-legged,
strong, handsome, reticent (sumo's first teen idol), became
the youngest *rikishi* ever to enter *makuuchi*, as *maegashira*
No. 14 in the 1990 Spring Basho. Never mind that he lost
eleven times and stumbled back down to *juryo*. He had made
history, and rejuvenated sumo. The kid had sex appeal! The
musty old Sumo Association suddenly had celebrities — the
hip, young, trendy kind — fighting for space in *Flash, Fo-*

cus, and *Friday* (Japan's versions of *People* and *Us*) with rock groups, recluses, serial killers, and porn stars!

Adding poignancy to the story of Little Spoon and Big Spoon was that they were the sons of a revered *oyakata,* Fujishima Formerly Takanohana, a former *sekitori* who had become — since his retirement and his emergence as a crafty sumo coach — an exalted Sumo Association dignitary. The fact that Fujishima's bouncing baby boys were competent wrestlers owed to his coaching. The blinding speed of their promotion up the ranks, however, was, well, a remarkable coincidence. And so what if their uncle, Fujishima's father-in-law, happened to be Futagoyama, President of the Sumo Association?

So, anyway, there I was, one day, watching the *juryo* matches, and up onto the *dohyo* steps Little Spoon. And then the NHK camera swings to Fujishima, sitting there beside the ring, judging the match. His son's match. Judging his son's match, along with all his other buddies in the Sumo Association.

And I flashed back to my previous incarnation as a crusading New England newspaper editor. "Just a god damn minute!" I shouted at the insensate television screen. "Mr. Chairman, I'm afraid Mr. Fujishima might be involved in a conflict of interest here!"

The reaction I got, sitting with a TV in an empty room, was less than gratifying.

Little Spoon and Tamaryu (his opponent) went ahead despite my protest, and fought a tenacious see-saw match, which ended dramatically as they tumbled off the *dohyo* together. The referee flashed his *goombai,* hesitantly, in Tamaryu's favor.

Not a smart move, because instantly one of the rings judges — tactfully, not Daddy himself — raised a hand, challenging the ref's call and forcing a *mono-ii* confab in the middle of the ring. Meanwhile, NHK ran back replays of the match. No matter how you looked at it, the damn thing was a toss-up. Tamaryu had been the aggressor throughout, but Takanohana, a stronger athlete who was a good student of his father's brilliant defensive tactics, had countered and neutralized every one of Tamaryu's assaults. At the end, Tamaryu backed Takanohana to the *tawara* and wrenched the younger wrestler powerfully toward the seats. As Little Spoon fell, he twisted and pulled Tamaryu with him. They both plummeted off the *dohyo*, landing at the same instant with a fleshy splat amid flying chopsticks and *bento* boxes.

NHK replayed the match three or four times, stopping the tape at the split second when both *rikishi* hit the deck. Meanwhile, the ring judges, Dad and his buddies, chewed the fat in the middle of the ring. Theoretically, they had two simple criteria to help them decide.

The first, the most important measurement, is the ring itself. If any part of a *rikishi*'s body touches the sand outside the ring, the match is over. The first wrestler who touches, loses.

However, it is possible to amend this consideration. When both *rikishi* touch outside at the same time, a wrestler who has executed a strong offensive move might still be declared the winner by virtue of his initiative. Once or twice, I've seen this judgment decided in a *rikishi*'s favor even after his foot, or a shoulder, appeared — by a fraction of a second, to have hit the dirt first.

If neither of these measurements are clear to the ring judges — after consulting, looking at marks in the sand, and reviewing the replay — they have the option of ordering an immediate do-over. This is a good face-saver for everyone.

These were the options available to the ring judges in deciding the victor in a meaningless second-division match between Takanohana and Tamaryu.

The first measurement, who touched first, was not applicable, because they'd hit the ground together. No advantage.

The second criterion fell slightly in Tamaryu's favor, because he had attacked — although indecisively — throughout the match. Advantage Tamaryu.

Still, it seemed too close to call. Why not give everyone a graceful compromise and have them wrestle again? Sorry. Life is not so simple.

When ring judges get together for *mono ii*, they have more matters to consider than merely which of these pugs dragged his piggies across the *tawara* first. In the back of their minds, they must also weigh, for example,

- The relative importance of the two *sumobeya* involved.
  In this case, Little Spoon, from Fujishima-beya, was a veritable prince among *rikishi*, one of a team of rising Fujishima pupils who would eventually supplant Kokonoe-beya as sumo's showcase stable. Tamaryu, on the other hand, hailed from Katanami-beya, a weak house with little influence and no prospects. Advantage Takanohana.

- The relative prestige of the two *rikishi* involved.
  Little Spoon was programmed for stardom, his recognition factor already comparable to Chiyonofuji, Konishiki, and the Beatles. Moreover, he was the keystone of the Sumo Association's efforts to regain the interest of Japan's fickle youth. When he set foot on the *dohyo*, a great feminine cheer went up in the arena. He was, simply, the most watched, most liked, most hoped-for wrestler in sumo. Tamaryu, on the other hand, was an aging field hand gradually slipping toward retirement. His value to the prestige and the future of the Sumo Association was, exactly, zero. Advantage Takanohana.

- The composition of the panel of judges. Fujishima, Little Spoon's father and *oyakata*, was one of the judges. Futagoyama, chief justice among all the judges, was Takanohana's grandpa. Katanami, Tamaryu's *oyakata*, was none of the above. Advantage Takanohana.

- Previous debts and obligations among all the parties involved. Without knowing all the byzantine connections that link the sumo world, it's impossible to determine who owed what to whom among the group that included Little Spoon and Tamaryu, Fujishima and Katanami, and all the judges on the *dohyo*. It would be safe to assume that Fujishima, whose position and wealth are near the pinnacle of the Sumo Association, held more markers than Tamaryu and his lowly coach. Advantage Takanohana.

It's possible to infer a number of other transactional factors into the conference that determined the outcome of that match between Little Spoon and Tamaryu. But the result would be the same: advantage Takanohana. In the underworld of business and politics with which I grew so familiar in the West, the issue was cut and dried. Regardless of how well or badly he might have performed — once the decision was ripped from the ref's hands — Takanohana had this victory in the bag.

A Sense of Honor

But wait! — as Billy Mays often exclaimed in his infomercials. There's more!

Within that little circle of pompous men in black robes, there was still another dynamic working. They were groping, in a few minutes of quiet intercourse, for something that sumo people call *rei*. You can translate the word differently according to the context, so that it comes out as "propriety," "order," "dignity," "politeness," "respect," or "balance." You can even define it as "class" or "the right stuff." In this case, the definition might be closer to "fairness," or even closer: "honor."

The quality that these five cloistered and mildly paranoid sumo judges held in common — which would be well-nigh impossible to find among any group of five corporate executives in any nation, including Japan — is a sense of honor. With that quality present, Tamaryu claimed at least one additional shred of advantage.

This "sense of honor" stuff sounds a little too noble to be true, but I think it's really there — fighting it out with baser instincts in the hearts of the sumo elders — on every close call. But you gotta balance that wishful inference with the fact that every *mono-ii* conference that ever occurred, like discussions among NFL officials after a disputed touchdown, is an impenetrable secret. You may impute motives (nice or nasty) to these old guys, but you can't verify anything. The sense that emerges from sumo insiders about the context of these meetings is that ring judges exercise a strange blend of deep myopia and extreme farsightedness.

In the near view, the ring judges focus on the events of this particular match at this moment. Regardless of the potential embarrassment to a member of their panel, or to Sumo Association's hierarchy, they will not reverse a decision in which there is clear physical (a toe-print on the sand) or visual (NHK's replay) evidence to the contrary.

Between this narrow plane of physical evidence and a distant peak that might be termed "the best interests of sumo," the ring judges don't see very much. It just isn't important to these guys how their decision affects the record of Takanohana or Tamaryu in this *basho*. It isn't even important whether fans or sportswriters see their decision as fair, or whether Fujishima's presence as a judge for his own son's match might look fishy to an outsider.

The fan is expected to believe that these judges are perfectly impartial because they mean to be impartial — as a matter of honor. The fan must believe — despite all evidence to the contrary — that what appears at the moment to be cheating will actually become, in the long run, a profound justice, a sort of transcendent fairness. Strip the judges, the sport, of this necessary suspension of disbelief, and you discredit sumo irreparably. Impose onto sumo the temporal concept of conflict of interest, and you take away the strange confusion of values — sports and religion — that makes sumo so intriguing for even those who don't know a rugby ball from a catcher's mask.

You must, despite the urge to scoff, embrace the dubious assertion that on the rare occasions when ring judges interfere with the outcome of a match and change it without any apparent regard for fairness, they perceive a higher morality. They're shining their *rei* on the masses.

For instance, the ring judges — Dad and the boys — decided the match in favor of Takanohana. Tamaryu, the apparent winner, bowed stoically and made his exit. He had had a sweet victory in his grasp. He was an old poop on his last legs but — until they snatched it away from him — he'd kicked sand on the rich kid and felt some of the old bounce return to his giddyup. But then they told Tamaryu, "No, you can't have this one," and he took it like a man. Tamaryu's loss was an injustice in the short term. But in the long term, we fans are advised to recognize a defeat that served Tamaryu and Katanami far better than an impertinent victory would have. Perhaps the ring judges realized that, in claiming a disputed victory over Little Spoon and thus slowing the rich kid's inevitable progress to the upper ranks, Tamaryu would suffer a small measure of disfavor from Uncle Futagoyama and other powerful members of the Sumo Association. Tamaryu was close to retirement; he was in line, perhaps, to take over management of a *sumobeya* — an expensive and difficult undertaking that requires financial aid and political favor within the Sumo Association. Any resentment that fell to Tamaryu would damage his prospects. It would also affect his *oyakata*, Katanami, and their small, impecunious *sumobeya*.

Consider, on the other hand, the blessings to Tamaryu as he bowed graciously to an unjust defeat. There was the gratitude of the Sumo Association, who could herald yet another victory for the nation's most popular sports star. There was an obligation, a favor owed to Tamaryu and Katanami by Fujishima, a giant in the sumo world. And there was the unspoken sympathy of all those who knew that Tamaryu accepted a humiliating reversal without a peep of complaint — with class. *Rei!*

"Yaocho Doesn't Exist"

Call it cheating or conflict of interest, the occasional tampering of the ring judges (in essence, the Sumo Association itself) sets a tone for the sport of sumo. The message conveyed is that, as long as motives remain "pure" and directed toward the preservation of order, certain results are negotiable.

Most of the day-to-day cheating in sumo (called *yaochozumo)* is done among the *rikishi* themselves, without the involvement or any sanction — positive or negative — from the Sumo Association. No one in the sumo world, no expatriate from the sumo world, will acknowledge the existence of *yaochozumo*, even though this word is one of the most oft-whispered in sumo.

Koji Kitao (formerly Futahaguro), who I think has a reasonable grievance against sumo's elders — because they threw him out of the sport — nevertheless carries no tales about cheating in sumo. There is, he insisted, no such thing.

"As far as I know, *yaocho* doesn't exist," said Kitao/Futahaguro, through his teeth. "It doesn't make sense to lose a match on purpose, because you don't want to be demoted. The differences in rank are so obvious, in the way you're treated, in the jobs you have to do, in the places you stay on trips. Everything in your life is so different at different ranks. It doesn't make sense to lose on purpose... "

On the other hand, weekly magazines like *Shukan Post* and *Shukan Shincho* have been, for decades, following up *basho* with expert analysis of which matches were phony, how they were lost intentionally, and why the deals were made. *Shukan Post* insisted, for example, that a dramatic three-way wrestle-off among Konishiki, Kirishima, and Hokutoumi (won by Hokutoumi) in the 1990 Spring *Basho* was bought and paid for.

Shukan Shincho, which took up the anti-*yaocho* cause from *Shukan Post* in the 2000's, eventually faced — and lost — a libel suit by the Sumo Association, because, predictably, *Shincho*'s lawyers could not find a single sumo wrestler to testify to *yaochozumo*.

Every sumo nerd, over beer, will regale you — if you ask — with tales of *yaocho*, citing whole tournaments that were riddled with graft.

Somewhere between Kitao/Futahaguro (who was, I think, conveying his own experience truthfully) and the weeklies (whose veracity, while not unimpeachable, cannot be completely scorned) lies the truth about *yaochozumo*.

On the record, *yaocho* does not exist. It never happened. It never will. Every single match in the history of sumo was on the up-and-up.

Accept this and you may also accept that jockeys never hold horses back in the stretch, and that prize fighters never go into the tank in fear for life and career. Illegal substances — from barbiturates to steroids to human grown hormone — have been completely eradicated in track and field, weightlifting, professional football, baseball, and bodybuilding. Blood-doping is nonexistent in bicycle racing. College athletes never receive hundred-dollar handshakes. College basketball players never shave points.

If *yaocho* did exist, however, it would not enjoy the vast underworld scale of operations attributed by the weekly magazines. If *yaocho* did exist, it would partake of the moderation that typifies sumo — watched over and regulated by the Sumo Association. It would serve to maintain balance in sumo, reverence for rank, and the proper order of things: *rei.*

If this were so, then it's reasonable to believe that the 1990 Spring *Basho* wrestle-off among Konishiki, Kirishima, and Hokutoumi might have been arranged — as *Shukan Post* claimed — with the blessing of the Sumo Association. Though two *rikishi* lost the *yusho*, each gained. In succumbing to Hokutoumi, Konishiki assured himself of a lead-pipe *yokozuna* nomination if he dominated the next *basho* (he didn't). Kirishima, while losing to Hokutoumi, assured his immediate promotion to *ozeki* (which he received). And Hokutoumi, who struggled but won, reasserted the primacy of the Kokonoe-beya as sumo's foremost stable, while subtly indicating that he — as a *rikishi* — was still subordinate to Chiyonofuji, his stablemate.

It all had the lovely, Confucian symmetry that the Sumo Association so cherishes. And yet, I cling to my doubt that this complicated wrestle-off was crooked — for one reason. To tamper with a series of matches so important and so public is indiscreet — a word difficult to associate with anything the Sumo Association has ever done. If there were deals involved in that wrestle-off, they were implicit — understood well beforehand among all the *rikishi*, all the *oyakata*, all the knowing elders of the Sumo Association.

The Last-Day Blues

Hence, my suspicion — with reservations — was that the
wrestle-off was legit. In fact, I trust most sumo matches to be
legit. I once thought, with Kitao/ Futahaguro, that all sumo
matches were honest. This belief persisted through five or
six *basho*, until I grew vaguely uneasy with the dullness that
seemed to grip the Kokugikan on the day — Day 15 — when
the atmosphere should be most exciting. This is a big day,
not just because the Elite are deciding the title, but because
another six, eight, ten *rikishi*, all up and down the *banzuke*,
are sweating out *kachikoshi*.

In any *basho*, there are *rikishi* who get through fourteen
days of wrestling at seven wins and seven losses. In order
to make *kachikoshi*, 8-7, and fend off demotion, they have
to win that last match. Often, they have to do it against a
higher-ranked *rikishi* with a better tournament record. Often, they have to overcome losing streaks, poor health, injuries, and ennui. They must summon all their grit and skills,
go out in the dirt weary and woozy, and bust a gut just one
more time.

So why, I said to myself after watching a year's worth of
Day 15s, are these last-gasp *kachikoshi* matches so sloppy, short, and desultory? Fatsoyama doesn't seem to care.
I learned from Kitao that demotion is the *rikishi*'s greatest
fear. So why did these matches so often seem to lack any
sense of urgency?

I began to form an answer to these questions when I began
to notice that *rikishi* who come to Day 15 at 7-7 almost never
lose. I figured I'd better find out for sure, so I started keeping
count. Between January '89 and July '90, there were 56 Day
15 matches that involved wrestlers who were 7-7 before the
match. Thanks to careful scheduling by the Sumo Association, only eight of those matches involved *rikishi* who were
both 7-7, therefore dooming one of them to certain *makeko-*

shi. The scarcity of head-to-heads between 7-7 *rikishi* isn't accidental. When one of the two *rikishi* has no chance for *kachikoshi* — sumo's version of certain death — it's not good management (although it's fun!).

I removed those eight head-to-heads from my statistics, and found that the *kachikoshi* rate for *rikishi* entering Day 15 at 7-7 was 39 wins, nine losses — a winning percentage of .813.

Now, it didn't make sense that a bunch of guys who'd gone through two weeks of win-one/lose-one sumo could suddenly boost themselves to a championship level of performance — even though motivated by desperation. Sixty percent, perhaps 67 percent was believable. Eighty percent was Never-never land — especially in light of the fact that 21 of these victories, more than half, came against equal or higher-ranked opponents.

Surprisingly, my little *ad hoc* effort in *yaocho* research was replicated in 2002, by Steven Levitt and Mark Duggan in their pop-economics bestseller, *Freakonomics*. Although not citing the earlier version of this book, Levitt and Duggan replicated and expanded on my research. They found that 70 percent of *rikishi* with 7-7 records on the final day of the tournament won. They also noted that this percentage tended to rise the more times the two wrestlers met, and it decreased when one of the *rikishi* was due to retire. The Levitt/Duggan study found that 7–7 *rikishi* won 79.6 percent of the time when statistics suggested a probability of winning only 48.7 percent of the time against that particular opponent.

More recently, in 170 matches between 2004 and 2009, these statistics have grown less dramatic. The winning percentage for 7-7 *rikishi* over this period has dipped to just under two-thirds. This still defies the laws of probability. But the interesting factor in this change, also noted by the *Freakonomics* authors, is that the usually impregnable Sumo

Association has evidently responded to increased scrutiny of its Day 15 matches involving .500 rikishi, not from *gaijin* like me and Leavitt & Duggan, but from the shrill and relentless Japanese weeklies.

Nonetheless, this slight dampening of Day 15 *yaocho* does not, I believe, represent a net reduction in match-trading. It simply means that, when a periodic outcry of *"j'accuse!"* rises up from *Shukan Something-or-Other*, the wrestlers, their elves, and their overseers simply shift as much *yaocho* as possible backward on the schedule — to Day 14.

Regardless of statistics, the truest proof of *yaochozumo* is the naked eye. On almost every Day 15 I've ever studied, I got this feeling that I was watching lousy, lazy sumo. The winners in these seemingly desperate *kachikoshi* matches were blasé, the losers were sluggish and then — it seemed — embarrassed, hurrying to get away.

One of the clearest examples of this melodrama occurred on the last day of the 2008 Kyushu (November) Basho. Throughout the Sumotori Rag, Baruto (Fred Thompson) seemed sullen and listless, even though a victory would be his tenth, an impressive *basho*. To understand Fred's despondency, it was only necessary to look at the schedule. Two *rikishi*, Ama (soon to become Harumafuji) and *yokozuna* Hakuho (UPS), had entered the last day at 12-2, tied for the *yusho*. Alas, they were not scheduled against each other. But if they both won, they would wrestle off for the title, a storybook ending to the *basho*. But for that ratings-boosting, crowd-thrilling sudden-death playoff to occur, Baruto would have to lose to Ama (which was by no means a sure thing) and Kotomitsuki, also 9-5 and a tough opponent, would have to lose to UPS.

Well, needless to say, the Sumo Association got the wrestle-off it wanted, because they had arranged it ahead of time. Kotomitsuki put on a nice effort before tanking his match against Hakuho. Fred Thompson's defeat was less decorous. He followed orders and lost, but did it so sloppily and with such an air of self-loathing that his quick retreat evoked, with every step, the specter of Marlon Brando in *On the Waterfront*.

"*I coulda had class. I coulda been a contender. I coulda been somebody, instead of a bum...*"

The Sumo Association's problem with foreign *rikishi* like Baruto — from Estonia — is that *gaijin* athletes, trained from childhood in their own countries to ask no quarter and give none in return, have difficulty understanding why they should ever lose a match on purpose. In every aspect of his body language that day, Baruto made clear his profound disagreement with the gentlemanly traditions of sumo.

Notwithstanding the scruples of a few *gaijin rikishi*, however, Kitao/Futahaguro was right. A *rikishi* will resist demotion at almost any cost. Fortunately, tradition assures that the cost isn't high and help is abundant. A *rikishi* in danger of *makekoshi* near the end of a *basho* often finds that his schedule has gotten easier.

But the schedule is still a risk. According to the unsubstantiated gossip that has circulated among sumo observers for decades, *yaochozumo* typically begins with two *sumobeya* flunkies, silently empowered to negotiate on behalf of two *rikishi* who are scheduled to wrestle one another. One *rikishi* needs a win. The other is off the bubble; either he has *kachikoshi* already, or he's already taken his eighth loss and can't be salvaged. Either way, he has a favor to give.

The two elves exchange pleasantries and discuss terms. No one in sumo — not the Sumo Association, not their *oyakata*, not even the two *rikishi* themselves — is ever informed of what transpires between the two elves. The *rikishi* are aware, however, that a meeting occurred, and that a favor was granted.

How to Take a Dive

The next day, in the consummation of that wordless contract, the voluntary loser applies one of several techniques to his own defeat.

If he's an inexperienced *dohyo*-diver, there is some danger that he could accidentally win — causing embarrassment to his *sumobeya* and incurring an obligation, for atonement, several fold greater than the original deal. Hence, the safest method for the *yaocho* novice is, literally, to take a dive: *hataki komi*, the matador. It's easy. At the moment of *tachiai*, the designated "loser" charges slightly crooked at the designated "winner." The winner anticipates this clue and deftly sidesteps the loser's misguided launch. He taps the loser up-side the head, thumps him on the back, and guides him into the dirt.

Olé!

The matador occurs with extraordinary frequency on Day 15.

For a slightly more sophisticated *yaocho*, the "salami squeeze" is popular —because it's not quite as obvious as the matador. When executing the salami squeeze, the designated "winner" allows the designated "loser" to achieve *morozashi* — both arms inside. The cleverness of this tactic is that, even though the eventual loser has dominant hand position, he wastes it. His hands, pathetically, seem to forget their function, and suddenly there he is, backpedaling helplessly. He looks like a man trying — to no avail — to lift an immense, uncooperative sausage. He pauses momentarily at the *tawara*, hugging the winner, groping at his back, reaching impotently for a *mawashi* that he just can't seem to find. "Goddammit, where is that belt?! Oops. Too late ...."

He's out. Match over. Another *kachikoshi*.

My favorite form of *yaocho* is "dirty dancing." Sumo's handful of great dirty dancers is so artful that they have restored much of my appreciation of Day 15. Dirty dancers are old-timers, Butterballs and Cabdrivers mostly, who bounce up and down the Fish Tank, doing each other favors.

Dirty dancing looks like a real match. The designated "loser" seizes a slight advantage at *tachiai*, and then applies his best technique, his strongest move — and he's got it! He won! Oh no, not quite. Look at that! He just missed!

They repeat this charade several times. The loser gets the winner in trouble, and then they strain, they grunt. At the last second, ever so subtly, the loser relaxes. The winner escapes the loser's grip just far enough to avert defeat. Finally, as the dance nears its end, the loser executes an almost perfect throw. Almost! He misses by a millimeter, and then — alas — having committed himself, he's off-balance, vulnerable... Whap!... And down.

When it's over, and you watch the NHK replay, and if you watch intelligently, you begin to see that the loser never really used his advantage and the winner was never in danger. They have performed an artful illusion. Hulk Hogan and Captain Lou Albano couldn't've pulled it off any niftier.

The Rite of Passage

When I began to watch these questionable sumo matches, applying my senses, skepticism, and statistics, I was upset with sumo — for allowing this flagrant deception, for fooling me. I don't like to be taken for a sucker. On reflection, however, my outrage waned.

I soothed myself with the perverse consolation that almost every sport we know and love not only contains cheating but — like the Sumo Association looking away from those wheeler-dealer flunkies — tolerates it. Drugs, scams, point-shaving, gambling, prejudiced judges — they're everywhere. Heck, Knute, they took steroids at Notre Dame!

I take consolation, however, from an awareness of *yaocho-zumo*'s context and limitations. I know almost every match in which it is likely to occur. I know that it is largely confined to the *maegashira* ranks and to the attainment of *kachikoshi*, by any means possible. I know that virtually 90 percent of all *yaocho* occurs within the last three days of a *basho*, with most of that action on Day 15. Even in a *basho* riddled with *yaocho*, I have spotted, at most, a dozen phony matches — in a total of at least 280. And I've even come to take a perverse enjoyment in inviting friends to watch Day 15 — so I can predict the results (with uncanny accuracy) of the day's most suspenseful matches. I keep thinking of the joke about the moron who lost a week's wages betting on instant replay.

As I've pondered *yaocho*, also, I've developed a grudging admiration for the Sumo Association's almost mystical power to oversee it without seeing it. Sumo's elders keep their little cheating problem in check first by the skillful use of the schedule, giving *rikishi* every chance to avoid a last-day crisis. Extending this sense of control beyond one *basho*, I've noticed that *yaochozumo* follows a kind of ebb and flow, proliferating for a while, until some silent signal from the Sumo Association curtails it abruptly.

It appears — Kitao/Futahaguro's disavowal supports the supposition — that many young *rikishi* are weaned gradually (perhaps reluctantly) into the ways of *yaocho*. The secret is kept away from those (like, perhaps, Futahaguro) who don't need help, from those who wouldn't benefit enough from it, and especially from those who might be indiscreet. By allowing it but holding the secret tightly within a chosen brotherhood, sumo's elders control *yaocho* more effectively than if they tried to ban it.

Yaocho's profoundest hold on *rikishi* — and the reason, I think, that the secret is so well guarded — lies in its use as a rite of passage into sumo's inner circle.

As he reflected on his ten years in sumo, one of Kitao/Futahaguro's most heartfelt remarks was this: "The *rikishi* bow to each other before the match and after. Sumo people say that sumo begins with politeness and ends with politeness. That's a beautiful tradition, one of the things I miss most of all."

In saying this, Kitao/Futahaguro used the word *"rei,"* for "politeness."

Eventually, in that spirit of "beginning with politeness," each *rikishi*, at some point, is initiated into sumo's secret brotherhood by accepting sport's politest offer. What higher act of *rei* than to concede the victory to an opponent who needs it? And what better sign of *rei* in the initiate than the gracious acceptance of the offer? And what better test of a *rikishi*'s commitment to the brotherhood than his willingness to subordinate his competitive passion to the greater good of all, the collective need? Especially when he knows that he won't get in trouble for it! And even better that he knows it will help break down those icy walls that stand between *sumobeya*, and will make him feel — once and for all — like one of the guys!

Yaocho prevents great upheavals in the ranks, and makes change a gentle process. All the new blood is filtered and diluted by the humbling process of *yaocho*. One of the sumo nuances that the observant fan eventually perceives is that a young *rikishi* proves his readiness to compete at the highest level not by showing that he can win in *makuuchi*, but by developing a talent for judicious defeat.

Conversely, *yaocho* also identifies dissenters, those whose pride inhibits them from losing even a meaningless match, even to help a colleague. Those *rikishi* aren't cast out indiscreetly (perhaps for fear that they might speak up), but their path becomes harder, their progress slower, their status always a little shaky. Among the most prominent of these uneasy princes in past years were Onokuni and Asahifuji. If they submitted to *yaocho*, they didn't do it often enough or with the proper alacrity. Some *rikishi*, I think — especially former collegiate wrestlers — are never initiated into the *yaocho* club at all, because they might not be trustworthy. Sumo gets them too late in life, too fully formed, and too ethically fastidious.

And some *sumobeya* are more inclined to play the game than others. The boys from Sadogatake-beya, for example, are always ready to make a deal. But the Kasugano *rikishi*, not so much.

As they govern all other aspects of their sport, sumo's elders govern *yaocho* with a politeness that borders on intimidation. No one, even a *yaocho* resister, ever steps very far out of line. To betray the group is tantamount to betraying one's family. When a *rikishi* resorts to *yaocho*, he's expected to use it sparingly, silently, with dignity (*rei*), and with a consciousness that *yaocho* serves not to further his private glory, but to keep the family in balance.

Yaocho is an invisible, but palpable presence in sumo. Look for it, and you'll never spot it. Even resisters — and I'm certain there are some — will deny its existence. By comparison, the Cheshire cat's smile is a bite on the ass. But *yaocho* is there, and will stay there because it ameliorates one of sumo's greatest problems, the loneliness and persistent mediocrity of most *rikishi*. When someone takes a dive on your behalf, it keeps you afloat. When you tank a match for another guy, you feel a little more deeply the sympathy of your group, your sense of belonging. If you're really talented, you can win day in and day out all by your lonesome. But cheating needs company.

Look at it this way. If Jake LaMotta had learned how to take a decent dive, Vicki might've stuck with him, and *Raging Bull* might've had a happy ending.

CHAPTER 12

THE STATISTICAL IMPERATIVE

Statistics are the lifeblood of sports.

To make the metaphor more apt, I should say that sports burn human energy like forests inhale carbon dioxide, and spew out stats the way the leaves bleed oxygen.

For example, one of my buddies in high school, Dick Albright (he was all bright, by the way; he went to M.I.T.), was the first kid I ever knew who made up a really elaborate imaginary game. Dick was doing this long before video games and was vaguely disdainful of Strat-O-Matic baseball. Dick's only tool in the creation of his own little baseball league was a standard deck of playing cards, including the jokers. He created a series of playing charts that corresponded with events on the field, ranging from various groundballs, fly-balls, and popups to pickoff plays, stolen bases, home runs, and sacrifices.

Dick was hardly the first to think of such a thing. *On the Road* author Jack Kerouac whiled away his childhood with a similar form of baseball solitaire whose teams were all named after automobile models — Chevvies, Pontiacs, Ramblers, etc. Another author, Robert Coover, wrote one of the great baseball novels of all time, *The Universal Baseball Association, Inc., J. Henry Waugh, Proprietor*, about a man so obsessed with his imaginary baseball league — using cards and dice — that he loses his capacity to distinguish his gameworld from reality.

Following these examples, I have — off and on since high school — wasted my own time with a variation of Dick's game, the Columbia Baseball League (CBL). In my first iteration, all eight shortstops in my league had names derived from the word "shortstop:" Shorty Stopp, Stoppy Short, Stortly Shopovinski, etc.

But the point of this exercise, for Dick, for me, for Jack Kerouac and the tormented J. Henry Waugh, was the stats, which were as important — sometimes more so — as playing the games. They usually took more time to compute (especially in the days before calculators) than the games themselves consumed. But they illuminated the games. They turned names into heroes and foreshadowed great clashes on a non-existent diamond. Stats followed the ups and downs of each player, game to game and season to season, chronicling their triumphs, recording their slumps and hot streaks, and explaining, eventually their demise.

Perhaps most important, sports statistics — whether real or imaginary — captivate fans, inculcate them with the nuance of sport, expand their intellectual engagement from just their favorite team to all teams and all players — as they compare, contrast, and pick arguments sometimes so arcane and sabermetric that they give pause to mathematicians.

Florence Nightingale, reportedly a Washington Senators fan, once said, "To understand God's purpose, we must study statistics, for these are the measure of his purpose."

As Robert Coover made clear, statistics bridge — or blur — the gap between reality and the gameworlds into which we choose, if we're lucky, to escape.

But sumo is a gameworld with almost no statistics. One reason its prestige as a sport is so tenuous, even in Japan, is that it suffers a stats gap, especially compared to baseball — Japan's other national sport.

As a regular diet, sumo is difficult for many hardcore fans to digest, and does not capture the initiate, the child, the hermit, the sideline lip-gnawer, or the gamesman with the same sort of spontaneity — even obsession — that occurs with baseball or golf, NHL or NFL. The action, the game itself, lures many fans, but there is a huge body of thinking fans who need to compute and compare statistics as badly as they need to watch the fleeting flashes of human struggle. There are millions of fans (well, maniacs) who feel torn between love of the games and a fascination for the games' wondrous, endless possibilities for trivial bookkeeping.

Even sumo nerds, usually as reluctant as the Sumo Association to suggest even the slightest change in the sport, have sensed this deficiency and tried to fill the stats gap, with other stuff. Instinctively, these interpreters of sumo's mystic meaning have used history as their portal to enlightenment, dragging readers into museums to look at *engishiki* dolls and into libraries to ponder mildewed passages in the *Nihongi*. Such studies tend to confirm an impression that sumo's history is vague and quaint, because vagueness and quaintness — read "cultural differences" — are precisely what feeds their viewpoint. The problem in this approach for the fan is that sumo's charming rituals — though explained in relentless detail and with glowering earnestness — come off as Shinto charades, imitations of some greater, deeper, more fearful rite within the imponderable psyche of Japan. But where's the Game in all this esoterica? It sends no message to the fan because it comes without superlatives — the Most, the Longest, Shortest, Quickest, Highest Total....

There just aren't enough numbers. You can't really compare Tsunenohana (1910-30) to Taiho (1956-71) to Chiyonofuji (1970-91) to Asashoryu (2000-?), not the way you can compare Ruth to Aaron to Oh to Bonds. Or Baugh to Bradshaw to Montana to Manning. Which means you can't work up a decent full-scale, table-thumping, "All right, asshole, let's look it UP!" bar-room shoutdown.

The Data Deficit

The main statistic in sumo is each *rikishi*'s won/lost record — a rather dismal number in itself since two-thirds of all *rikishi* end their careers below .500.

As a pale facsimile of stats, sumo information also provides such items as height and weight, and the guy's hometown ("Folks, here's an interesting stat! Since 1750, Fatsoyama is only the third *rikishi* to make it to *makuuchi* from the town of West Tokushima!"). The pre-*basho* info kit also tells the stat-hungry fan how many *yusho* (usually none) each *rikishi* has won, how many Fighting Spirit, Technique and Outstanding Wrestler prizes he's won instead of the *yusho*, how old he was (usually fifteen) when he entered sumo, how old when he was promoted to the upper divisions, what his rank was in the last *basho* and, of course, the name of his *sumobeya*. This all comes off as more of a resumé than a statistical profile.

During the matches, occasionally, a commentator will reel off some fascinating statistical tidbit — perhaps noting that at age 31, Kirishima was the sixth (or fifth, or seventh — whatever) oldest *rikishi* in history to gain promotion to *ozeki*.

Terrific, but answer me this: what's his batting average with runners in scoring position after the seventh inning?

What were his 100-meter splits?

What's his hang time?

I'm not a stats freak. I bore easily and math was never my forté (although I can still calculate an ERA in my head). What I represent — as anyone can plainly see — is a healthy, mainstream interest in sports numbers. I am one of millions who believe you can't enjoy sports fully without you got a set of fundamental stats. So I asked myself how I could introduce new and useful numbers to the numberless wasteland of sumo. The answer, which came to me in a kind of self-illuminating Siddharthan literary epiphany, was moronically simple!

Rating the Rikishi

It's obvious to anyone who contemplates the notion of introducing new statistical measurements to the sport of sumo that no such innovation would earn the blessing of the Sumo Association. However, in order to enlist support from even one of sumo's multitude of less official guardians, any new statistics must still recognize and incorporate the Sumo Association's rankings. Bearing this in mind, I said: "Why not assign a numerical value to all the *rikishi* in sumo's upper division? Next, why not make those values parallel to the rankings established every two months in the Sumo Association's *banzuke*?"

So I did.

My *rikishi* rating (RR) system gives points, from 1 to 20, to each *rikishi*, according to his place on the official pecking order. The maximum, 20 points, goes only to *yokozuna* who are at the very pinnacle of the sumo world. The lowest rating, one point, applies to the bottom of the Fish Tank and the Border Patrol (roughly from about *maegashira* No. 9 to *maegashira* No. 16) and to *juryo* wrestlers who receive one-day invitations to compete in *makuuchi*.

This 20-point rating system, as I've applied it to day-to-day competition in each *basho* for more than 20 years, breaks down in the following order:

YOKOZUNA: 16-20 points

As you might guess, the only *yokozuna* who has ever enjoyed an RR of 20 was Chiyonofuji. This happened twice, and he only earned it after he had won two straight *yusho* and had been undefeated in the previous *basho*. Under less brilliant conditions, a *yokozuna* who wins tournaments, or contends consistently, is worth 18-19 points. Gravy Train *yokozuna* are worth only 17 points and can sink as low as 16. Asashoryu, the best *rikishi* since 2000, peaked several times at 19 points. His Mongolian arch-rival Hakuho has hit 18.

OZEKI: 13-17 points

The rule of thumb for *yokozuna* applies to *ozeki* wrestlers. A steady contender deserves 17 points. An otherwise dominant *ozeki* coming off a bad *basho* can sink as low as 15 points. An *ozeki* permanently resigned to the Gravy Train — Kaio and Chiyotaikai being perhaps the all-time examples — deserves only 13 or 14 points.

SEKIWAKE: 11-15 points

Occasionally, a *sekiwake* emerges before the basho as an *ozeki* candidate and a genuine *yusho* contender — as Ama/ Harumafuji did in the 2008 Kyushu Basho. In that rare case, you have a 15-point *sekiwake*, more point-worthy than a Gravy Train *ozeki*. Also, *sekiwake* who aren't really in the running for *ozeki* promotion, but are keeping a grip on the

Tightrope from *basho* to *basho* — as Ama/Harumafuji did through every tournament in '08 — are bonafide 14-pointers. New *sekiwake*, up from *komusubi*, are usually assigned 12 points. There are exceptions, like Kotoshogiku, for example, a habitual visitor to both *komusubi* and *sekiwake*, who merits 13 points for sheer persistence. On the rare occasion when a Cannon Fodder competitor gets a battlefield promotion from *maegashira* all the way to *sekiwake*, without stopping in the Meatgrinder, the reasonable expectation is that he will be annihilated and sent back down. Hence, the appropriate rating is 11 or 12.

KOMUSUBI: 10 points

Komusubi is a plateau. The two guys in the Meatgrinder are always rated at 10 points.

MAEGASHIRA: 1-9 points

In assigning points to the rank-and-file *rikishi*, I give the maximum 9 points to one or two guys on top of the Cannon Fodder squad and then reduce numbers at regular intervals all the way down. However, I adjust this according to my assessment of the *rikishi* whom the Sumo Association has — sometimes willy-nilly — placed at these levels.

For instance, in the Aki Basho in September, 2008, I rated West *maegashira* No. 1, Miyabiyama, at only 8 points, because I regarded him as a weak representative in that position. His final record turned out to be 4-11. As a contrasting example from the 1989 Autumn Basho, I gave all three of the top-rated *maegashira* — Kirishima, Mitoizumi and Akinoshima (who retired with the designation "Yokozuna Killer") — the 9-point max, because they were probably the best three *rikishi* to ever occupy those positions. Together, in that rare *basho*, despite the crippling pressure of the Cannon Fodder schedule, this exceptional trio compiled a 24-21 record, and beat the Elite seven times.

In practice, the numerical scale I've invented — which parallels the Sumo Association's assessment of the wrestlers' competitive strength — turns into scores. When a *rikishi* wins, he tallies (on the Benjamin scorecard) points equal to his opponent's *rikishi* rating (RR). For instance, beat one of the two *komusubi*, and you get 10 points. Beat Asashoryu and you get — at least — 17 points. Beat Border Patroller Tosanoumi and you get one point.

The loser, in each case, scores nothing.

Over the course of the fifteen days of competition, the result is the ideal consummation of every sport: a score for ever player!

For example, in the 2009 New Year Basho, Asashoryu (Hinganai) had a 15-1 record, won the championship (in a wrestle-off) and scored 168 points, compared to runner-up Hakuho (UPS), with a 14-2 record and 157 points. In points, Harumafuji (8-7) and Baruto (9-6), tied for third place with 97, while Kotooshu — with a better record of 10-5, had only the fifth-best point total, at 83.

According to Sumo Association standings, third place actually belonged to Tamanoshima (*maegashira* No. 15) and Homasho (*maegashira* No. 16) who were both 11-4 — but who, on the Benjamin scale, scored only 15 points each in 15 matches. Neither of these two lowly 11-4 *maegashira* faced an opponent worth more than three points. Comparatively, the easiest match for both Harumafuji and Baruto was against *maegashira* No. 3 Takekaze, whose value was six points.

Last place, by the way, went to either Masatsukasa, who was 4-11 with four points, or Bushuyama, who was 2-13 with five points.

The virtues of scoring lie not only in such obvious benefits as How Much a *rikishi* scored, but also in How Much he

Coulda scored. When you keep score, a myriad variety of comparisons begin to develop. For example, in that same *basho*, Hakuho's only loss until the wrestle-off with Asashoryu, was to *ozeki* Harumafuji (12 points). This means UPS Coulda reached Day 15 with 151 points (instead of 139) and avoided a wrestle-off by winning his match with Hinganai — which he did. Hakuho's final 15-match Coulda was 169; his actual score, good for only a tie and a rematch with Asashoryu, was 157.

Obviously, a scoring system helps compare schedules. In the 2009 March Basho, Hakuho scored 170 out of a possible 170 points as he won an undefeated *yusho*. Two *rikishi*, Asashoryu and Homasho, tied for runner-up with 11-4 records. But *yokozuna* Asashoryu tallied 112 of a possible 169 points. Homasho, a Fish Tank *maegashira*, had a Coulda total of only 54 points, scoring 37. In that *basho*, by further comparison, the low scorer was rock-bottom *maegashira* Toyozakura, who went 4-11 and scored five of only 17 possible points. The difference between Asashoryu's 170-point schedule and Toyozakura's 17-point schedule defines vividly the immense gap between the Elite in sumo and the guys in the Fish Tank.

But also in the March '09 *basho*, a prime example of how a point system highlights differences in difficulty-of-schedule was Hokutoriki. At No. 1 *maegashira*, he faced a serious test, with a Coulda that was virtually identical to the *basho*'s two *yokozuna*. He blew the test spectacularly, winning only two matches, scoring nine points out of a possible 171 (or 5.3 percent).

By maintaining a day-to-day score sheet during a *basho* (which I do), the fan has an additional touchstone for the drama of competition. In the first week of a *basho*, there often emerges an undefeated Fish Tank *rikishi* who finds himself standing side-by-side, in the Sumo Association's measure (won-lost record), with the mightiest *yokozuna*.

So it stood, for example, for Futeno on Day 9 of the 2008 Aki Basho (Sept.). With an 8-1 record, Futeno, a No. 10 *maegashira*, was running seemingly neck-and-neck in the *yusho* race with *yokozuna* Hakuho. But Futeno's *rikishi* rating was 2 points, Hakuho's was 17. Futeno, with a schedule entirely confined to the Fish Tank, had scored 10 of a possible 14 points. Hakuho's total that day was 56 points, out of a possible 64. Futeno finished the tournament with a respectable record of 11-4, with 17 points and a Coulda of 31. Hakuho scored 139 of a possible 147 and won the *basho*.

Point totals, reflecting the quality of opponents, show the occasional amazing phenomenal fish, like Futeno, Tamanoshima, or Homasho, in his true light — way down in the standings where he belongs. Beyond the individual tournament, the faithful sumo statistician — using the Benjamin system — inevitably accumulates data that compare *rikishi*, as competitors, over the long term. Among the stats I've created to compare *rikishi* scientifically, not only in one *basho* but over many *basho*, the most important are as follows:

OAR (Opponents' Average Rating). By averaging the values of all Fatsoyama's opponents, we know precisely how tough his schedule really is. In nine *basho* from January 2008 to May 2009, Harumafuji and Hakuho had sumo's toughest schedules, with OAR of, respectively, 10.66 and 10.60. The easiest nine-*basho* ride was for Takamisakari, who's average opponent was worth only 2.47 points.

APM (Average Points per Match). By dividing the numbers of points by the number of matches, we see — at a glance — the strength and consistency of a *rikishi*'s performance, day in and day out. Hakuho, the best in my '08-'09 nine-*basho* sample, had an APM of 9.17. Asashoryu, with a slightly easier schedule, scored only 7.77. Takamisakari, the worst, scored just 1.00 point per match.

APB (Average Points per Basho). By extending this simple statistic back through the same nine *basho*, the statistician derives a splendid, simple device for identifying the best *rikishi* over that period. It is the sumo equivalent to the National Football League's quarterback ratings (only easier to figure out).

For example, in the rating period from January 2008 through May 2009, the Top Ten rated *rikishi,* measured by APB, were as follows:

1. Hakuho (9 *basho*) — 140.56 points
2. Harumafuji (9) — 111.33
3. Asashoryu (7) — 103.00
4. Kotooshu (9) — 79.44
5. Kisenosato (9) — 75.00
6. Kotomitsuki(9) — 70.89
7. Kaio (9) — 70.22
8. Kotoshogiku (9) — 62.22
9. Chiyotaikai (9) — 59.33
10. Baruto (9) — 57.67

By comparison, in the same span, competing in a minimum of six *basho*, the worst five APB:

31. Tamanoshima (7 *basho*) — 12.86
32. Tochinoshin (6) — 12.50
33. Toyohibiki (6) — 12.00
34. Kakizoe (7) — 11.63
35. Tosanoumi (6) — 8.00 (Pathetic, huh?)

This scoring system, I believe, is simple. The permutations and resulting analyses are probably infinite.

I don't propose to examine those permutations here, but I've noticed some interesting possibilities for the serious stats geek. One, for example, is the comparison of a *rikishi*'s potential points per *basho* (OAR) with his actual point totals (APM). The closer the two numbers, the more likely the *rikishi* is maxing out his potential. A big gap, on the other hand, suggests that this guy is chronically overmatched, or absurdly overestimated by the old farts in the Sumo Association who organize the *banzuke*. Three examples: In the same '08-'09 period studied above, Hakuho had an OAR of 10.60 and an APM of 9.17. a remarkable fall-off of only 1.43 points. Comparatively, UPS' fellow *yokozuna* Asashoryu (OAR: 10.58, APM: 7.78), had a gap of 2.80 — which is still pretty impressive. Far less impressive was Miyabiyama, who had a Top-Ten OAR of 9.56, but only scored 3.23 points per match, an embarrassing gap of 6.42. These numbers make it pretty clear that the Sumo Association gave Hotcakes every possible chance to make the big time, and the little Butterball wasn't up to the job.

Another number with potential that I've never quite figured out is PPP (Potential Points Percentage), which divides the total points per *basho* by the total value of a *rikishi*'s opponents. In nine *basho*, for example, the best PPP was Hakuho's at .865 and the worst was Hokutoriki at .261. But so what? This might be a meaningless statistic.

Indeed, all sports statistics flirt perilously with meaninglessness. In trying to make sumo slightly more digital, I have merely striven to show (a) that there is vast potential in this untrod field of math and (b) that it's a do-it-yourself effort. Since the official sumo folks are sure to stick to their own paltry arithmetic, the thinking fan is free to style himself or herself as a statistical entrepreneur. The numbers in this chapter represent a pittance of venture capital.

Use it or ignore it, but listen. There are people out there now drawing up a draft lists, operating sumo rotisserie leagues, and even pitting imaginary *rikishi* against one another, just like Dick Albright and Jack Kerouac. And if one of you, alone and palely loitering in your living room with an empty bottle, a broken heart, and NHK, should happen to start up an imaginary sumo league (the Universal Sumo Association, Inc.?), well, don't forget me! Even though I tell myself I've outgrown that sort of thing, I'd still love to see your power matrices, probability tables, and stress charts, and I'd like to know whether — as your engine of chance — you decided to use dice, or playing cards, or one of those new doo-hickeys... you know, a computer.

CHAPTER 13

WHITHER SUMO...
Especially with
all these gaijin?

This above all: Sumo will never change.

The sport declined alarmingly in the 1980's, but made an improbable comeback the following decade, when the emergence of the two young hunks, Wakanohana and Takanohana (The Spoons) triggered an extended "sumo boom." But Little Spoon's retirement in 2002 at age 29 led to a post-millennium fallow period whose duration no one can guess.

Things got so bad that by 2009, at the Haru Basho in Osaka, there were empty seats on the weekends. As Vizzini in *The Princess Bride* would say, "InconCEIVable!"

If the Sumo Association had anything in common with the commissioners of almost any other professional sport, they would have reacted with a sense of urgency. They might have pondered a few new enticements for fans, ticket discounts, better merchandise, cheerleaders, maybe even better athletes and a rule change or two. Not the Sumo Association.

The Mongol Hordes

Since Little Spoon hung it up, the biggest trend in sumo has been an influx of foreign wrestlers that turned from a trickle to a flood in the mid-2000's. More than just filling in for young Japanese athletes who overwhelmingly prefer other sports, these *gaijin* effectively took over the sport. Immigrant jocks from beyond the Sea of Japan were so thoroughly dominant over homegrown *rikishi* that, by 2009, it was no exaggeration to declare that sumo had become Mongolia's de facto national sport.

As of July 2009, *gaijin* among the sumo Elite outnumbered Japanese *rikishi*, 6 to 5. However, this near standoff didn't truly depict the pre-eminence of outsiders. By the second *basho* of '09, the Sumo Association had gone seven years without one Japanese *rikishi* worthy of promotion to *yokozuna*.

Starting in 2002 and extending into 2009, the *yusho* score between foreign and Japanese *rikishi* was 39 to 7. Of the *yusho* claimed by *gaijin*, 34 went to the two Mongolian assassins, Hakuho and Asashoryu. The last Japanese *yusho* winner, possibly for years to come, was Tochiazuma, who won the Hatsu Basho in January, 2006.

Starting in the following *basho* and continuing 'til March 2008, the Mongols won 13 straight *yusho*, their streak broken at the Natsu Basho '08 by Kotooshu, a Bulgarian. The Mongolians began another winning streak in the next *basho*.

As of July 2009, there were three Japanese *ozeki*, Kaio, Chiyotaikai and Kotomitsuki, all over the age of 33 (Kaio was pushing 37). None was capable of challenging ever again for a *yusho*. The best up-and-coming young *rikishi* was newly minted *ozeki* Harumafuji, from Mongolia. Japanese fans hoping for a Great White (native-born) Hope had slim pickings. Only Kisenosato, Tochiozan and Goeido, each 22 years old, were showing much promise. But there were more Mongolians moving up the *banzuke*, ready to muscle them aside.

The Sumo Association greeted the Mongol hordes with, seemingly, open arms. Sumo Association press releases bragged blithely about the flourishing diversity of their once-insular sport. The old farts noted that the arrival of Mongolians, Russians, Georgians, Estonians, etc., had been foreshadowed by the Polynesian pioneers of previous decades, Takamiyama, Konishiki, Akebono, and Musashimaru.

In fact, before Takamiyama (Jesse Kuhaulua), there had been a few *rikishi* of Korean descent, but those were pre-diversity days and, besides, we're talking Koreans here. Koreans are to Japanese as Yankees are to Red Sox. Hence, sumo's first real *gaijin* snuck in through the servants' entrance and did their utmost to "pass" for Japanese.

Those backdoor Koreans, in a significant sense, established a pattern for sumo's pretense of internationalism. The aesthetic essence of being a sumo wrestler is to look as traditional — meaning Japanese — as possible. I've always contended that the strength, the beauty, the charm of sumo is that it cannot be effectively exported to any other culture. Indeed, one of the first jobs an *oyakata* must undertake with a foreign wrestler — before he even teaches him *morozashi* and *yorikiri* — is to grow out his hair, swell out his gut, sign him up for lessons in *kana, kanji,* and *Nihongo,* teach him how to use chopsticks, make him bow at anything that moves and, this above all, transmogrify him into the spitting image of those godlike Ukiyo-e *rikishi* depicted in the 1800's by artist Utagawa Kuniyoshi.

The success of any foreign *rikishi* in sumo correlates with his willingness to be the nail, not the hammer. He has to become as Japanese as any alien being can possibly become. Jesse Kuhaulua figured this out and worked hard to fit in, opening the door for the next Hawaiian sumo aspirant, Konishiki — who probably set the whole integration plan back ten years. Konishiki never quite got the drift. Though he deserved to be elected *yokozuna* several times, Konishiki was denied because his behavior remained blatantly American. He understood the system, but couldn't help but bridle at the arbitrary rulings, mean-spirited reprimands, and gratuitous scoldings regularly handed down by the old farts. Throughout his tumultuous career, Konishiki remained outspoken (in excellent Japanese), especially when confronted by unfairness.

Hawaiian No. 3 — who wisely joined Jesse's Azumazeki-beya — was Akebono. Akebono did all the bowing and scraping that Konishiki's proud nature could not accommodate. Akebono established a model of *faux* Japaneseness that all subsequent *gaijin* — if they were smart — have emulated. Akebono learned Japanese swiftly and mumbled it fluently through a thousand sedative sumo interviews. His sumo training was rigidly traditional, and he faithfully mastered all the standard Japanese forms of obeisance. He carried himself — despite his height of 6'8" — humbly. In 1996, he surrendered his U.S. passport, assumed Japanese citizenship, and changed his name from Chad Rowan to Taro Akebono. He was, in every sense, the Sumo Association's Gunga Din.

Akebono was so much more pleasing to the Sumo Association than Konishiki — or even Takamiyama — because, in the memorable words of Strother Martin in *Cool Hand Luke*, he "got his mind right." Although unable to change his unfortunately alien appearance, Akebono completely acquiesced to the code of *rikishi* behavior imposed by sumo's Strother Martins. He gave the Sumo Association, unlike Konishiki, no excuse to deny him sumo's highest honors.

For foreigners following in Akebono's size 19 footsteps, the pattern has continued, and *gaijin* have multiplied like immense, carnivorous hamsters. But the opportunity for Japanization bestowed upon all these outsiders shouldn't be seen as a sign of the Sumo Association's post-millennial open-mindedness. The old farts started admitting *gaijin* — more than they ever anticipated — because they have no choice. They've got 700 slots to fill among more than 45 *sumobeya*, and they can't get local kids to sign up anymore.

Sumo in Japan is beginning to look like boxing in the United States — a Third World sport too dirty, difficult, and dangerous (in Japanese: *kitanai, kitsui, kiken*) to attract the elite athletes who once filled the gyms and battled to become contenders. In America today, there are no middle-class boxers. Long ago, the exodus of ethnic whites from boxing — as Irish and Italian families grew more affluent — led to the coining of the term, "Great White Hope." Nowadays, as black athletes find more opportunity in football, basketball, and other, less bloody, sports, they're also forsaking the boxing ring. Only kids with no other possibilities still look to boxing for a path out of poverty.

Parallel developments have become increasingly evident in sumo. Even before the foreign invasion, sumo was not the preferred sport of elite athletes in Japan's population centers in the Kanto and Kansai plains. Going back as far as the great *yokozuna* Futabayama, born in 1912 in Oita on the southern island of Kyushu, sumo represented a rare avenue for boys from the boondocks to make their way in the world.

Taiho, sumo's winningest *rikishi* ever, was from the northern island of Hokkaido, as were Chiyonofuji and Hokutoumi, Kokonoe-beya's twin killers of the 1980's. Likewise, Asahifuji was from Way Up North in Aomori while Terao, perhaps the most popular *rikishi* of his era, grew up Way Down South in Kagoshima.

More recently, rather than dividing sumo into the meaningless East/West divisions of ancient tradition, it would be far more feasible — and entertaining — to pit an all-star team of *rikishi* from Way Up North (Hokkaido, Aomori, Tohoku, Akita, Niigata, etc.) against their equally abundant counterparts from Way Down South (Fukuoka, Oita, Kochi, Kumamoto, Wakayama, etc.).

The Mongolians could wait for the winners and then, alas, kick the hell out of them.

Ay, here's the rub. There are Mongols, Mongols everywhere because the Sumo Association can no longer sell — even to the rubes from Shikoku and the hayseeds from Tohoku — the proposition that the sumo life represents a higher standard of living. Certainly, if a recruit from, say, Niigata (Way Up North) ascends doggedly in seven years from his typical unpaid sumo apprenticeship, and, in nine years, reaches *makuuchi* at age 24, he'll be making about $135,000 a year — which is three-tenths of the minimum salary ($442,000) given a 19-year-old rookie in Major League Baseball, not counting the bonus the baseball player received for signing his first minor-league contract.

In sumo, a *yokozuna* earns the maximum salary — usually augmented by prize money — of about $300,000 a year. This still falls short of the Major League's rookie minimum, but it sounds pretty good until compared to the salaries — as of about 2010 — of stars in virtually every other professional sport. For instance, at the same time Asashoryu in sumo was pulling down three-tenths of a million, Red Sox pitcher Daisuke Matsuzaka in baseball was earning $10 million. Yankee outfielder Hideki Matsui was paid $13 million, Colts quarterback Peyton Manning $14 million, Yankee third baseman Alex Rodriguez $28 million, and Lakers' star Kobe Bryant $31 million.

Bear in mind that no baseball, football, basketball, or hockey player — or professional athlete in any sport — is required to live in a dormitory, do kitchen patrol, clean toilets, and provide intimate W.C. assistance to senior colleagues who have grown too fat to wipe their own asses.

Cracks in the Façade

The influx and dominance of foreigners in sumo, as Japanese athletes sought any other option available, was one of many cracks in the Sumo Association's façade as the 21st century entered its second decade.

Indeed, the Sumo Association was still doing many things well. It was rich. It was still more influential politically than almost any other non-government organization in Japan, and probably more powerful than the government itself. Its TV alliance with NHK, one of the world's largest television empires, was etched in granite. Its problems with the tabloid press were typically contentious, but the old farts still had cozy relationships with Japan's newspaper giants, Yomiuri, Asahi, Nikkei, Mainichi, Kyodo News, and *The Japan Times*, as well as all the private television broadcasters. The Sumo Association could still command the high ground in any controversy and bully its position to the top of the news.

Best of all, the Sumo Association had perpetuated the festival atmosphere that prevails at each *basho* and serves as the biggest reason for fans to fill the arena. Sumo continued to be a terrific show, despite the evident, but easily ignored mediocrity of the competition.

However, beyond the dearth of Japanese talent on the *dohyo*, the Sumo Association had other problems that threatened to linger for years into the future. The weekly magazines had become so persistent, in accusations about matters like hazing, links to the Mob, and *yaochozumo*, that the Sumo Association could no longer keep such stories entirely out of the mainstream press. Whistleblowers had appeared among the sumo ranks, a development unthinkable as recently as 2002. Drugs were mentioned. We're not talking steroids, just marijuana, but any such suggestion was a huge shock in a sport where, ever since Oda Nobunaga organized the first *basho* in the 1500's, the drug of choice has been *saké*.

Perhaps most alarming, with the flood of foreigners, the rock-ribbed discipline characteristic of all things sumo — in message, demeanor, style, and jock behavior — had regressed. *Rikishi* were acting up. A Russian pothead was kicked out. Two ex-*rikishi,* reportedly ready to spill the beans about *yao-cho,* died mysteriously. Worst of all, Asashoryu was swooping into that stupid samurai pose just before every match he wrestled.

Hin ga nai, man!

An American Solution

This above all: Sumo will never change.

But I can't help myself. I occasionally imagine Japan's sumo enthusiasts suddenly realizing that they've got to change the sport before it's too late. To do this, though, they can't hope for any cooperation from the ossified old farts in the Sumo Association.

It's a familiar dilemma. American professional sports have faced such crises frequently. The solution often involves the formation of a rival league. In baseball, for example, at the turn of the 20th century, the "National" league was challenged by a rival "American" league. From this clash emerged the World Series and the two-league structure that has thrived for more than a hundred years.

In my lifetime, the National Football League has faced competition from, successively, the All-American Football Conference, the American Football League, the World Football League, and the XFL — not to mention Canadian football and the Arena League. The NFL survived all these challenges, but only after considerable expense, a few traumatic rule changes, several embarrassments that included losing Super Bowl III, and the absorption of a number of the rival-league teams into the NFL.

In basketball, the National Basketball Association's greatest threat came from the upstart American Basketball Association. The inevitable merger blessed the NBA with an infusion of fan enthusiasm and a wave of talented players, among them future Hall of Famers George "The Iceman" Gervin, Artis Gilmore, and Julius "Dr. J" Erving.

As such examples suggest, a really cool way to solve sumo's bad habits and popular decline, as I see it, would be to give the Sumo Association some serious competition. Call it the National Sumo League (NSL).

As I envision this fantasy league, its first priority is to retain all the pageantry and foofaraw that has always made sumo such a visual feast. Although I make fun of the Shinto pretense and the prancing and pawing by *rikishi*, I am loath to give it up. I'd make sure the NSL does all that stuff exactly the same.

Behind the scenes is where the big changes would come.

THE SCHEDULE: Just like the Sumo Association, the NSL would hold six 15-day *basho* a year, in the months not already occupied by the Sumo Association. This would give sumo fans a *basho* every month. Heaven!

Of course, the Sumo Association would be highly unlikely to allow a rival league to hold its *basho* at the sacred Ryogoku Kokugikan in Tokyo, but that's cool. My plan is to hold

only two *basho* a year in Tokyo, where there are plenty of
venues outside Ryogoku. Ideally, the NSL could rent the Tokyo Dome in non-baseball months — when the Giants and
Nippon Ham Fighters aren't using the field.

Right now, the only cities besides Tokyo that are anointed
as *basho* sites by the Sumo Association are Kansai's two me-
tropolises, Osaka and Nagoya, plus Fukuoka on the southern
island of Kyushu. By contrast, the NSL's popular outreach
program (POP) would introduce serious sumo to all those
Japanese cities that never get a real *basho*. The NSL sumo
schedule would cycle through perhaps a dozen cities, including Yokohama, Sendai, Kyoto, Hiroshima, Matsuyama, Na-
gasaki, Aomori, Niigata, Sapporo, etc., — with, perhaps, the
occasional expedition to Honolulu, Seoul, or Ulan Bator.

Most important, by eliminating a lot of the shady middle-
men who infest the Sumo Association's commercial dealings,
the NSL would offer a brand of sumo that has fewer frills
and much cheaper tickets. Ideally, instead of splurging on one
day at the sumo matches, the middle-class fan could afford a
"season ticket" for all 15 nights, for the whole family.

Yes, I'm talking about night sumo. It worked for Wrigley
Field, Monday Night Football, and the Rumble in the Jungle.
Why not sumo, yo? I also think that, in late summer and
early fall, sumo could go back outdoors like the old days. Al
fresco under-the-lights sumo matches, in 90-degree tempera-
tures! Huge, glistening bodies crashing together with a splat
so mighty that the closest fans are sprayed with sweat and
slobber while they lick sno-cones and sip piña coladas!

Finally, at the end of every *basho*, after the commissioner
finished bestowing the trophies and prizes, he would look
into the TV cameras and call out the Sumo Association. Six
times a year, just like clockwork, with fans, TV commentators and a half-dozen hysterical weekly tabloids egging him
on, the NSL commish would challenge the old farts to a Sumo

Super Bowl, our guys against your guys.

Bring it on!

RECRUITMENT: The first source of athletes for the National Sumo League would be all those vaguely discontented veteran *rikishi* trapped in all those grungy *sumobeya* controlled by the Sumo Association. The great tradition of upstart sports leagues is to raid the established teams and offer their best players a deal they cannot resist.

If a *yokozuna* was earning a cool $300,000 a year, the NSL would drop in and offer him a far cooler half-million. If a promising young *rikishi* was languishing in the *komusubi/sekiwake* ranks, tell him he'll enter the NSL at *ozeki*, at twice the Sumo Association's *ozeki* salary.

Beyond the fun of poaching talent, a new, improved sumo association in Japan would work tirelessly to bring Japan's best young athletes, from all sports, back to Japan's national pastime. This would be a welcome departure from current practice.

Today, the Sumo Association can't attract the best high school and university talent in Japan because sumo life consists almost exclusively of drudgery without money. To an unfortunate extent, the Sumo Association has resigned itself to scouring the hills and hinterlands for fat boys with not much hope for a productive future — in sports or any other occupation. In return for dropping out of school and committing themselves to the bizarre monasticism of the *sumobeya*, all the Sumo Association offers these kids is room and board — not much of the former and too much of the latter. And maybe, if they stick it out for ten years or so, a nice case of pancreatitis.

By contrast, the National Sumo League would pay up front, in the form of a five-figure signing bonus, and after that, a weekly paycheck. Recruits would be old enough to know better, largely high school or university graduates. The NSL would scout universities that have sumo clubs, but the league would also look for talent in sports like rugby, American football, baseball, basketball, judo, and freestyle wrestling. Potential *rikishi* would not have to be huge, because the NSL — like sumo in older times — would emphasize athleticism over sheer bulk.

By undertaking a vast overhaul of the "sumo lifestyle," the NSL would be able to extend its outreach overseas to athletes from non-Third World nations, including the United States. Without the requirement that they live like giant friars who've taken a vow of poverty, American collegiate wrestling champions and football players might consider a sumo career. The same would apply to a vast talent pool of young wrestlers, rugby players, and other athletes from Europe to Asia to Australia.

However, as league commissioner, one of my objectives for the NSL would be to concentrate recruiting heavily in Japan. Sumo is Japan's jewel. Sumo's audience is Japanese, and its competitors — with a handful of exceptions — should be Japanese.

TRAINING: Herein lies the revolution.

The typical training regimen in sumo, put simply, is inefficient, unpleasant, and grossly unhealthy. It promotes muscle development only indirectly while exerting tremendous strain on a *rikishi*'s respiratory, circulatory, and gastric systems. Nonetheless, the Sumo Association's network of *sumobeya* — concentrated in several Tokyo neighborhoods — practices this unwholesome regimen with very little deviation. This proximity among *sumobeya* allows the Sumo Association to look over every *oyakata*'s shoulder and make sure there are few deviations from the norm.

In the NSL, there would be no dorm-like *sumobeya*. *Rikishi* would use their paychecks to rent their own apartments. They would train in specially equipped gyms operated by their coaches. The gyms wouldn't necessarily be located in the same neighborhood, or even in Tokyo. They would be located wherever each sumo "team" decides to set up shop. Indeed, as a means of restoring and expanding sumo's popularity, the NSL would disperse its heroes into as many Japanese cities as possible.

Instead of more than 45 *sumobeya* with anywhere from two to 25 *rikishi*, the NSL would begin with eight sumo "teams," of 20-25 *rikishi* each. Rather than 700 *rikishi*, most of them little more than indentured servants, there would be about 200, all of them expected to eventually compete for championships.

Each *rikishi* would have a good breakfast before he started practice. There would be morning practice, followed by lunch, followed by afternoon practice. Partying at night would be discouraged; sleep — perhaps even a curfew — would be recommended. Coaches would use modern methods and equipment to build strength, muscle, agility, and skill among their *rikishi*. As in most professional sports, technical eclecticism would be encouraged. Coaches and their assistants would apply expertise not only in sumo, but in related forms of wrestling and other disciplines, like judo, basketball, yoga, modern dance, and gymnastics. Above all, each coach would be free to coach his own way, with no oversight by the league.

The health of the *rikishi* would be the league's foremost consideration. Although there would be six *basho* a year, each *rikishi* would be allowed a maximum of five *basho* in a row. Each NSL team would employ a dietician, a full-time trainer, and a team doctor. The NSL would adopt medical standards similar to those in the best professional leagues.

It would enforce the strictest drug-testing standards of any sport in the world.

After each *basho*, *rikishi* who competed would be required to rest at least two weeks before resuming practice.

Rikishi would be free to date, to wed (either sex), to have families, to buy homes, drive cars, and live like normal people. They would not be required to wear bathrobes 24 hours a day. They would be personally responsible for their behavior and would get no cover from the NSL if they screwed up.

THE SHOW: OK, in the NSL, the bathrobes (*yukata*) would be optional, but they'd all still have to wear the same hairdo, with the greasy kid stuff and the gingko-leaf topknot.

Even if you treat the jocks like grownups, sumo still has to look like sumo!

The show in the arena would look the same in every respect, but it would be shorter. The NSL's daily TV spectacle would be limited to two divisions, *juryo* and *makuuchi*, each with 40 *rikishi*. The individual battles between *rikishi* would remain the primary focus of the *basho*. However, as NSL commissioner, I would introduce some sort of point system similar to the one I've explained in Chapter 12. The point system would illuminate differences between the wrestlers' skill levels but would also pose — for the first time in sumo — the possibility of team competition.

In an eight-team NSL, each team could be affiliated with a different community in Japan or — more in keeping with Japanese tradition — a giant corporate sponsor. They could even have nicknames: the Yokohama Whales, the Mitsubishi Manatees, the Shitamachi Sasquatches, the Gifu Godzillas…

The possibilities are endless.

All this would take place on TV — probably one of the commercial channels — in prime time. Today, the main bouts of each *basho* take place on NHK from 4-6 p.m., when most gainfully employed people can't get to a television. As far as I know, no one from either the Sumo Association or NHK has ever proposed that sumo might be better off by broadcasting at almost any other time slot.

I'm only guessing, but it seems reasonable to assume that sumo's TV audience, shifted into prime evening viewing hours, would at least quadruple.

This audience might grow even larger with a few simple enhancements.

Music, for example. Each *rikishi* could be introduced with his own theme song: "Born To Be Wild," "Woolly Bully," "Big Bottoms," "Also Sprach Zarathustra." The possibilities are endless.

Girls, for example. One subtle change the NSL might make inside the arena would be replacing the old, dull ushers with cute girls, mincing down the aisles in a costume of *happi* coat and bikini bottoms, leading the patrons to their seats and winking at the TV cameramen — who would be among the most grateful people in Japan.

A less subtle innovation would come in the preliminaries. These would include a slate of minor-league matches among apprentice *rikishi*, but also a few *onna-zumo* bouts. The girl (*onna*) wrestlers, ideally, would wear designer-color, tushie-flattering *mawashi* (with matching toenail polish) and — of course — sports bras. But they'd be deadly serious. Really! Think Serena Williams and Mia Hamm.

INCOME: Payments for TV rights, especially with the addition (I hope tastefully and subtly) of commercials, would provide a substantial share of the revenue needed to make the NSL a profitable concern.

Ticket sales would help, of course, and the NSL would exploit merchandising at an unprecedented scale. The untapped possibilities for sumo apparel, sumo souvenirs, sumo gifts, gewgaws, and gadgets boggle the mind. Example: Throughout his 21 years in sumo, during which he won 1,045 matches and 31 yusho — making him more or less the Ted Williams of sumo — there was never a Chiyonofuji t-shirt. There are no sumo t-shirts.

By comparison, the Red Sox have sold upwards of 10,000 t-shirts a year (at about $22.95 each) honoring pitcher Tim Wakefield, a swell guy but not exactly a star. The numbers for really popular American players, like Albert Pujols, stagger the imagination.

The Sumo Association does sell souvenirs, the best of which are *tegata*, framable placards bearing a *rikishi*'s signature and in red ink — I love this part — his handprint. But put these same things on a t-shirt and you're more than doubling your revenue potential.

And then there are bubble-gum trading cards. In the history of sumo, there has never been a single trading card. I know this is hard to believe in the country than invented Pokemon but... well, suffice it to say that the Sumo Association had nothing to do with Pokemon.

There is also enormous commercial potential in items like commemorative sumo plates, and commemorative limited-edition *sumotori* coins from the Franklin Mint, preferably pitched by some celebrity spokesperson like Flavor Flav or Wilford Brimley on cable TV for $19.95.

But the real goldmine for the NSL, beyond t-shirts, trading cards, and TV, would be parimutuel betting.

Few sports are better suited to well-organized legal betting than sumo. As in horse-racing, there are long gaps between matches — plenty of time to rush to the ¥2,000 window and lay your lunch money down on Fatsoyama's nose. Or just sit there and call OTB! Sumo fans could bet all 40 matches in a day's competition, or like canny horseplayers, they could pick and choose. The NSL could chum the waters and expand the handle by setting up Daily Doubles, Trifectas, Perfectas, you name it.

Japan, like most countries, has a flourishing underworld of bookmakers, all of whom would love to take bets on sumo. They've never done it, however, because *yaochozumo* poisons the well. In the NSL, *yaocho* would be strictly forbidden, for a lot of good reasons, but mostly because there would be betting. One of the ironic assurances that any sport is on the up-and-up is the presence of gamblers. There are few locales on earth more honest than a blackjack table in Las Vegas.

Even better, you could bet on NSL sumo all over the place. The Japan Racing Association (JRA) already has a network of off-track betting offices all over Japan. The JRA would be thrilled to add the NSL's action to their portfolio.

And then there's your overseas market. Legal bookmaking venues in Britain — although in a fairly spastic fashion — have been taking bets on sumo for years. The introduction of match-by-match gambling on sumo would vastly expand this handle. Any country with satellite TV and off-track betting could join the party. Once the NSL qualified for the Las Vegas sports books, it would be virtually immune from failure.

Just a Game

For a *gaijin* sports fan in Japan, the NSL is an idea that could make you homesick: Teams, bets, ushers in bikinis, rock 'n' roll! I tell ya, if I could actually start up a rival sumo league in Japan, I'd be rich!

OK, back to reality.

It's not in the cards. There aren't any cards to begin with. Even if some foolhardy entrepreneur somehow raised the capital and got the NSL going, Japan wouldn't accept it. If you conducted a survey, sumo fans might agree to the need for a thorough housecleaning and a dose of Kennesaw Mountain Landis. But try giving them a real new deal, and they would — I promise — recoil in horror.

The Sumo Association knows this. They are safe from any possibility of protest and any hint of reform. The old farts will continue shuffling along in their cozy habits of brainwashing, hazing, ostracism, gross nepotism, and favoring Hippos over all other aspirants. There is selfishness, injustice, and tyranny in sumo, and I've bridled at them all. I'll do it again — out loud, with you if you want. But all my discontents boil down, basically, to recreational kvetching. I can't work up any lasting outrage, because, after all, it's just a game. There are bigger problems elsewhere in the world.

Sumo is comfortably bogged down. It will remain just so, both impervious and dependable — like a familiar friend, like the last scene in *Casablanca*, like that first wonderful sentence of *The Catcher in the Rye*. With all its perversities, sumo remains more fun than hassle. It will always invite you — hey, seduce you — to fog your eyes and imagine yourself right up there with the fat guys — hugging Twin Peaks' epic boobs, steering Kirinishiki's world-class love-handles, admiring the sensuous curve of Kotomitsuki's tummy, grinding thighs with Baby Huey, busting Asashoryu's nasty chops, rolling in the dirt with Fred Thompson, staring down the barrel of Takamisakari's werewolf charge, or aching spitefully to grab a chair-leg and knock that shit-eating grin off Mitoizumi's face!

Sumo lets you put yourself there and feel yourself on the *dohyo* — because it's the way most of us would fight if we had to: one-on-one, overweight, and awkward. Sumo touches us because its combatants are more human, more oppressed, and more exposed than most of us ever want to be. Most of us dare not feel superior to these underdressed blimps because we've been there at least once — pants down, red in the face and groping for our last vestige of dignity.

Meanwhile, like all athletes, these guys are our heroic stand-ins. They serve, bare-assed and wounded, in our place — just like us... only larger.

It takes a while to absorb the nuances of sumo, and to disregard its distractions. It takes longer to tolerate its defects. But if you give yourself that time, accept those flaws, and allow yourself the empathy that *rikishi* strangely inspire, then, by and by, you'll find yourself in tune, and swaying to the beat; and uttering the same cathartic cry that echoes from two eager throats in our little living room 90 days a year...

"Come on, Lardass! *Jikan desu!* Rip that pig's face off!"

Acknowledgments

Writers, especially when the topic is blood, sweat and blubber (one of many rejected titles for this book, by the way), just want to have fun. So, it's been a blessing to have editors at Tuttle who've been willing to play along with my madness. The first of these, editor of the original *The Joy of Sumo*, was Ray Furse, who encouraged the project, stepped out of my way while I wrote the manuscript, and finally waged the necessary internal battles to make sure the book came out the way we wanted it. Ray's partner in my defense was the wonderful Barbara Brackett.

My editor on this revision, Bob Graham, has been patient with my temperament and deft in steering the project. Most important, he has been serious about making sure that the whole thing — production and prose — has been fun.

A few other thanks are in order, especially to my agent, Jack Scovil, who freed me from my commitment to fiction long enough to indulge my perverse interest in fat men wrestling. Thanks also to Naoko Funabashi, who started up this long-delayed revision by buttonholing Bob Graham at a Colby College parent gathering. I will be eternally grateful to my illustrator for *The Joy of Sumo*, Greg Holfeld, for his superb and insightful art and for his eagerness to plunge back into sumo all over again. I wish I could have given him more work.

Finally, nothing I do is possible without the sustenance and enthusiasm of my wife, my own true love and my toughest audience, Junko Yoshida.

Glossary

Although this book is distinctly not a comprehensive guide to sumo terminology (especially of the dumber variety), I was forced to include a number of actual Japanese words as I wrote it. In order to help the reader cope with this imposition, these terms are compiled and defined — after a fashion — below.

aki basho: Fall tournament

ankogata: A sumo body type that suggests flab; endomorph.

banzuke: The Sumo Association's bi-monthly roster of rankings; inscribed in fine calligraphy and printed on rice paper, it's one of the classiest sumo souvenirs you can find.

basho: A sumo tournament, 15 days in length.

beteran: A "veteran" *rikishi*; more accurately, one who is seen as old, dull, and over-the-hill.

chankonabe: The main diet of sumo wrestlers; a cholesterol cocktail.

chikara-mizu: "Power water." No, not Gatorade. A ladle full of water each *rikishi* drinks and spits before the match.

chonmage: The sumo hairdo — greasy kid stuff with a ginkgo-leaf topknot.

dohyo: The raised sand and mud platform on which the fat guys wrestle.

fundoshi: A Japanese jock strap.

furo: A nightly bath, every salary-man's birthright — which his spouse must have ready for him, at exactly the right temperature, even if he doesn't get home 'til 4 a.m. Possibly the leading cause of divorce in Japan.

gaijin: A foreigner in Japan.

gakusei-zumo: An educated sumo wrestler.

genki: Fit as a fiddle and ready for love.

geta: Wooden platform shoes.

goombai: The referee's lacquered "war fan," which he points in the direction of the winner's corner to show the outcome of a match.

gyōji: The referee; an ugly cheerleader; human costume jewelry.

hanamichi: Literally, "primrose path." Actually, vinyl tile. The "east" and "west" aisles down which *rikishi* waddle on route to the *dohyo*.

hanten: A quilted house-jacket worn in the wintertime in homes without central heating.

haru basho: Spring tournament

hataki: A form of boxing in sumo, with blows directed

mainly at the opponent's face and head.

hataki-komi: The "matador" move, in which one wrestler leaps aside to avoid his opponent's charge, then pushes his opponent down as he charges by.

henka: A sidestep to dodge the other *rikishi* at *tachiai* — frowned on by purists, but requiring agility, deception, and timing.

heya: A sumo stable where *rikishi* live and train.

hidari-uwate: Sumo jargon. A left-hand grip over the other guy's belt.

hidari-yotsu: A left-hand belt grip.

higashi: East, the more prestigious division.

ichimon: A group of *sumobeya* related by family, history, or proximity. In French, *"cahute;"* in English, *"cahoots."*

jikan desu: "Time's up!" "All aboard!" "Dodgeball!" The *gyoji*'s last message to the *rikishi* before *tachiai*.

jo-jin: Cannon fodder. *Rikishi* between *sekiwake* and *maegashira* number 4 who face the most brutal schedule in any *basho*.

jonidan: The second lowest division in sumo, between *sandanme* and *jonokuchi*.

jonokuchi: The lowest division; raw recruits and indentured servants.

jūryō: The second of the three broad rankings of sumo wrestlers; between *makuuchi* and *makushita*.

kachikoshi: A majority of wins (at least eight) in a 15-day tournament; insurance against demotion in the ranks.

kadoban: Make or break for an *ozeki* who was *makekoshi* in his last *basho*. If he doesn't win eight matches next time out, he is demoted. Really embarrassing!

kana, kanji, and Nihongo: Three forms of the Japanese language — respectively, phonetic writing, Chinese ideograms, and spoken Japanese.

Kennesaw Mountain Landis: The retired judge appointed commissioner of Major-League Baseball after the Chicago "Black Sox" gambling scandal of 1919.

kensho-kin: Money in envelopes handed to *rikishi* after winning a match.

kesho-mawashi: Sumo apron. The fancy half-skirt, usually adorned with bad art or thinly veiled advertising, in which *rikishi* parade before each day's wrestling.

kimarite: Technique; the official winning "move" in any match.

kinboshi: "Gold star," with a raise in salary, awarded to a *maegashira* who beats a *yokozuna*.

komusubi: The fourth highest individual rank in sumo and the lowest of the four *sanyaku* ranks; the borderline between the exalted stars and the rank-and-file.

kotatsu: A Japanese table that warms the feet with a cunning combination of heating element and blanket. One of

Japan's greatest inventions.

maegashira: The lowest, and largest, category of individual sumo ranks in the upper *(makuuchi)* division; the rank-and-file fat guys.

makekoshi: A minority of wins (seven or fewer) in a 15-day tournament; after this, you get demoted in the ranks.

makushita: The lowest of the three broad rankings of sumo wrestlers; also, the third specific rank just below *makuuchi* and *juryo.*

makuuchi: The highest of the three broad rankings of sumo wrestlers; above *juryo* and *makushita.*

mawashi: The sumo wrestler's belt, or sash.

migi-yotsu: A right-hand belt grip.

mono ii: Review of a referee's call by the panel of judges.

morozashi: Both hands on the other fat guy's belt and inside his arms; the death grip.

natsu basho: Summer tournament.

nekodamashi: Sumo clapping, supposedly to distract one's opponent.

nigate ishiki: Pre-competition dread; a premonition of defeat.

Nihon Sumo Kyokai: The Japan Sumo Association.

nishi: West, the less prestigious division.

obāsan/obaasan: Granny.

obentō: Box lunch.

obi: A belt for a *yukata,* necessary because *yukata* don't have buttons down the front.

ojii-san: Gramps.

omiyage: An obligatory gift.

onna-zumo: Girl sumo, an occasionally serious variation, but nowadays mostly confined to a few strip joints in Tokyo's red-light Kabuki-cho district.

oshibori: Washcloth.

oshidashi: Victory by pushing.

otaku: Nerd, geek, propeller-head, trainspotter.

oyakata: The master and coach of a sumo stable, formerly a wrestler himself.

ōzeki: The second highest individual rank in sumo, just below *yokozuna.*

rikishi: The best term for sumo wrestler; "big strong bastard."

Ryogoku Kokugikan: The main sumo arena in Japan, in Tokyo's Ryogoku neighborhood.

sagari: A silly fringe with vague historical significance, hanging down from a sumo wrestler's belt.

sandanme: Sumo's fourth rank, just below *makushita.*

sanyaku: The top four individual ranks in sumo's upper division — including *yokozuna, ozeki, sekiwake,* and *komusubi.*

sekitori: A term for sumo wrestler in the upper two ranks, *makuuchi* and *juryo.*

sekiwake: The third highest individual rank in sumo, below *yokozuna* and *ozeki.*

shikiri: The Sumotori Rag.

shikō: Foot-stomping.

shikona: A *rikishi's* ring name, or *nom de guerre.*

shimpan: Ringside judges, usually senior *oyakata* with deep ties to the Sumo Association.

shita: Below.

shini-tai: "Dead body." A *rikishi*

beaten so obviously that he is declared the loser even though, technically, he landed outside the *tawara* before the other guy. A term used very rarely.

somebody-no-kachi: The victory announcement, in which "somebody" is replaced by the winner's name and *"kachi"* means he "won."

something-dashi: Any winning move that involves pushing.

something-tenage: Any winning move that involves an arm throw.

soppugata: A sumo body-type that suggests athleticism; ectomorph.

sumōbeya: A sumo stable; Japan's version of "Animal House."

sumōtori: Yet another term for sumo wrestler.

tabi: Old-fashioned Japanese socks.

tachiai: The face-off and collision that begins each sumo match.

tawara: The circle of sand-packed rice-straw bales within which the fat guys wrestle; cross the *tawara* first and you lose.

tegata: Placard with a *rikishi*'s handprint and autograph. A very cool sumo souvenir.

Tojo, Hideki: Japanese Imperial Army general who served as Japan's Prime Minister for much of World War II, from 18 October 1941 to 22 July 1944.

Tokugawa: The family name of numerous *shogun* who ruled Japan from 1603-1867.

torinaoshi: A do-over, following *mono ii*, when the five ring judges can't determine who

won the match. Great fun!

toshiyori: Sumo elder; old fart.

tsukebito: Sumo flunky; sparring partner; low-ranked *rikishi* with no talent, who clings to sumo life by waiting on higher-ranked *rikishi*.

tsunatori: Promotion of a sumo wrestler from *ozeki,* the second highest rank, to *yokozuna,* the highest rank.

tsuppari: A form of boxing in sumo, with open-handed blows directed mainly at the opponent's neck and chest.

tsuridashi: Victory by carrying the opponent off the *dohyo;* the Big Hernia.

tuchis: Yiddish for "ass," "tushy," the permanent vertical smile.

uchigake: Gobbledegook.

utchari: Victory by last-second reversal of positions.

uwa: Above.

yakitori: Barbecued food on sticks, usually chicken, or chicken entrails, or parts of the chicken that make entrails, by comparison, seem appetizing.

yaocho-zumō: An arranged match; a tank job; a dive.

yokozuna: The highest individual sumo ranking; superstar.

yorikiri: Victory by grabbing the belt with two hands, lifting, grunting and pushing; the missionary position.

yukata: A cotton bathrobe; the sumo wrestler's daily (and nightly) garb.

yūshō: The championship of a 15-day tournament.

zōri: Dress sandals.

Index

A

Akebono ("The Great Pumpkin") 37, 134, 227, 228-229

Akinoshima 49, 64, 116, 135, 136, 164, 165-168, 217

Akinoumi 10

Aminishiki 86

angles, importance of 120-121, 126

ankogata 44, 47, 49

aprons 68-70

armpit-wiping 95

Asahifuji 45, 60-61, 64, 67-68, 95, 133-152, 155, 176, 187, 209, 232

Asasekiryu ("Scarlett Ohara") 40, 90

Asashio 52

Asashoryu ("Hinganai") 35, 39-40, 50, 53, 87, 88, 92, 134, 163, 176-177, 186, 214, 216, 218-222, 226, 230, 232, 242

Average Points Per Basho (APB) 221-222

Average Points Per Match (APM) 220-222

B

backstage 57-72

banzuke (poster showing official rankings) 43, 173-175, 188, 202, 215, 222, 227

Baruto ("Fred Thompson") 42, 89, 126, 177, 204-205, 218, 221

basho 13, 14, 15, 22, 25-26, 54, 61, 66-68, 82, 98, 101, 110, 133-144, 168, 171-188, 231, 233-234

blubberbutts 44

body shapes 43-55

bowing 159-161, 198-199, 208-209, 228

boxer, the 107, 125

boxing 104, 107, 229

box seats 20-21

bulldozer, the 106-107, 108, 125

Bushuyama 218

butterballs 52-53, 177, 207

C

cabdrivers 53-54, 207

chankonabe 14, 61, 93

cheating 189, 199-210

chikara mizu 79, 161

Chiyonofuji ("The Wolf") 32-33, 45, 47, 50, 52, 61-63, 68, 83, 88, 92, 95, 102-103, 106, 109, 116-117, 119, 126, 133-152, 155, 168, 179, 195, 201, 214, 216, 230, 240

Chiyotakai 54, 176, 183, 216, 221, 227

choking 63-64

chonmage 40-41

concentration 96, 119-120, 185-187

cultural pageant, sumo as a 16

D

Daishoyama ("Dimples") 38
-*dashi* 125-126
death, early 39
diet 14, 20-21, 61, 93, 141
dive, taking a 189, 199-210
dohyo 20, 21, 22, 23, 26, 29, 62, 67, 69, 72, 76, 78-79, 88, 90, 98, 123, 125, 127, 128, 129, 155, 159, 161, 185, 231, 242
drugs 232

E

East and West divisions 69, 175, 180, 232
Eastern Europe, *rikishi* from 37, 41-42
elderly fans 22
emotion 155-159
expelled from sumo 71

F

false starts 110-111
feet, importance of 119-120
female fans 8, 19, 90
finger-licking 91
finish, the 123-129
food 14, 20-21, 61, 93
foreign *rikishi* 37, 60-63, 204-205, 225-243
Fujinoshin ("The Sweathog") 37, 78, 87
Fujishima 193-199
Fukuoka 22, 234
Futabayama 10, 229
Futagoyama 91, 93, 136. 151, 193, 198
Futahaguro (Kitao) 65-66, 71, 81, 140, 142, 199-200, 202, 205, 208-209
Futeno 220

G

gaijin fans 9, 11, 14, 15, 19, 21, 22, 35, 44, 47, 88, 114-115, 131, 187, 241
gakusei-zumo 168
gambling 135, 240-241
grips, favorite 45-47
Goeido ("Route 66") 35, 227
goombai (war fan) 78, 88, 98, 110, 121, 125, 127, 129, 134, 144, 193
Grouping urge 43-55
gyoji see 'referee'

H

Hakuho ("UPS") 40, 50, 95, 108, 126, 134, 178-179, 182, 186, 204-205, 216, 218-222, 226
hanamichi 72
Hananokuni 35
hands, importance of 116-119
Harumafuji (Ama) 66, 86, 95, 104, 106, 108, 176-177, 180, 183, 186, 204, 216-217, 218-221, 227
hatake 107
hataki attack 129
hataki komi 127, 206
henka 109
hidari-uwate 116
hidari-yotsu 45-47
Hinganai see 'Asashoryu'
Hippos 50-51, 54, 107, 118, 129, 154, 242
Hokutenyu 179
Hokutoriki 49, 219, 222
Hokutoumi 35, 50, 89, 92, 95, 102, 108, 135, 138-140, 142, 143, 149, 179, 200-201, 230
Homasho 163, 218, 219, 221
honor 196-199, 207
hooker, the 107

I

injuries 169, 176, 183, 202
interview, post-match 163-168
Itai ("Ouch!") 35, 130
Iwakiyama ("Mount Baldy") 40, 53

J

Japanese fans 10, 21, 22
Jikan desu! 26, 64, 243
Jocks 49-50, 54
jonidan 25
jonokuchi 25, 82
Jumpers 99-104
juryo division 26, 33, 38, 82, 101, 181,
    183-185, 192, 216, 238

K

kachi 124-125
kachikoshi 67, 172-174, 176-179, 181-
    182, 202-207
Kaio 54, 69, 85, 87, 94, 130, 176, 216,
    221, 227
Kakizoe 52, 181, 221
kesho-mawashi 68-70
kimarite 123-129
Kimura, Shonosuke 144, 149, 151
Kimurayama 53, 90, 95
Kirinishiki 242
Kirishima 35, 52, 66-68, 126, 127,
    177-179, 180, 200-201, 215, 217
Kisenosato ("The Eagle") 40, 109,
    221, 227
KITSH 79-96
Koboyama 182
Kokkai ("Ralph Kramden") 42, 54
Kokonoe 135-136, 138, 143, 151, 195,
    201, 230
kokoro 80
komusubi 26, 174-175, 177-179, 180,
    217, 218, 235
Konoshiki 51, 61-63, 68, 83, 85-86,
    87, 90, 91-93, 102, 109, 116, 129,

131, 135, 136, 162, 163, 165, 167,
    179, 195, 200-201, 227, 228
Kotofuji 131
Kotogaume 164-165, 177
Kotoinazuma ("Baby Huey") 35, 37
Kotomitsuki 176, 204-205, 221, 227,
    242
Kotonishiki 130, 135
Kotooshu ("Fat Elvis") 42, 176-177,
    218, 221, 227
Kotoshogiku 217, 221
Kotozakura 142
Kuhaulua, Jesse see 'Takamiyama'
Kushimaumi 61, 89, 127
Kyokudozan 120-121, 127

L

locker room 65-68, 161

M

maegashira 26, 82, 174-175, 177,
    178, 180-183, 185, 192, 207, 216,
    217-219
Maenoumi ("Mighty Mouse") 168
makekochi 173, 179, 182, 202-205
makushita 25, 184
makuuchi division 26, 33, 39, 50, 54,
    82, 101, 173-174, 181, 183-185,
    186, 188, 192, 209, 216, 230, 238
Masatsukasa 218
matador, the 108-109, 127, 206
mawashi 37, 38, 40, 47, 71, 82, 93-94,
    106, 110, 117-118, 121, 122, 146-
    148, 161, 162, 206
migi-yotsu 45-47, 116, 167
Mitoizumi 38-39, 41, 90, 91, 94, 110,
    217, 242
Miyabiyama ("Hotcakes") 66, 182-
    183, 222
Mongolia, *rikishi* from 39-40, 104,
    163, 226-231
mono ii 127-129, 192-199

morozashi 118, 127, 148-149, 206, 227
Musashimaru 22, 227

N
Nagoya 22, 120, 133-152, 155, 234
names 32-42
Nankairyu 106-107, 108, 111
National Sumo League (NSL) 233-241
NHK-TV 15, 19, 22, 25, 27, 44, 45, 51, 114-115, 124, 125, 134, 163-168, 193, 197, 207, 223, 231, 238-239
nigate ishiki 63-65
nodawa 104

O
obaasan 22
Oda Nobumaga 232
Oginohana 62, 66-68
ojiisan 22
omiyage 21
Onokuni 51, 118, 127, 129, 142, 176, 179, 209
Opponents Average Rating (OAR) 220, 222
origins of sumo 15-16, 157, 232
Osaka 22, 234
oshibori 95-96
oshidashi 124, 125-126
otaku 14
Owakamatsu 102
oyakata 13, 34, 61, 67, 142, 166, 192, 193, 196, 199, 201, 205, 227, 236
ozeki 26, 50, 52, 54, 67, 82, 109, 140, 173-176, 178, 179, 182, 201, 215, 216, 226, 235
Ozutsu ("The Goldfish") 33-34, 37, 52, 86

P
politics, 191-192, 231
posing 73-79

post-match rituals 153-169
Potential Points Percentage (PPP) 222
pre-match rituals 76-96
pre-match silence 70-72
pre-match warmups 71
prize money 160-161
promotion 91, 108, 134, 138-140, 151-152, 176, 201

R
rankings 173-185
Receivers 99-104
referee 78, 98, 102, 110, 121-123, 124-125, 127-129, 130, 134, 144, 149, 160, 193
rematch 129
rikishi 14, 15, 17, 32-33, 34-36, 42, 43-47, 70, 72, 76-78, 106, 108, 143, 162, 164, 172, 174-175, 185, 199, 201, 205, 214-215, 228-229, 232, 237, 243
rikishi rating 215-223
ring judges 77, 107, 110, 123, 125, 127-128, 130, 154, 192-199
ripsnorter in Nagoya, the 133-152
Ryogoku ("Trashcan") 37, 135
Ryogoku Kokugikan 10, 20-21, 22, 23-24, 63, 93, 233-234
Ryukozan ("Humpty Dumpty") 39

S
sagari 110
salaries 230-231, 235
salt throwing ritual 26, 39, 41, 78-79, 88-90
sandanme 25
sanyaku 175, 177, 179, 181
sekitori 33, 61, 65, 193
sekiwake 26, 82, 174-175, 177-179, 183, 216-217, 235
self-abuse 93-94
shiko 83-85
shimpan see 'ring judges'

Shinko 61, 65-66, 70, 81, 93, 105, 155, 186-187

Shinto 16, 47, 79, 88, 161, 233

shitate grip 43-46

shuffling ritual 79, 87

soppugata 44, 47, 49

souveniers 240

sponsors 160

sports fans 31-32

sportmanship 155-159, 163

squatting ritual 79, 85-87

staring 91-93

statistics 211-223

stoicism 155-159

stomping ritual 79, 83-85

strangler, the 108, 125

styles of *tachiai* 106-109

Sumo Association 13, 15, 16, 27, 36, 38, 43, 44, 46, 55, 63-65, 83, 90, 91, 99, 108-109, 110, 123, 124, 125, 128, 133, 136, 138-144, 151, 154-155, 157, 162-164, 168, 171, 180, 183, 185, 187-188, 192-199, 200-201, 202-207, 213, 215, 216-218, 222, 227, 228-233, 234-236, 239-240, 242

sumobeya 20, 34, 38, 42, 77, 79, 128, 129, 136, 142-143, 159, 171, 173-175, 178, 195, 199, 205-206, 209-210, 214, 229, 235, 236-238

sumotori 33

sumotori rag, the 73-96, 144

T

tabi 121

*tachia*i 67, 72, 76, 83, 90-91, 93-95, 97-111, 144, 181, 182, 206-207

Taiho 60, 137, 214, 232

Takahanada 38

Takamisakari ("Mad Dog") 36, 41, 87, 91, 94-95, 130, 155, 183, 220-221, 242

Takamisugi 120-121

Takamiyama 34, 61, 135, 227-228

Takanofuji 53

Takanohama ("Frankenstein") 34

Takanohana ("Little Spoon") 38, 134, 192-199, 225

Takanohanada 34, 38, 191-193

Takatoriki 129-131

Takekaze 35, 218

Tamakairiki 89

Tamanoshima 94, 124, 218, 220-221

Tamaryu 102, 192-199

Tamawashi 35

tawara 23, 69, 89, 103, 119, 120, 125, 127, 147, 149, 151, 194, 195, 206

taxonomy, sumo 43-55

teahouses 20-21

team competition 238-239

-tegata 240

television, Sumo on 8-9, 11, 12, 14, 15, 17, 22, 37, 114-115, 124, 163-168, 238-239

-tenage 126-127, 147

Terao 102, 119-120, 129, 177, 230

thoroughbreds 44

tickets 20-21, 234, 239

Tochiazuma 226

Tochinoshin 221

Tochinowaka ("Big Al") 38, 92, 135, 182

Tochiozan 69, 90, 227

Tochitsuhasa 86

Tokitenku 35, 163

Tokyo 10, 20, 22, 73-76, 234, 236, 227

torinaoshi 129

Tosanoumi 184, 218, 221

Toyohibiki 221

Toyonoshima 53, 87, 124

Toyonoumi 26, 34

Toyozakura 35, 68, 219

training 236-238

tsukebito 65, 94, 160

Tsunenohana 214

tsuppari 107
tsuridashi 126, 127

U
ushers 20
utchari 127
uwate grip 45-46
*uwate*nage 147, 149

W
Wakanohana ("Big Spoon") 34, 38,
  192-193, 225
Wakanosato 69
Wakasegawa 168
washcloth 95
water, drinking 26, 79, 161
weightlifting 126, 136
winning move, the 123-129
withdrawal, after a match 159-163

Y
yakuza, links to the 232
Yamamotoyama ("Twin Peaks") 41,
  51, 54, 84, 95, 129
yaocho 142-143, 189, 199-210, 232,
  241
yokozuna 26, 37, 39, 50, 61, 67, 70,
  71, 82, 108, 138, 155, 163, 173-
  176, 178, 179, 180, 187, 201,
  215-216, 219-220, 229, 230, 235
  promotion to 91, 108, 134, 138-
  140, 151-152, 176, 201, 226, 228
yorikiri 125, 147, 227
Yoshikaze ("Tokyo Rose") 40
yusho 61, 67, 137, 140-141, 173, 176,
  179, 187-188, 201, 204, 214, 216,
  219, 226-227, 240

Z
zori 121

Credits

Cover, photo insert pp. 1, 2B, 6B, 7T, 7B, 8T, 9T, 13T, 13B, 14T, 14B, 15, 16T, 16B © AFP/Getty Images; photo insert pp. 2T, 3T, 3B, 4-5, 6T, 8B, 10-11, 12 © Getty Images; photo insert p. 9B © Sports Illustrated/Getty Images

Cover Design by Opalworks